THE EVERYTHING® JUICING BOOK

Dear Reader,

More and more research supports the theory that juicing boosts health, increases longevity, and prevents and treats hundreds of conditions and diseases ranging from acne and arthritis to allergies and cancer. Unfortunately, despite the best of intentions, most of us find it difficult to consume enough fruits and vegetables every day for overall good health.

Juicing is an easy, convenient, delicious, and nutritious way to consume a high level of essential vitamins, minerals, and disease-fighting antioxidants and phytochemicals, delivering nutrients to the body in a form that is immediately absorbed and assimilated. Cooking and processing destroys natural nutrients in foods, but juicing helps preserve those nutrients.

Whether you're already an avid juicer or are just trying it for the first time, *The Everything® Juicing Book* offers a step-by-step guide to making nutritious juices, whether you want to increase your energy or treat a serious condition. The 150 delectable juice recipes in this book were created by coauthor Patrice Johnson, a Cordon Bleu-trained chef. Each one is guaranteed to delight even the most discriminating taste buds.

Carole Jacobs & Chef Patrice Johnson

Welcome to the EVERYTHING® Series!

These handy, accessible books give you all you need to tackle a difficult project, gain a new hobby, comprehend a fascinating topic, prepare for an exam, or even brush up on something you learned back in school but have since forgotten.

You can choose to read an Everything® book from cover to cover or just pick out the information you want from our four useful boxes: e-questions, e-facts, e-alerts, and e-ssentials.

We give you everything you need to know on the subject, but throw in a lot of fun stuff along the way, too.

We now have more than 400 Everything® books in print, spanning such wide-ranging categories as weddings, pregnancy, cooking, music instruction, foreign language, crafts, pets, New Age, and so much more. When you're done reading them all, you can finally say you know Everything®!

QUESTION

Answers to
common questions

FACT

Important snippets
of information

ALERT

Urgent
warnings

ESSENTIAL

Quick
handy tips

PUBLISHER Karen Cooper

DIRECTOR OF ACQUISITIONS AND INNOVATION Paula Munier

MANAGING EDITOR, EVERYTHING® SERIES Lisa Laing

COPY CHIEF Casey Ebert

ACQUISITIONS EDITOR Katrina Schroeder

SENIOR DEVELOPMENT EDITOR Brett Palana-Shanahan

ASSOCIATE DEVELOPMENT EDITOR Elizabeth Kassab

EVERYTHING® SERIES COVER DESIGNER Erin Alexander

LAYOUT DESIGNERS Colleen Cunningham, Elisabeth Lariviere, Ashley Vierra, Denise Wallace

Visit the entire Everything® series at *www.everything.com*

THE
EVERYTHING®
JUICING BOOK

All you need to create delicious juices for optimum health!

Carole Jacobs, former nutrition editor, *Shape* magazine
and Chef Patrice Johnson with Nicole Cormier, RD

Avon, Massachusetts

An Everything® Series Book.
Everything® and everything.com® are registered trademarks of F+W Media, Inc.

Published by Adams Media, a division of F+W Media, Inc.
57 Littlefield Street, Avon, MA 02322 U.S.A.
www.adamsmedia.com

ISBN 10: 1-4405-0326-5
ISBN 13: 978-1-4405-0326-9

Printed in the United States of America.

20 19 18 17 16 15 14 13 12 11

Library of Congress Cataloging-in-Publication Data
is available from the publisher.

This publication is designed to provide accurate and authoritative information with regard to the subject matter covered. It is sold with the understanding that the publisher is not engaged in rendering legal, accounting, or other professional advice. If legal advice or other expert assistance is required, the services of a competent professional person should be sought.

—From a *Declaration of Principles* jointly adopted by a Committee of the American Bar Association and a Committee of Publishers and Associations

Many of the designations used by manufacturers and sellers to distinguish their products are claimed as trademarks. Where those designations appear in this book and Adams Media was aware of a trademark claim, the designations have been printed with initial capital letters.

The Everything® Juicing Book is intended as a reference volume only, not as a medical manual. In light of the complex, individual, and specific nature of health problems, this book is not intended to replace professional medical advice. The ideas, procedures, and suggestions in this book are intended to supplement, not replace, the advice of a trained medical professional. Consult your physician before adopting the suggestions in this book, as well as about any condition that may require diagnosis or medical attention. The author and publisher disclaim any liability arising directly or indirectly from the use of this book.

This book is available at quantity discounts for bulk purchases.
For information, please call 1-800-289-0963.

Contents

Acknowledgments

Thanks to Katrina Schroeder at Adams Media, and Robert G. DiForio at D4E0 Literary Agency.

Top Ten Reasons to Juice

1. Juicing can help you get your nine recommended daily servings of fruits and vegetables.

2. Juicing is good for digestive health. It aids digestion and can ease conditions such as acid reflux and ulcers.

3. Juicing can help alleviate allergies and respiratory disorders.

4. Juicing can boost your immune system and help your body resist and fight infections.

5. Juicing can help reduce high blood pressure and high levels of bad cholesterol.

6. The fruits and vegetables you use in juicing are very high in antioxidants, which are revered for their anti-aging properties. But antioxidants also improve circulation, contribute to cardiovascular health, enhance brain function, and reduce the negative effects of stress.

7. Juice is high in beneficial vitamins and minerals. It can also help you get enough fiber, protein, and unsaturated fats.

8. Commercial juices often contain added sugars and preservatives. By juicing your own fruits and vegetables, you can tailor your juices to your tastes and needs.

9. Juicing is a low-calorie way to boost your energy level so you can enjoy life more.

10. Juice is simple to make and it tastes delicious!

Introduction

"EAT YOUR VEGETABLES!" IS a familiar battle cry around dinner tables—but Mom hasn't been the only one insisting we eat our peas (carrots, turnips). Since 1990, the U.S. Department of Agriculture has recommended we consume at least two servings of fruits and three servings of vegetables daily, while the United States Cancer Institute suggests we eat five servings of fresh vegetables and three servings of fruit every day—which they have dubbed "the daily eight." Despite those repeated urgings, studies show that most Americans still fall short of the mark, increasing their risk of developing a variety of chronic conditions and serious diseases.

Although most people understand the importance of eating more fruits and vegetables, they often lack the time, energy, or motivation to make it happen. For such people, juicing can be the difference between great health and chronic illness.

Juicing is also an easy and convenient way to consume your daily quota of fruits and vegetables, assimilate vital nutrients more rapidly, hydrate your body, and enjoy a steady stream of energy—all without growing your own organic farm or taking fistfuls of supplements every day. During the juicing process, the cell walls of the fruits and vegetables are sliced open to release a cornucopia of nutrients—including amino acids, chlorophyll, enzymes, minerals, and vitamins—all of which are quickly absorbed by the body once the juice is consumed.

Juicing for health and well-being is not a new trend. It has a rich and illustrious history that dates back to biblical times, when fruits and vegetables were eaten raw and fruits were made into beverages by island peoples.

Today, thanks to the advent of high-tech juicers that make juicing easier, faster, and more fun, juicing has never been more popular. Millions of people have turned to juicing to ward off everyday disorders like colds and migraines, promote longevity, shed excess pounds, enhance memory, reduce stress, treat skin diseases, develop more beautiful and lustrous hair, build stronger nails, and prevent and treat a host of conditions and diseases.

Naturally low in calories and high in fiber, fruits and vegetables facilitate weight loss and are packed with antioxidants and phytochemicals that help prevent serious diseases. Research shows that people who consume generous amounts of fruits and vegetables have a reduced risk of stroke, Type 2 diabetes, some types of cancer, cardiovascular disease, and hypertension.

This combination health guide and cookbook provides all the information you need to become a juicing genie. You'll learn about the best fruits and vegetables ideal for juicing, important tips on the care, handling and storage of fruits and vegetables, and the nutritional and health benefits of specific fruits and vegetables. You'll also get a crash course in juicers as well as 150 recipes that demonstrate how to spin fruits and vegetables into delectable and nutritious juices. Those of you who thought you hated fruits and vegetables are in for a delightful taste sensation!

CHAPTER 1

The Juicing Revolution

More than two-thirds of all deaths in the United States are directly related to nutritional deficiencies, so it's no surprise that many people are turning to juicing to ensure optimum nutrition and health. The juices from fresh fruits and vegetables provide every nutrient needed for health and longevity, condensing the nutrients from several pounds of produce into a quart of beverage. Ninety percent of the antioxidant action in produce is in the fruit, not the fiber. Juicing removes the fiber from produce, allowing the body to more quickly absorb and assimilate nutrients.

The History of Juicing

Juicing is a delicious and nutritious way to replenish the body's stores of minerals and vitamins. Juicing is hardly a new trend. The first written words on juicing are found in the Dead Sea Scrolls, which date from before 150 B.C. to about 70 A.D.

Since the Dawn of Time

History shows that succulent fruits that were especially easy to find, including lemons, oranges, and pomegranates, have been made into beverages by many different cultures since the dawn of time. Island cultures created nutritious drinks from tropical fruits. In Peru, passionfruit was smashed and combined with water to produce a refreshing drink. The Dead Sea Scrolls describe how the Essenes, a desert tribe in ancient Israel, pounded figs and pomegranates into a mash that provided "profound strength and subtle form."

The Need for Juicing in the Twentieth Century

The biggest advocate of juicing in the twentieth century was Dr. Norman W. Walker, an English researcher and author. His book, *Raw Vegetable Juices*, published in 1936, introduced juicing to the modern age.

Today, the benefits of fresh juice are more important than ever. The modern diet has strayed dramatically from the natural diet that our ancestors followed. Commercial farming methods have robbed the soil of important mineral contents, resulting in fruits and vegetables that are severely lacking in vitamins and minerals.

The late Dr. Linus Pauling, winner of two Nobel Prizes, attributed most disease, illness, and ailments to mineral deficiencies in the diet and soil. He claimed that the increasing incidence of disease could be blamed in part on the adoption of commercial farming procedures in the United States, which rob the soil and produce of mineral content.

Pauling charged that crops are raised in toxic soil laced with commercial crop fertilizers that contain petroleum and other unhealthy chemicals, genetically altered foods are grown and harvested in unnatural settings, and farm animals are raised in unsanitary conditions and fed steroids to pump up their market weight. In addition, some scientists believe the world's seafood supply, once a reliable source of minerals, has become so contaminated by environmental poisons that some health experts advise against eating such popular seafood as tuna, shrimp, and scallops.

ALERT

Convenience and fast foods, which are seriously lacking in nutrients, have become a wobbly source of fuel for many time-crunched Americans. Many commercial products are made with refined white flour, which loses 90 percent of its vitamin and mineral content during the refinement process.

Over the past sixty years, there's been a sharp decline in the variety of foods that are being grown. Modern day agriculture emphasizes growing a handful of reliable and profitable crops over the smorgasbord of varieties grown by farmers in centuries past, which provided a fuller spectrum of vitamins and minerals. Today, the typical American eats fewer than twenty different kinds of food. In addition, modern food processing relies on overcooking, packaging and storage, and shipping procedures that transport food states, countries, and even continents away from where it was grown, thus robbing it of its nutritional value.

Juicing can help put nutrition back in your life. It condenses the nutrients of many different types of produce into one glass.

The Culinary Joys of Juicing

If you love fresh fruits and vegetables, you probably don't need anyone to tell you that drinking them in juice form is equally delicious. But you may not realize that becoming a juicer will open you up to an endless array of new tastes, flavors, and textures.

Instead of crunching into a boring old apple, orange, or banana—you already know what they taste like—you can combine them in a juicer and create an exciting new drink. Toss in a handful of pitted cherries, a splash of lemon or lime juice, or a pinch of your favorite herbs, and voila! You have a totally new and different juice (and new added nutrients) with very little effort.

A Family Affair

Juicing is also an easy and delicious way to encourage your family to eat their veggies without having a showdown at the dinner table. In fact, once you set up a juicer in the kitchen, good luck getting your kids to stay away. They'll be so fascinated by the chance to create their own personal drink that reminding them to eat their veggies may become a thing of the past.

The Juice Pharmacy

Juicing is an easy way to replenish necessary vitamins and minerals without growing your own organic farm or taking fistfuls of supplements every day.

During the juicing process, the cell walls of fruits and vegetables are sliced open to release nutrients, including amino acids, chlorophyll, enzymes, minerals, and vitamins, all of which are quickly absorbed by the body once the juice is consumed.

A-to-Z Nutrients

If you're looking for something nutritious to consume, it doesn't get much better than fresh squeezed juice, an easy, delicious, and convenient way to get your fruits and vegetables. Here are just a few of the many nutrients you can get in a single glass of juice.

Amino Acids

The building blocks of protein, amino acids comprise more than half of your body's non-water weight. If you don't have enough, your body can't provide the many functions necessary for health

Antioxidants

The latest and trendiest heroes of the nutrition world, antioxidants are substances that protect your cells against the effects of free radicals. Free radicals are molecules that are produced when your body breaks down food or when you are exposed to environmental toxins like tobacco smoke, radiation, and pollution. Free radicals can damage cells and may play a role in heart disease, cancer, and multiple other diseases.

Carbohydrates

Fruits are high in both simple and complex carbohydrates, quickly absorbed molecules that provide you with a ready source of energy. Complex carbohydrates, found in root vegetables and potatoes, are broken down more slowly than the simple carbohydrates found in sweeter fruits like apples, oranges, and cherries. By releasing a more gradual supply of sugar, complex carbs help maintain steady glucose levels, which is especially important for diabetics.

ESSENTIAL

Medical science is only beginning to identify the hundreds of thousands of different antioxidants found in fruits and vegetables. A few of the more common antioxidants include beta-carotene, lutein, and lycopene, although many vitamins, including vitamins A, C, and E, also contain antioxidants. New research indicates that antioxidants help promote endurance, slow aging, and improve mental functions.

Chlorophyll

Chlorophyll helps your body's organs (especially your liver) eliminate toxins by improving cellular and organ detoxification. Chlorophyll also has anti-cancer properties and can prevent carcinogens from binding to the DNA in your body's cells. It also protects against the formation of calcium stones in the kidneys and helps break them down and eliminate them.

FACT

Chlorophyll helps the body maintain a proper acid-alkaline balance. This is especially important today because most Americans eat a diet that is extremely high in acids and low in alkaline foods. Studies show that a high-acid environment in the body may predispose it to cancer.

Juicing dark, leafy green vegetables is one of the best ways to consume an adequate amount of chlorophyll, especially chard, collard greens, romaine lettuce, kale, parsley, and wheatgrass. Cabbage, celery, cucumbers, green pepper, spinach, turnip greens, and watercress are also high in chlorophyll, and can be mixed and matched to create delicious and energizing juices.

Essential Amino Acids

These essential eight acids are not manufactured by the body and can only be supplied from the food you eat. Amino acids are responsible for thousands of bodily functions, including repairing and building muscle, blood, and organs; manufacturing hormones; and maintaining a healthy immune system, mental functions, circulation, sleep, memory, and physical and mental energy.

ALERT

A deficiency in just one amino acid can cause accelerated aging, hormonal imbalances, sleep problems, impaired brain function, allergies, and gastrointestinal problems, and lessen your body's ability to repair and regenerate itself. Juices, especially those made with dark, leafy greens and sprouts, provide the body with a wide range of amino acids that are easily digested and absorbed.

Enzymes

These biochemicals act as catalysts to trigger a wide variety of functions in your body, including regenerating and maintaining fluids, cells, tissues, and organs. Researchers have identified about 1,000 enzymes, many of which are found in fresh fruits and vegetables. Enzymes are destroyed by heat—another reason why raw fruits, vegetables, and juices are so healthy. Without enzymes, your body can't carry out necessary functions or make the most of nutrients found in other foods.

Fats

While fat is often vilified, you actually couldn't live without a little bit of the good type of fat. Unsaturated fat is found in vegetables like avocados, olives, nuts and seeds, and heart-healthy oils and butters derived from olives, almonds, walnuts, safflowers, sunflowers, and others.

Fiber

Fiber is a type of carbohydrate found in fruits and vegetables that resists your body's efforts to digest it via enzymes and acids. Soluble fiber forms a gel-like substance in your digestive track that binds cholesterol so it can't be reabsorbed. Insoluble fiber, often called nature's broom, decreases the time food spends in your intestines before it is eliminated as waste. All fruits and vegetables are loaded with fiber.

Minerals

Minerals are found in abundance in fresh fruits and vegetables, especially organically grown produce. Minerals like calcium and magnesium are important for building and repairing bones, teeth, hair, and nails. Potassium, sodium, chloride, and calcium are essential for regulating the body's balance of electrolytes. Trace minerals, or those the body needs in minuscule amounts, including chromium, copper, fluoride, boron, and selenium, play an important role in many bodily functions, including metabolism and hair and nail growth.

Omega-3 Fatty Acids

Omega-3 fatty acids are the real heroes of the fat world. They are found in fruits and vegetables and in higher concentrates in oily fish such as salmon, tuna, and mackerel. Omega-3 fatty acids decrease the risk of heart attacks by causing blood platelets to become less sticky and reducing the inflammation found in autoimmune diseases such as arthritis and colitis.

Phytochemicals

Phytochemicals are non-nutritive plant chemicals that have protective or disease preventive properties. There are more than 1,000 known phytochemicals, although scientists believe there are thousands more yet to be discovered. Fruits and vegetables produce phytochemicals to protect themselves from illness and attack, and recent research has demonstrated that phytochemicals can also protect humans from diseases. Some of the most well-known phytochemicals found in produce include lycopene in tomatoes, isoflavones in soy, and flavonoids in fruits.

Most phytochemicals have antioxidant activity and protect cells against oxidative damage and reduce the risk of developing certain types of cancer. Phytochemicals with antioxidant activity include allyl sulfides (found in onions, leeks, and garlic); carotenoids (found in fruits and carrots); flavonoids (found in fruits and vegetables); and polyphenols (found in tea and grapes).

Isoflavones, found in soy, imitate human estrogens and help reduce menopausal symptoms and osteoporosis. Phytochemicals such as indoles, found in cabbage, stimulate enzymes that make estrogen less effective, and may also reduce the risk of breast cancer. Other phytochemicals that interfere with enzymes include protease inhibitors (found in soy and beans) and terpenes (found in citrus fruits and cherries). Saponins, a phytochemical found in beans, interferes with the replication of cell DNA, thereby preventing the multiplication of cancer cells. Capsaicin, which is found in hot peppers, protects DNA from carcinogens. The phytochemical allicin, found in garlic, has antibacterial properties.

The phytochemicals in cranberries bind to cell walls to prevent the adhesion of pathogens to human cell walls. This explains why cranberries not only prevent urinary tract infections but also improve dental health—plaque can't stick to the teeth.

Protein

Protein is found in virtually every cell in your body, from your skin and hair to your nails, as well as your bones, muscles, and cartilage. It's necessary for the manufacturing of hormones, enzymes, and other chemicals in your body. Protein is classified as a macronutrient because your body needs large amounts of it. Vitamins and minerals, on the other hand, are called micronutrients because you only need them in small amounts for health. Because your body can't store protein, you need to consume a sufficient amount in your daily diet to replenish supplies, which means you must consume it on a regular basis. Scientists believe that vegetable sources of protein, such as beans, nuts, and whole grains, are the best choices. They offer healthy fiber, vitamins, and minerals without the unhealthy saturated fat found in animal protein sources. Tofu and other soy foods are an excellent red meat alternative, provided you don't overdo it. Two to four servings a week is considered a healthy amount.

Vitamins

Vitamins are substances necessary to sustain life. Fruits and vegetables provide a wide array of essential vitamins, including most of the following vitamins recognized in the United States: biotin, carotenes, folate (folic acid), vitamin A, vitamin B complex, vitamin B1 (thiamin), vitamin B12 (cobalamin), vitamin B2 (riboflavin), vitamin B3 (niacin), vitamin B5 (pantothenic acid), vitamin B6 (pyridoxine), vitamin C, vitamin D, vitamin E, and vitamin K.

FACT

Needed only in small amounts, the body must get vitamins from food because they are either not made in the body or made in quantities that are too small for growth, vitality and well-being. A deficiency of a particular vitamin causes disease symptoms that can only be cured by that vitamin.

Water

Our cells are primarily composed of water, which is necessary for their proper function. Raw juice, unlike coffee, soft drinks, or alcoholic beverages, supplies the water you need to replenish lost fluids. It also provides necessary vitamins, minerals, enzymes, and phytochemicals. Juice helps the body maintain proper alkaline balance, which is necessary for immune and metabolic function.

Nutritional Benefits of Juicing

Freshly squeezed fruits and vegetables are the kings of the food kingdom, for several reasons. Fruits and vegetables provide a wealth of nutritional benefits that could never be squeezed into a vitamin supplement. Also, no other health food on earth can be so quickly digested and absorbed by the body.

Why Not Just Eat or Cook with Produce?

There's absolutely nothing wrong with eating fruits and vegetables, or cooking them and enjoying them with meals. But there are several reasons why juicing is a more effective way of ensuring you get the most bang from your buck when you're dealing with fresh produce.

✓ Juicing filters out the fiber contained in fruits and vegetables and leaves you with a concentrated array of nutrients, making it an easier and convenient way to consume a greater volume of produce than you could ever comfortably consume in raw or cooked form.
✓ Unlike most forms of cooking, juicing does not destroy any of the nutrients in fruits and vegetables.
✓ Fresh produce doesn't contain any of the unhealthy fillers or ingredients that prepared produce may contain. You don't have to read any labels or do any guesswork to know your juice is 100 percent natural.
✓ Because juicing removes the fiber from produce, the result is juice that is almost completely self-digesting. The nutrients are absorbed almost immediately by your body.
✓ Juicing makes it easy to achieve what's sometimes called rainbow nutrition, or consuming the widest possible variety of fruits and vegetables every day. The color of each fruit or vegetable signals its unique vitamins, minerals, trace minerals, antioxidants, anti-carcinogens, detoxifying agents, digestive aids, natural blood purifiers, blood thinners, immune stimulants, and memory enhancers.
✓ Juicing makes it easy to get the recommended five daily servings of fruits and vegetables for health and disease prevention.

ALERT

According to the National Institutes of Health, most people get less than 75 percent of the recommended daily allowance (RDA) of essential nutrients. Because nearly all the necessary vitamins and minerals for health are found in fruits and vegetables, juicing is a fast, easy, delicious, and guaranteed way to cover your nutritional bases.

The Synergy Connection

Many nutrients need to work with other nutrients to enjoy maximum performance and really strut their nutritional stuff. For instance, vitamin E is most effective when it's combined with vitamin C and the mineral selenium, while beta-carotene boosts the benefits of zinc and many other nutrients.

Looking for fast energy? Fruits and vegetables have the highest rate of bioavailability of all foods. That means your body can make full use of the nutrients in juice within forty-five minutes to two hours after you drink it. As a side bonus, juicing also helps reverse digestive problems caused by food additives, preservatives, overcooking, and processed foods.

Juicing for Enzyme Action

Fresh juice contains tons of enzymes—chemicals in fruits and vegetables that are catalysts for the biochemical reactions behind every function the body performs. Fruits and vegetables have digestive enzymes that help the body digest carbohydrates, fats, fiber, and proteins, and convert large food chemicals into smaller ones that are more easily absorbed and used by the body.

Health and Disease Prevention Benefits of Juicing

One of the most healthful properties of juicing is that it allows your body to easily assimilate key enzymes, vitamins, minerals, phytochemicals, antioxidants, and minerals like iron, copper, boron, potassium, sodium, iodine, and magnesium. In whole fruits and vegetables, these nutrients are trapped in indigestible fiber, which prevents them from being immediately assimilated by the body.

Juicing and Disease Prevention

Juicing can eliminate acid reflux disease, stomach ulcers, gallstones, and other digestive disorders. It can also reverse diabetes and stabilize blood sugar within just a few days.

Juicing can also boost your immune function and make you increasingly immune to colds, the flu, and other infectious diseases. In addition, it can normalize your sleep, increase your energy and stamina, and enhance cellular energy, helping you ward off any number of infectious diseases. The powerful alkalizing effect of juicing can also help restore bone density and reverse osteoporosis.

FACT

The natural medicine in nature's juices can help prevent cancer, halt tumor growth, and destroy cancer cells. Type 2 diabetics who incorporate juicing into their daily regimens often find they can go off or dramatically decrease their insulin medication. If you've had a heart problem, juicing can reverse blocked arteries, clear out the cardiovascular system, and prevent heart attacks.

If you have some pounds and inches to lose, juicing can also help detoxify your body and help you lose weight quickly and permanently without starving. In addition, juicing can also keep your body's organs and tissues hydrated and healthy and detoxify the liver, gallbladder, kidneys, heart, and brain using safe, natural cleansing processes. Juicing can enhance learning and creativity and improve memory and cognitive function.

The Anti-Aging Benefits of Juicing

Research has shown that certain nutrients slow the visible signs of aging, prevent many disorders, and extend life expectancy. While you've been told time and again to get your daily vitamins and to eat lots of fresh fruits and vegetables every day, when was the last time you actually got two servings of fruit and seven servings of vegetables in your daily diet?

The Problem with SAD

Unfortunately, the standard American diet (SAD) does not provide the nutrients your body desperately needs to function properly. In fact, it contributes to the acceleration of aging more than any single factor and increases the incidence of free radical exposure.

FACT

Free radicals start in the environment, are ingested with food, and then form within your body. Pesticides, insecticides, fried foods, barbequed foods, charbroiled foods, alcohol, coffee, and artificial additives are all sources of free radical exposure.

Juicing ensures you get sufficient amounts of phytochemicals, substances in plants that are considered among the most powerful ways to fight disease. While most people would find it difficult to eat enough raw fruits and vegetables to get the necessary amounts of phytochemicals, no one would have trouble drinking enough juice to get sufficient amounts of these powerful nutrients.

Juicing for Weight Loss

The many enzymes in fruits and vegetables play an integral role in maintaining a healthy metabolism, which means juicing can also help improve a sluggish metabolism and make it easier for you to shed unwanted pounds, have sufficient energy to exercise regularly, and keep the lost pounds off. Because fruits and vegetables provide a lot of fiber and water, they also aid weight loss by filling you up with very few calories.

The Fountain of Youth?

If you're looking for a way to age gracefully, you may want to try juicing. Research shows that the concentration of antioxidants in juice combats the damaging effects that free radicals have on skin and muscle.

Juicing has been proven to help keep skin wrinkle-free and muscles well toned. In addition, increasing the intake of antioxidants by juicing can slow the onset of age-related illnesses.

Juicing and Alzheimer's

But perhaps the most exciting news about juicing concerns its ability to ward off Alzheimer's disease. A recent study conducted by Vanderbilt University shows that drinking fruit and vegetable juice more than three times a week can dramatically cut your chances of developing Alzheimer's.

Juicy Truths and Myths

Before you delve into the details of juicing and invest in a juicer, take a moment to separate the truth from the bunk about juicing.

Some claim juicing is a waste of time, energy, and money, and that you're much better off just eating the whole fruit and skipping the juicing. The fact is that while fruits and vegetables are extremely nutritious when they are eaten raw and whole, the fiber they contain means the nutrients take longer to absorb and assimilate.

FACT

> Most fruits and vegetables undergo a great deal of abuse before going into a can or bottle. When fruits and vegetables are frozen as concentrates, chemical processes destroy much of their nutrients and enzymes, and make them a far cry from freshly made "living" juices.

According to the Department of Agriculture, 90 percent of the antioxidant action in fruit is in the juice, not the fiber. It's hard for most people to eat enough raw fruits and vegetables to equal what they'd get in a quart of juice. Remember that a quart of vegetable juice equals five pounds of tomatoes!

CHAPTER 2

Gearing Up for Juicing

Juicing is extremely simple, but it pays to invest in a quality juicer and learn the ins and outs of juicing techniques before attempting to create your own beverages. Your pre-juicing education should include learning how to take care of your juicer so it lasts for years, the best (and the worst) fruits and vegetables for juicing, additional accessories that can make juicing faster and more enjoyable, the importance of buying organic and locally grown produce, and how to store your juice to ensure maximum nutrition and flavor.

Types of Juicers

A juicer is a mechanical device that can be operated, either manually or electrically, to extract juice from vegetables, fruits, and leafy greens. There are different types, depending on the fruit or the vegetable.

ALERT

Don't confuse a blender with a juicer; they are two different animals. You'll need a juicer for the recipes in this book. A juicer has a mechanism that will separate the pulp from the juice, whereas a blender grinds the produce and the pulp has to be manually strained.

Centrifugal Versus Masticating Juicers

Centrifugal juicers are one of the oldest types and have a simple design with a shredder and a strainer. A spinning basket shreds the produce and then forces the juice through a fine strainer by centrifugal force. This process adds oxygen to the juices and makes them a little frothy.

In masticating juicers, the produce is squeezed through gears that crush the produce and force it through a fine strainer. The pulp is continuously extracted, and because the machine doesn't generate heat or friction, nutrients are preserved.

FACT

Both types of juicers work efficiently, so the best type is the one that works best for your needs. Although few stores will let you test-run a juicer before purchasing to ensure it's a good fit, you can find video demos and information online to help you make a decision.

Buying the Perfect Juicer

Cost is one of the biggest factors in choosing a juicer. Though high price doesn't necessarily mean high quality, there is always a certain amount of correlation between the two. Juicers range anywhere from $75 to $350—and you usually get what you pay for.

Factors to Consider

Besides cost, there are other important factors to be considered before putting down money for a juicer:

- **Ease of use.** Look for an easy-to-use juicer that does not require much time and effort to operate and clean.
- **Reliability.** Buy a trusted brand that does not require you to replace parts often.
- **Horsepower.** Make sure your juicer has at least 0.5 horsepower to avoid burning out.
- **Multiple speeds.** Buy a quality juicer that has at least two speeds—high for harder jobs and slow for easier ones. Inexpensive juicers have only one high speed. In addition, make sure your machine has electronic circuitry that maintains blade speed during juicing.
- **Feed tube.** Look for a juicer with a large feed tube to avoid having to cut produce into teensy pieces. Also, make sure the tube is easy to use at your height.
- **Versatility.** Make sure your machine can handle tough, hard vegetables and fruits like carrots, pineapple skins, watermelon rinds, and beets, as well as delicate greens like lettuce, parsley, and herbs.
- **Output.** Check out how much juice your model can extract from the given quantity of food, choosing machines that remove at least 90 percent of the juice from the pulp. Some models yield more pulp than juice: Models that extract the pulp to an outside container leave less pulp behind than those that separate the pulp inside the machine.
- **Size.** Make sure you buy the right size juicer for your needs. If you plan to create juice just for yourself, choose a juicer with a beaker that holds a cup.
- **Continuous juicing.** Choose a machine that ejects pulp into a receptacle rather than a juicer that keeps the pulp in a center basket. Juicers with center baskets require that you stop the machine and wash out the basket frequently in order to continue juicing.
- **Simplicity.** Choose a juicer that has only a few parts to clean. The more parts a juicer has, and the harder and more complicated it is to wash, the longer it will take to clean and reassemble—and the less likely you'll be to want to use it again. Also, make sure all the washable parts

of your juicer are dishwasher safe. In general, centrifugal juicers are easier to clean than masticating juicers.

- **Quality.** Make sure your juicer sits securely and solidly on your counter and doesn't jiggle around when you use it. You want to feed your body, not your floor!
- **Noise.** Choose a juicer that is quiet. Some brands are so loud you may need to wear earplugs to use them. In general, centrifugal juicers and more expensive models tend to be quieter than masticating models.

FACT

Some of the popular and reliable brands of juicers include Champion, Omega, Nutrisource, Lequip, Juice Fountain, Samson, Solo Star, Green Star, and Green Power. You can find reviews from *Consumer Reports*, but you might also want to get first-hand reviews from friends and family who already own juicers.

Care and Feeding of Your Juicer

Like any home appliance, your juicer will last much longer if you respect its size, limitations, and quirks, and keep it clean and in good working order after each use. If you're buying a used model, you may want to have a veteran juicer look it over before you use it for the first time. The last thing you want to do is butcher fruits and vegetables and render them useless for your juices. Plus, it's always better to be safe than sorry when it comes to dealing with appliances that have motors and sharp blades.

Juicing Do's and Don'ts

Here are a few tips and trade secrets to ensure smooth juicing:

✓ Wash all produce before juicing. Remove bruises, mold, blemishes, and dings.

✓ Go organic. The price is more than worth the health benefits. Otherwise, you'll have to peel everything before placing it in the juicer and lose out on lots of nutrients. Non-organic produce is sprayed with pesticides that penetrate the peels and skins of produce—the largest source of nutrients in produce.

✓ Always peel oranges, tangerines, bananas, avocados, kiwifruits, pineapples, and grapefruit, even if they're organic.

✓ Don't remove the stems and leaves of most produce, including beet stems and leaves, strawberry caps, and small grape stems. They contain a high concentration of nutrients and won't hurt you or your juicer.

✓ Cut most fruits and vegetables into strips or sections that fit easily into your juicer's tube without forcing or jamming. With experience, you'll learn what size works best for your particular machine.

✓ Insert a grocery store-sized plastic bag in the pulp receptacle of your juicer to catch the pulp during juicing. When you've finished making your juice, you can either throw away the pulp, or save it for cooking or composting, and there's no need to wash the pulp receptacle after each use.

Necessary Accessories for Juicing

In addition to a quality juicer, you'll also need some other simple equipment, some of which you may already have around the house. If you don't have a selection of sharp knives for peeling, chopping, and coring, now's the time to invest in them.

Juicing Essentials

Buy a stiff brush for scrubbing vegetables like carrots and beets. Also invest in a quality peeler that removes the least amount of skin possible so you aren't peeling away nutrients found in the skin and directly under.

You'll also need a sieve for straining juices, measuring cups and spoons, and flexible rubber spatulas. Make sure everything is plastic, not wood, to avoid transferring potentially dangerous bacteria into your juices.

Be Clean and Safe

Counter tops, cutting boards, utensils, and any other equipment that comes into direct contact with fresh produce should be thoroughly washed with hot water and soap. Rinse and sanitize them with a mild bleach solution, then air-dry them. Immediately place peeled or cut fruits and vegetables on a separate clean plate and avoid putting them back on the cutting board.

If you've been using a wooden cutting board, now's the time to heave it and replace it with a heavy plastic cutting board that fits in your dishwasher for easy cleaning. Wooden cutting boards are porous and absorb bacteria and allow it to grow. The same goes for sponges, which soak up bacteria.

The Importance of Organic

Whenever possible, use organic fruits and vegetables for juicing. Organic produce is grown without synthetic fertilizers and chemical biocides. Every year, the conventional U.S. agriculture industry goes through more than 1 billion pounds of pesticides and herbicides. Only 2 percent of that actually kills insects; the remaining 98 percent goes into the soil, air, water, and food supply—including the nonorganic fruits and veggies you eat! Buying and consuming organic produce is one way to circumvent this health hazard.

Because organic farming does not use chemicals to preserve produce, it focuses on growing crops in season. By using organic produce grown in the United States, you'll use fruits and vegetables that are grown in season rather than imported from foreign countries where organic standards may not be as high and where carcinogenic sprays are still legal.

No chemicals or pesticides are used in the organic growing process. In 2002, the National Organic Program, administered by the U.S. Department of Agriculture, prohibited the use of chemicals in organic farming and stipulated management practices "with an intent to restore and then maintain ecological harmony on the farm, its surrounding environment, and ultimately, the whole planetary ecosystem."

When choosing organic produce, look for labels marked "certified" organic. This guarantees that the produce has been grown according to the strict standards set forth by the National Organic Program, including inspection of farms and processing facilities, detailed record keeping, and testing the soil and water for pesticides to ensure government standards are met. Labels reading "transitional organic" mean the food was grown on a farm that has recently converted or is in the process of converting from conventional to organic farming practices.

The Argument for Organic Produce in Juicing

It's especially important to buy organic when purchasing produce that is particularly vulnerable to pesticide contamination. This includes apples, apricots, bell peppers, cherries, celery, grapes, green beans, cucumbers, peaches, spinach, and strawberries.

You should also steer clear of produce that's been irradiated, or subjected to gamma ray radiation to kill pests and germs and prolong shelf life. Irradiation can lead to the formation of dangerous chemicals in produce called radiolytic products, which include formaldehyde and benzene.

Although the FDA has approved irradiation, the average dose to decontaminate some produce has been measured at levels that are 5 million times what you'd receive in a chest x-ray. That's a dangerous amount of radiation, and it also kills off vitamins and minerals. The process of irradiating fruits and vegetables is especially dangerous because the large amount of water in produce triggers a greater production of free radicals—toxins that damage cells and lead to multiple diseases and premature aging.

The Importance of Buying Local

In addition to buying organic produce, you'll also get more nutritional bang from your buck if you buy produce that was grown locally or regionally. Experts agree that fruits, vegetables, and greens provide peak nutrition when they are ripe. Unfortunately, more than 60 percent of the commercial produce in the United States is picked before it's ripe, which means the produce you buy doesn't have its full nutritional component.

ALERT

Early harvesting practices are common in the three states responsible for growing and producing the bulk of the country's produce—California, Texas, and Florida. Once harvested, much of the produce is packed and shipped elsewhere. That means it is days or weeks old—and yet still not naturally ripe—before it hits your supermarket shelves.

Dangerous Additives

In addition to early harvesting practices, modern agriculture has introduced fungicides, coolants, and chemicals to enhance the appearance of produce and slow the rate of perishing. Local and regionally grown produce doesn't have to be picked before it ripens because it isn't traveling far to get to the supermarket. This gives it a chance to ripen on the vine, ensuring you get maximum nutrition from your produce.

If your supermarket doesn't carry local organic produce, try your local health food store or a local farmer's market. You can also request that your supermarket begin stocking local organic produce. You probably aren't the only patron who wants it.

Grow Your Own

If all else fails, you can always grow your own organic produce. The good news is it's not as complicated or difficult as you may think. If you don't have a green thumb, there are tons of books, magazines, and websites out there to help you such as *The Everything® Grow Your Own Vegetables Book*.

When you begin juicing, you'll already have the beginnings of a compost heap, a necessity in organic gardening. Find an out-of-the-way place in your garden and make a pile of leaves and grass. Save your fruit peels, cores, seeds, and pulp along with coffee grounds and filters, tea bags, and other compostables in a milk carton and mix them with the leaves. Throw a handful of dirt on top of the pile and stir it with a shovel. Nature will do the rest!

You're in Control!

The best thing about backyard organic gardens is that you're in control of the fertilizers, pesticides, herbicides, and growing aids you use. Avoid toxic weed killers and pesticides, and opt for all-natural alternatives that will not harm the soil, animals, or your family. Limit weeds and reduce the need for chemical-laden weed killers by weeding regularly and using natural or reclaimed ground cover between your food plants. Store-bought weed prevention products are also available in ready-to-use natural and organic versions, including Preen Organic Vegetable Garden Weed, Perfectly Natural Weed N Grass Killer, Weed Pharm Organic Weed Control, and Green Light Organic Spot Weeder.

If you have access to a deck, a roof, or even a small patch of ground, you can grow your own produce. Herbs can be grown on a windowsill, and tomato and bell pepper plants can thrive in a container on a balcony or patio. Hanging containers are a great way to grow smaller vegetable and fruit plants or herbs without taking up any floor space.

Organic Gardening Resources

For complete details and lots of encouragement on growing your own backyard or patio organic garden, check out these helpful websites:

- *www.the-organic-gardener.com*
- *www.your-vegetable-gardening-helper.com*
- *www.organicgardening.com*, the companion site to the magazine *Organic Gardening*
- *www.organic-gardening.net*
- *www.organicgardeningguru.com*
- *www.organicgardeninfo.com*

Rodale's New Encyclopedia of Organic Gardening is a classic basic reference for home gardeners. You might also want to join a local gardening club to stay abreast of what grows best in your soil.

The Un-Juiceables

Unfortunately, not every fruit or vegetable—or even every part of every fruit or vegetable—lends itself to juicing.

Fruits with Low Water Content

Fruits that don't do well in juicers include those with a low water content, including bananas and avocados. You can still include these in your juice, but run them through a juicer alone before adding them to the main juice.

Produce that Doesn't Yield a Lot of Juice

Fruits that don't separate easily from their pulp in juicers include papaya, coconut, strawberries, cantaloupe, honeydew, peach, plums, and prunes. For best results, juice separately and add to the juice mixture.

FACT

Dried fruits, including raisins, figs, and dried fruit, also won't work well in your juicier. However, if you're gung-ho for fig juice, soak 1 cup figs in 1 quart water for 8 to 10 hours. You'll wind up with a pretty tasty beverage.

Parts of Produce Your Juicer Won't Like

In addition to produce that doesn't have enough water content to juice, there's also a category of leaves, stems, and skins of otherwise juiceable produce that should never go into your juicer. They include:

- ✓ The peels of oranges, grapefruit, tangerines and nectarines contain bitter oils that may cause digestive problems. (Lemon and lime peels can be juiced if they are organic.)
- ✓ Hold the pits, stones, and hard seeds from peaches, plums, apricots, cherries, and mangos. They are too big and hard for your juicer to digest and could cause damage. Softer seeds from oranges, lemons, watermelons, cantaloupe, and grapes can be juiced without hurting you or your juicer.

- ✓ Apple seeds contain small amounts of cyanide, a poison that may cause problems for children, the elderly, and adults with food sensitivities.
- ✓ The peels of mangos and papayas contain irritants that may be harmful if eaten in large quantities.
- ✓ Larger stems from grapes will dull your juicer blade.
- ✓ Carrot and rhubarb greens are bitter and contain toxic substances.
- ✓ The peels of any produce grown in a foreign country where carcinogenic pesticides are legal and still used should never be juiced.

Of course, you never want to juice any part of a fruit or vegetable that has a bruise, splotch, mold, or ding. For the best results, make sure everything you put in your juicer is freshly washed, scrubbed free of dirt, and completely free of blemishes.

Extending the Life of Juice

Juice is a very fragile creation that spoils quickly. To get maximum nutrients from your juice, drink it immediately if possible. Juice spoils quickly, often after just twenty-four hours—even when refrigerated.

ALERT

Juice from melons, cabbages, and cruciferous vegetables should never be stored or refrigerated. If you make juice containing these fruits and vegetables, consume it immediately and toss any remaining juice.

Storage Tips

If you can't consume your homemade juice creations right away, store them in the refrigerator in an airtight, opaque, and insulated container. Light, heat, and air will zap nutrients and turn juice brown.

Fresh From the Freezer

If you can't find fresh fruits for your favorite juices, you can substitute dry-packed frozen fruits, available in your local supermarket and packaged without added sugar or syrup. You may lose a bit of the fresh taste. Some nutrients may also be lost, although many remain intact when produce is dry-packed.

Also consider buying large quantities of your favorite fruits when locally available and freezing them yourself for later use. Drinking juice from frozen fruit is better than drinking no juice at all.

FACT

To freeze fruit in a jiffy, clean, slice, peel, or section fruits into pieces no bigger than an inch, spread across a baking sheet, cover with plastic, and put in the freezer until frozen. Transfer fruit to a heavy, resealable plastic bag, date it, and use within two months.

While frozen fruit is fine for juicing, you won't want to use canned fruit unless you're really desperate. Besides being soft and mushy, the fruit in cans is loaded with sugar and often packed in sugary syrup—neither of which will enhance the taste or texture of your juice.

CHAPTER 3

Basic Juicing Ingredients

Organic produce is the best choice for juicing, and growing fruits and vegetables in your backyard garden is the easiest way to ensure they haven't been contaminated by dangerous herbicides or pesticides. If you don't have the time or space to grow your own, purchase locally or regionally grown organic produce in your local health food store, farmer's market, or supermarket. Organic produce doesn't expose you to the dangerous chemicals used in commercial agriculture, ensuring that you'll get maximum nutrients from the fruits and vegetables you juice.

Best Juicing Fruits

Fruits, whether they grow on trees, in the ground, or on bushes, are packed with vitamins and acids that naturally cleanse and purify the body. Called the body's cleansers, fruits contains both simple and complex carbohydrates and release energy over an extended period of time.

Fresh fruits are also great stores of solar energy, ripening more slowly than most other foods and soaking up large sources of vitamin C, which strengthens the immune system, helps ward off infection, and builds strong bones, teeth, and nails.

Focus on Citric Acid

The acids in fruits are what give them their tart, or puckery, flavor. Citric acid is found most abundantly in lemons and other citrus fruit, including lime, grapefruit, orange, cranberry, strawberry, raspberry, pineapple, peach, and tomato. Acids scour away strong bacteria and waste in the body's tissues and facilitate healing.

Enzymes in Fruits

All fruits contain powerful enzymes that have powerful antibacterial qualities. Enzymes help cleanse the gastrointestinal system by digesting and neutralizing excess protein and fat. If consumed regularly, fruit enzymes can also help flush out the tissues, organs, and muscles by ridding them of these same excesses.

The Fluid Connection

In addition to acids and enzymes, fruits also provide a highly purified source of liquids to the body. This helps dilute acidity and build strong bones and teeth.

Fruits of the Tree and Vine

From apples to watermelon, fruits of the tree and vine provide an abundance of life-enhancing and disease-fighting vitamins, minerals, antioxidants, and phytochemicals.

Fruits of the Tree

Tree fruits are as American as apple pie and are a highly versatile player in juicing, contributing a wide range of flavors, colors, and textures. Here are some of the most popular fruits:

- **Apples.** Rich in vitamins A, B-1, B-2, B-6, C, folic acid, biotin, and a host of minerals that promote healthy skin, hair, and nails, apples also contain pectin, a fiber that absorbs toxins, stimulates digestion, and helps reduce cholesterol. Apples are extremely versatile and blend well with other juices. Yield per pound: six to eight ounces of juice.
- **Apricots.** Apricots are high in beta-carotene and vitamin A and are a good source of fiber and potassium. Yield per pound: six ounces of juice.
- **Cherries.** Rich in vitamins A, B, C, folic acid, niacin, and minerals, cherries are potent alkalizers that reduce the acidity of the blood, making them effective in reducing gout, arthritis, and prostate disorders. Yield per pound of pitted cherries: six to eight ounces of juice.
- **Grapefruit.** Rich in vitamin C, calcium, phosphorous, and potassium, the pink and red varieties of grapefruit are sweeter and less acidic than white grapefruit. Grapefruit helps strengthen capillary walls, heal bruising, and reduce skin colds, ear disorders, fever, indigestion, scurvy, varicose veins, obesity, and morning sickness. Yield per pound: six to eight ounces of juice.
- **Lemons.** Lemons are high in citric acid and vitamin C, so a little goes a long way in juicing. Their high antioxidant content and antibacterial properties relieve colds, sore throats, and skin infections, and also help reduce anemia, blood disorders, constipation, ear disorders, gout, indigestion, scurvy, skin infections, and obesity. Yield per pound: four to five ounces of juice.
- **Oranges.** A rich source of vitamins C, B, K, biotin, folic acid, amino acids, and minerals, oranges cleanse the gastrointestinal track, strengthen capillary walls, and benefit the heart and lungs. Oranges help reduce anemia, blood disorders, colds, fever, heart disease, high blood pressure, liver disorders, lung disorders, skin disorders, pneumonia, rheumatism, scurvy, and obesity. Yield per pound: six to eight ounces of juice.

- **Limes.** Similar to lemons in nutrients but not as acidic or cleansing, limes can be substituted for lemons in juice recipes. Yield per pound: four to five ounces of juice.
- **Peaches and nectarines.** High in beta-carotene and vitamin B, C, niacin and minerals, peaches and nectarines cleanse the intestines and help relieve morning sickness. Yield per pound: one to three ounces of juice.
- **Pears.** Rich in fiber and vitamin C, B, folic acid, niacin, and the minerals phosphorous and calcium, pears help reduce disorders of the bladder, liver, and prostate as well as constipation. Yield per pound: four to six ounces of juice.
- **Plums.** High in vitamin C, A, copper, and iron, the benzoic and quinic acids in plums are effective laxatives. Plums help with anemia, constipation, and weight loss. Yield per pound: four ounces of juice.
- **Grapes.** High in caffeic acid, which helps fight cancer, grapes are also packed with bioflavonoids, which help the body absorb vitamin C. Grapes also contain resveratrol, a nutrient that helps prevent liver, lung, breast, and prostate cancer, and saponins, a nutrient that binds with cholesterol and prevents the body from absorbing it. Yield per pound: eight ounces of juice.

Tropical Fruit Magic

You can find a bounty of tropical fruit in your local supermarket, even if you live in a cold climate, including:

- **Avocados.** Although frequently mistaken for a vegetable, the avocado is actually a member of the pear family. Rich in vitamins A, C, and E, avocados should be blended or juiced separately and added to juices. Ripe avocados can be refrigerated for up to five days. Yield per pound: two ounces of juice.
- **Bananas.** Bananas are a great source of potassium, an essential electrolyte, as well as magnesium and vitamin B6. Because of their low water content, bananas should be juiced or blended alone, then added to juices. Yield per pound: two ounces of juice.

- **Kiwifruit.** Kiwi are rich in vitamins A and C and contain nearly as much potassium as bananas. Their fuzzy skins contain valuable anti-oxidants and can also be used in marinades for tenderizing meats. Yield per pound: four ounces of juice.
- **Mangos.** Like other orange-colored produce, mangos are packed with beta-carotene. Yield per pound: five ounces of juice.
- **Papayas.** Papayas are loaded with papain, an enzyme that promotes digestion and has been shown to protect the stomach from ulcers. Papayas are also rich in vitamins A and C, and have an abundance of natural sugars. Papayas can also help reduce acidosis, acne, heart disease, tumors, ulcers, and blood disorders. Yield per pound: one to three ounces of juice.
- **Pineapple.** A great source of potassium, calcium, iron, and iodine, fresh pineapple is worth the hassle required to prepare it for juicing. Using a strong knife, slice off the top and bottom of the pineapple so it sits flat on your cutting board, and then slice off the peel. Yield per pound: six ounces of juice.

Melon Madness

Melons are the juiciest fruit by far and a natural for fresh, homemade juices. They come in many varieties, including canary, cantaloupe, casba, Crenshaw, honeydew, and mush. They are sweet and fun summertime thirst-quenchers.

All varieties are rich in vitamins A, B complex, and C, and promote skin and nerve health. Melons provide enzymes and natural unconcentrated sugars that help aid digestion.

Best Melons for Juicing

Cantaloupe, honeydew, and watermelon are among the most popular melons in the United States.

- **Cantaloupe** is high in beta-carotene, vitamin C, and potassium. It alleviates disorders of the bladder, kidney, and skin and reduce constipation. Yield per pound: eight ounces of juice.

- **Honeydew** is high in potassium and vitamin C. It produces delicious juice that promotes energy. It alleviates disorders of the bladder, kidney, and skin and reduces constipation. Yield per pound: six ounces of juice.
- **Watermelon** is high in electrolytes and rich in vitamin A and the mineral potassium. It quenches thirst and also helps cleanse the kidney and bladder. Watermelon helps reduce aging, arthritis, bladder disorders, constipation, fluid retention, kidney disorders, pregnancy, prostate problems, and skin disorders and promotes weight loss. Yield per pound: six to eight ounces of juice.

Berry Delicious

Red, blue, purple, or black—no matter what the color or size, berries are wonder foods that are loaded with phytochemicals, antioxidants, and other vitamins and minerals that help prevent cancer and many other diseases. Cranberries and blueberries also contain a substance that may prevent bladder infections.

FACT

Eating a diet rich in blackberries, blueberries, raspberries, cranberries, and strawberries may help to reduce your risk of several types of cancer. The blue color in blueberries comes from anthocyanins, phytochemicals that help protect your body from cancer. Blueberries and raspberries also contain lutein, which is important for healthy vision.

- **Cranberries.** High in vitamin C, B complex, A, and folic acid, cranberries help prevent bladder infections by keeping bacteria from clinging to the wall of the bladder. Cranberries also help reduce asthma, diarrhea, fever, fluid retention, disorders of the kidney, urinary tract and lungs, and skin disorders, and facilitate weight loss. Yield per pound: four to six ounces of juice.
- **Blueberries and blackberries.** Both berries are packed with saponins, which improve heart health, as well as disease-fighting

antioxidants, vitamin C, minerals, and phytochemicals. Yield per pound: three ounces of juice.

- **Raspberries.** Raspberries are packed with vitamin C, potassium, and are sixty-four calories per cup. Yield per pound: four to five ounces of juice.
- **Strawberries.** Strawberries are packed with vitamin C, iron, calcium, magnesium, folate, and potassium—essential for immune system function and for strong connective tissue. Strawberries also provide just fifty-three calories a cup. Yield per pound: four to five ounces of juice.

Best Vegetables for Juicing

From asparagus to zucchini, your biggest problem when it comes to juicing with vegetables is trying to decide which ones to use.

The Difference Between Fruits and Veggies

Unlike fruits, which all have a seed or pit of some sort, the only thing that vegetables have in common is that they all grow in the ground. In addition, unlike fruits, which have to be ripe to be juiced, vegetables don't need to be ripe to taste great or to yield maximum nutrients. In fact, the sooner you pick or buy them and use them in homemade juices, the better they taste!

Cabbage Patch Kids

From broccoli and cauliflower to Brussels sprouts, kale, cabbage, and bok choy, the members of the cruciferous or cabbage family pack a nutritional wallop. They contain phytochemicals, vitamins, minerals, and fiber that are important to your health. Studies show that sulforaphane—one of the phytochemicals found in cruciferous vegetables—stimulates enzymes in the body that detoxify carcinogens before they damage cells.

Here's a rundown of the most delicious and nutritious root crops for juicing:

- **Broccoli.** Packed with fiber to help regularity, broccoli is also surprisingly high in protein, and it's packed with calcium, antioxidants, and vitamins B6, C, and E. Because of its strong flavor, broccoli works best combined with other vegetables in juices, rather than juiced alone. Wash well and use within four days to get maximum nutrients. Yield per pound: six ounces of juice.

- **Cabbage.** Another member of the fiberific cruciferous family, cabbage comes in many different varieties, from white cabbage, which also comes in red and green, to Savoy cabbage, with delicate, crinkly leaves. Other members of the cabbage family you can use in juicing include kale, collard greens, Brussels sprouts, and Chinese cabbage. All have large stores of vitamins B6 and C. Kale and collard greens also have a lot of vitamin A and calcium. Members of the cabbage family are also packed with minerals. Yield per pound: six ounces of juice.
- **Cauliflower.** Like other cruciferous vegetables, because of its strong flavor, cauliflower works best as a contributing player rather than a solo act. High in vitamin C and fiber, it has a more delicate taste than other cruciferous veggies. Use within four days or refrigerate for up to a week. Yield per pound: six ounces of juice.

Earthy Root Veggies

Classified by their fleshy underground storage unit or root, which is a holding tank of nutrients, root vegetables are low in fat and high in natural sugars and fiber. Root veggies are also the perfect foods to eat when you need sustained energy and focus.

Powerhouse Veggies

Some of the most nutritious root veggies include those with orangey skins, including carrots, squash, and sweet potatoes. The orange skin signifies they contain beta-carotene, a powerful antioxidant that fights damaging free radicals.

Here are some delicious and nutritious root vegetables to include in your juices:

- **Beets.** Both the beet greens and beetroots are juiceable and highly nutritious. The roots are packed with calcium, potassium, and vitamins A and C. Choose small to medium beets with fresh green leaves and roots. Use greens within two days and beets within two weeks. Yield per pound: six to seven ounces of juice.

- **Carrots.** The king of juicing vegetables, carrots lend a mild, sweet taste to juice combos and taste equally delicious on their own. Carrots are packed with vitamins A, B, C, D, E, and K, as well as calcium, phosphorous, potassium, sodium, and trace minerals. Fresh carrot juice stimulates digestion; improves hair, skin and nails; has a mild diuretic effect; and cleanses the liver, helping to release bile and excess fats. Remove foliage when you get home, because it drains moisture and nutrients from the carrots. Refrigerate and use within a week. Yield per pound: six to eight ounces of juice.

- **Celery.** High in vitamin C and potassium with natural sodium, celery has a mild flavor that blends well with other veggies. Its natural sodium balances the PH of the blood and helps the body use calcium better. Choose firm, bright green stalks with fresh green leaves. Refrigerate for up to a week. Yield per pound: eight to ten ounces of juice.

- **Fennel.** Similar to celery in nutrients and high in sodium, calcium, and magnesium, fennel has a licorice-like taste that enhances the taste of juices made from vegetables with a strong flavor. Choose fennel bulbs the size of tennis balls with no bruising or discoloration. Refrigerate and use within five days. Yield per pound: six to eight ounces of juice.

- **Garlic.** A member of the lily family, this aromatic bulb, high in antioxidants for reducing cholesterol and heart disease, adds flavor and tang to vegetable juices. Use one or two cloves per quart. Choose firm, smooth heads and store in a cool, dry place. Use within two weeks.

- **Ginger.** Technically a rhizome and native to Asia, ginger has a sweet, peppery flavor that enhances juice. Buy large, firm nodules with shiny skin. Refrigerate and use within a week.

- **Parsnips.** Cousins to the carrot, parsnips are packed with vitamin C, potassium, silicon, and phosphorous. Choose large, firm parsnips with feathery foliage. Refrigerate and use within a week. Yield per pound: four ounces of juice.

- **Potatoes.** High in vitamins C and B and potassium, potatoes add a light flavor to juice. Store in a cool, dry place and use within two weeks. Yield per pound: five to six ounces of juice.
- **Radishes.** Small but mighty in taste and loaded with vitamin C, iron, magnesium, and potassium, radish juice cleanses the nasal sinuses and gastrointestinal tract and helps clear up skin disorders. Use a handful in vegetable juice to add zing. Refrigerate and use within a week. Yield per pound: two to four ounces of juice.
- **Turnips and turnip greens.** Ounce for ounce, turnip greens have more calcium than milk. The root supplies calcium, potassium, and magnesium. Together, they neutralize overly acidic blood and strengthen bones, hair, nails, and teeth. Store turnips at room temperature, scrub well, and use within two weeks. Refrigerate greens and use within a week. Yield per pound: four ounces of juice.
- **Sweet potatoes and yams.** High in beta-carotene, vitamin C, calcium, and potassium, these two vegetables have a similar taste and can be substituted for one another in recipes. Store in a cool, dry place. Yield per pound: four ounces of juice.
- **Green onions.** Green onions are high in disease-fighting antioxidants and have the mildest flavor of the onion family, making them ideal for juicing. They also have antibacterial properties that fight infections and skin diseases. Green onions should be firm and deep green in color. Refrigerate, and use within a week. Yield per pound: two to three ounces of juice.

Fresh from the Vine

From acorn squash to zucchini, vegetables straight from the vine deliver a cornucopia of nutrients and fiber. Vine vegetables are also especially easy to grow in small, compact gardens, or in containers on patios.

- **Cucumbers.** With their mild flavor, cukes complement other juices and go well with herbs. Cucumbers are high in vitamin A and silica, which help repair connective tissue and skin. Buy firm, dark green cucumbers with a slightly bumpy skin. Use within four days. Yield per pound: eight ounces of juice.

- **String beans.** High in vitamin B, calcium, magnesium, potassium, protein, and sulfur, string bean juice is good for your overall metabolism and your hair, skin, and nails. It has a strong flavor and it tastes best when combined with other veggie juices. Yield per pound: four to six ounces of juice.
- **Summer squash and zucchini.** Rich in vitamins B and niacin, calcium, and potassium, summer squash has a bland flavor that works best with other vegetable juices. It helps cleanse and soothe the bladder and kidneys. Store in a cool, dry place. Use within a few weeks. Yield per pound: four to six ounces of juice.
- **Tomatoes.** Tomatoes are a good source of lycopene, which has been proven to have anti-cancer properties, and vitamin C and potassium, which cleanse the liver and add to the body's store of minerals, especially calcium. Fresh tomato juice also stimulates circulation. Store at room temperature. Yield per pound: eight to ten ounces of juice.
- **Bell peppers.** High in vitamin C, red peppers are also high in vitamin A and are much sweeter than the green variety. Peppers contribute to beautiful skin and hair, while red peppers stimulate circulation and tone and cleanse the arteries and heart muscle. Store at room temperature. Before juicing, wash gently with a mild castile soap, pull out the large clump of seeds, and remove the cap. Yield per pound: five to six ounces of juice.

Leafy Greens

Your juice isn't complete without a dose of leafy greens. Research shows that leafy greens are one of the most concentrated sources of nutrition. They supply the iron, calcium, potassium, and magnesium, vitamins K, C, E, and many of the B vitamins in abundance.

Leafy greens provide a variety of phytonutrients, including beta-carotene and lutein, which protect cells from damage and eyes from age-related problems. A few cups of dark green leaves also contain small amounts of omega-3 fatty acids and nine times the RDA for vitamin K, which regulates blood clotting, protects bones from osteoporosis, and may reduce risk of atherosclerosis by reducing calcium in arterial plaques.

A Dieter's Delight

Because greens have very few carbohydrates and a lot of fiber, they take the body a long time to digest. If you're on a diet, leafy greens can be your best friend; they fill you up, but they have very few calories and no fat. In fact, most greens have so little impact on blood glucose that many low-carb diets consider them free foods.

FACT

Studies show leafy greens pack a powerful nutritional punch by helping reduce heart disease, lung cancer, and colon cancer. A team of researchers from the Harvard School of Public Health found that individuals who consume leafy greens daily had a 23 percent reduction in coronary heart disease.

Leafing Through the Leafy Greens

Leafy greens run the gamut in taste, from arugula—which ancient Romans considered an aphrodisiac because of its peppery taste—to iceberg lettuce, which is crunchy and sweet with a very mild flavor. Here are some of the most popular leafy greens used in juicing:

- **Lettuce.** Deep green lettuce is a good source of calcium, chlorophyll, iron, magnesium, potassium, silicon, and vitamins A and E. All types help rebuild hemoglobin, add shine and thickness to hair, and promote hair growth. Iceberg contains natural opiates that relax the muscles and nerves. Lettuce juice is strong and works best in combination with other vegetables. Wash carefully and refrigerate in original plastic. Use within a few days. Yield per pound: four ounces of juice.
- **Parsley.** Packed with chlorophyll, vitamins A and C, calcium, magnesium, phosphorous, potassium, sodium, and sulfur, parsley helps stimulate oxygen metabolism, cell respiration, and regeneration. Wash, refrigerate, and use within five days. Yield per ounce: one to two ounces per three-inch bunch of parsley.

- **Spinach, kale, and Swiss chard.** Popeye was right all along. You'll be strong to the finish if you eat your spinach, kale, and chard, which are similar in nutritional value and provide ample supplies of iron, phosphorous, fiber, and vitamins A, B, C, E, and K. Wash thoroughly and bag loosely in the refrigerator. Use within four days. Yield per pound: four ounces of juice.
- **Watercress.** This delicate leafy green veggie has a slightly pungent taste and is packed with vitamin C, calcium, and potassium. It also contains acid-forming minerals, which make it ideal for intestinal cleansing and normalizing, and chlorophyll, which stimulates metabolism and circulatory functions. Refrigerate and use within five days. Yield per pound: two to four ounces of juice.
- **Wheatgrass.** The juice from wheat berries contains many anti-aging properties, including vitamins A, B complex, and E, chlorophyll, a full spectrum of minerals, and various enzymes. Refrigerate and use within four days. Yield per pound: six to eight ounces of juice.

Special Added Attractions

You can boost the taste and nutritional value of juice with supplements that include soy and nutritional powders and herbal additions.

Best Soy and Powder Additives

Soy and powders can give your juices a rich, flavorful taste and texture and boost the nutrient value. They include:

- ✓ **Silken tofu**, a soy product, adds flavor and texture and is rich in isoflavones, which may prevent cancer and osteoporosis, and help reduce heart disease.
- ✓ **Flaxseed** is high in omega-3 acids found in oily fish as well as lecithin, which facilitates digestion.
- ✓ **Wheat germ**, high in vitamin E, thiamine, and copper, adds protein and fiber to juice.
- ✓ **Bee pollen** is high in protein, vitamins A, B, C, and E, calcium, and magnesium.

Best Herbal Helpers

Herbs lend phytochemicals and fresh taste and aroma to juices.

- ✓ **Basil** provides vitamins C and A, plus beta-carotene.
- ✓ **Chives** provide calcium, phosphorous, and several vitamins.
- ✓ **Cilantro** is renowned for its anti-cholesterol, anti-diabetic, and anti-inflammatory effects.
- ✓ **Dill** is rich in anti-oxidants and dietary fibers that help control blood cholesterol levels.
- ✓ **Mint**, including peppermint and spearmint, has the ability to cut off the blood supply to cancer tumors.
- ✓ **Oregano** is among the best sources of vitamin K, and it has antioxidants that prevent cellular damage caused by oxidation of free radicals.
- ✓ **Rosemary** provides carnosic acid, which shields the brain from free radicals and lowers the risk of stroke and neurodegenerative diseases.
- ✓ **Tarragon** is packed with minerals and vitamins C, B6, A, and E, and may help transfer nutrients to your muscles.

CHAPTER 4

Juicing for Weight Loss

High levels of fruits, vegetables, and beans promote weight loss because they are low in calories and high in volume and critically important nutrients. Because they fill you up without loading you up with fat and calories, produce leaves less room for more fattening and less nutritious foods. Studies show eating a lot of fruits and veggies also helps turn off cravings for processed food and helps reduce binging on fattening foods. Unlike crash diets that rob your body of essential nutrients, juicing promotes safe and healthful weight loss.

Best Nutrients for Weight Loss

Many people who want to lose weight pay more attention to how many calories they consume than to the amount of nutrients in their foods—an approach that often boomerangs. Research shows that low-nutrient diets are likely to hinder weight loss efforts by robbing your body of essential vitamins, minerals, and other nutrients required for weight loss.

ALERT

Research published in the *American Journal of Clinical Nutrition* linked a low intake of essential nutrients with lowered metabolism and an increased waist circumference—proof that eating a diet low in nutrients as well as calories can sabotage weight loss and actually lead to weight gain.

Ten Nutrients that Speed Weight Loss

If you feel tired, can't seem to focus, have little or no sex drive, and can't lose weight no matter how few calories you consume, the problem probably stems from how few nutrients you're taking in. Fortunately, the most essential nutrients for weight loss are easy to consume via juicing. The following nutrients, all abundant in fruits and vegetables, will help speed weight loss and give you the energy and stamina you need to maintain a healthy diet and exercise program.

1. **Fiber.** Although it's essential for health and weight loss, most people consume less than half the twenty-five or more grams of fiber required. Low fiber intake is also associated with a host of diseases, including heart disease, Type 2 diabetes, and some types of cancer. Getting more fiber via juicing will also help you feel full longer and decrease your craving for sugary, fattening foods. By increasing your fiber intake gradually, you'll avoid the unpleasant side effects of consuming more fiber, such as intestinal upset, bloating, and gas.
2. **Omega-3 fatty acids.** Too little of this good fat can lead to a host of problems ranging from dry, itchy skin to heart disease. Omega-3 fatty acids

also help increase satiety so you feel full longer and won't be tempted to snack on fattening foods. In addition, omega-3 fatty acids help you look and feel younger by giving your skin the moisture and oils it needs to prevent premature wrinkling.

3. **Folic acid.** Folic acid can help reduce the risk of heart disease and colon cancer and speed up a sluggish metabolism. In addition, studies show that pregnant women who consume too little folic acid are at a higher risk of having children with neurological defects.

4. **Calcium.** Despite the "got milk?" campaign, most Americans still consume less than half the recommended daily allowance (RDA) of 1,000 milligrams a day. Calcium strengthens bones, teeth, and nails and helps prevent osteoporosis, and it also regulates blood pressure, which helps you shed unwanted pounds.

5. **Vitamin D.** This wonder vitamin can help facilitate weight loss as well as prevent numerous chronic diseases, including diabetes, various cancers, multiple sclerosis, rheumatoid arthritis, and hypertension. It is available in supplement form, but you can also get it the old-fashioned way: by getting some fresh air. Your body absorbs ultraviolet sunlight, which it then converts to vitamin D.

6. **Iron.** If you feel tired, sluggish, and have little or no motivation to diet or exercise, you may be suffering from a common condition called iron-deficiency anemia. About one in five people suffers from a lack of iron. Juicing and eating lots of citrus fruit and salad veggies increases your body's absorption of iron. Having more energy means you'll be more likely to exercise regularly and burn more calories.

7. **Vitamin C.** Vitamin C increases your body's absorption of iron, which gives you more energy and stamina. It also helps reduce infections that can cause anything from colds to pneumonia, all of which interrupt healthy eating and exercise programs.

8. **Pantothenic acid.** This B vitamin plays a role in the metabolism of fat and has been shown to facilitate weight loss.

9. **Vitamin E.** This vitamin also plays a role in fat metabolism. A deficiency of vitamin E is also associated with higher body fat levels.

10. **Zinc.** Research indicates that zinc deficiency is associated with a higher level of body fat.

Micronutrients that Enhance Weight Loss

Your body needs a host of micronutrients to perform at maximum capacity. Think of your body as a motor in a race car. Without the right fuel, your engine won't run fast or hot enough to burn off unwanted fat.

Micronutrients that Zap the Pounds

The following micronutrients—or substances you need in very small amounts in your body—work in specific ways to enhance the loss of body fat, preserve muscle mass, and regulate levels of blood sugar and insulin:

- **Chromium** is an essential nutrient for normal sugar and fat metabolism —and one of the most critical micronutrients for weight loss. It lowers blood sugar and insulin levels and increases the level of "good" (HDL) cholesterol, which lowers total cholesterol and triglycerides and helps regulate appetite, reduce cravings, and shed pounds. This trace mineral also improves your resistance to insulin, the hormone in your body that controls sugar. Proper insulin functioning promotes thermogenesis, or burning calories by raising body heat. When your body is deficient in this trace mineral, your blood sugar levels become elevated and you begin craving sugary foods.
- **Alpha lipoic acid (ALA)**, often called the universal antioxidant, enhances the body's ability to metabolize food into energy.
- **DMAE** (dimethylaminoethanol), a naturally occurring nutritional substance with powerful anti-inflammatory properties, improves skin firmness and muscle tone. It is a crucial micronutrient to consume to keep skin tight if you plan to lose a substantial amount of weight.
- **Glutamine**, the body's most abundant amino acid, drives muscle-building nitrogen into the muscle cells, where it is synthesized for growth. It is also converted into glucose when the body needs more energy. When the body is in a highly inflammatory state, it breaks down valuable muscle tissue to get the extra glutamine it needs, resulting in loss of muscle mass. Lean muscle mass is a metabolic tissue that burns far more calories than flab—even when you're just sitting around!
- **Carnitine** and its derivative, acetyl-L-carnitine, are two of the most important nutrients for weight loss. Carnitine promotes metabolism,

while acetyl-L-carnitine transports fatty acids from the blood into the cell for energy production. Carnitine needs the presence of adequate omega-3 acids to do its job.

- **Coenzyme Q10**, or ubiquinone, is a powerful antioxidant/anti-inflammatory that enhances metabolism, promotes weight loss, increases energy and endurance, and maximizes the burning of foods for fuel, which normalizes fats in the blood.
- **Conjugated linoleic acid (CLA)** decreases body fat, especially in the abdomen, and helps block the absorption of fat and sugar into fat cells. In addition, it helps the insulin receptors remain intact, thus increasing insulin sensitivity.
- **Gamma linolenic acid (GLA)**, an important omega-6 essential fatty acid, is necessary for regulating weight loss, blood pressure, and many other bodily functions.
- **Maitake mushroom extract** facilitates weight loss by controlling blood sugar levels and preventing metabolic imbalances that increase the risk of cardiovascular disease, diabetes, and metabolic disturbances.

ALERT

To lose weight, your body also needs at least eight glasses of water daily to use stored fat, promote colon health, and flush away toxins released during weight loss. In addition to helping your body function, drinking a glass of water before each meal also helps you feel full more quickly so you naturally consume fewer calories.

In addition to getting essential vitamins, minerals, and micronutrients, you can also speed weight loss by drinking sufficient juice. Two to three glasses of fresh fruit or vegetable juice daily is a delicious way to give your body all the nutrients it needs for weight loss.

Best Vegetables for Shedding Pounds

The average American consumes a diet that contains just 8 percent fruits, vegetables, and beans—one reason Americans are getting fatter every year.

To lose weight, it's necessary to consume the right nutrients and eat in a way that makes you feel full and satiated.

Fiber for Weight Loss

Fruits and vegetables are great weight loss foods because your body uses practically every calorie for metabolism rather than storing it. Some of the best vegetables to help speed up weight loss are those that include lots of fiber, including leafy greens like collard, spinach, and Swiss chard, and cruciferous vegetables like Brussels sprouts, broccoli, and cabbage.

FACT

New studies show that not all produce is created equal when it comes to helping you lose weight. Certain fruits and vegetables contain more nutrients per calorie than others, helping your body function while discarding excess pounds. Cabbage, lemons, and grapefruit are good examples.

Vitamins for Weight Loss

Vegetables that are high in vitamins C and E and pantothenic acid help regulate fat metabolism. Good sources of vitamin C include kale, parsley, broccoli, Brussels sprouts, watercress, cauliflower, cabbage, spinach, turnips, and asparagus. Veggies high in vitamin E include spinach, watercress, asparagus, carrots, and tomatoes. Pantothenic acid, a B vitamin that facilitates fat metabolism, is found in cruciferous veggies like broccoli, cauliflower, and kale.

Minerals for Weight Loss

Your body needs certain minerals found in abundance in certain vegetables to maintain weight loss. Chromium, a trace mineral that regulates metabolism, is found in green peppers, parsnips, spinach, carrots, lettuce, string beans, and cabbage. Magnesium, which regulates energy, is found in spinach, parsley, dandelion greens, garlic, beets and beet greens, broccoli, cauliflower, carrots, and celery. Zinc, associated with lower body fat levels, is found in turnips, parsley, garlic, carrots, spinach, cabbage, lettuce, and cucumbers.

Fruits that Help You Slim Down

Fruits, like vegetables, are also loaded with nutrients that support or enhance weight loss. Vitamin C, important for fat metabolism, is found in abundance in strawberries, papaya, citrus fruit, mangos, and cantaloupe. Vitamin E, also essential for fat metabolism, is found in tomatoes.

Certain fruits that are antioxidant super foods are also super weight-loss foods. At the top of the list are strawberries, raspberries, and blueberries—all of which are low in calories, filling, and packed with antioxidants that promote weight loss. In addition, berries also supply a lot of energy that helps you burn off fat more quickly.

Minerals in Fruits that Facilitate Weight Loss

The mineral chromium, which regulates insulin, is found in apples. Magnesium, which is involved in energy regulation, is found in blackberries. Fruits are good sources of zinc, a mineral associated with low body fat levels. The best fruits for zinc include grapes and tangerines.

Herbs for Weight Loss

In addition to fruits and vegetables, several herbs and even a few weeds may help you lose weight. They include bladderwrack and hawthorn, which regulate thyroid and adrenal gland function; chickweed, a traditional appetite suppressant; and juniper berries, which are a diuretic and detoxification agent.

Why Juice for Weight Loss

Juicing for weight loss is so healthy that it's fast replacing dangerous crash diets and starvation diets. It supplies your body with the concentrated nutrients it needs to manage ailments, boost your immune system, and facilitate digestion. In addition, you can eliminate that annoying water weight that accumulates before and during your menstrual cycle by juicing a delicious combination of celery, cucumber, cranberry, and watermelon—all natural diuretics.

Juicing for Rainbow Nutrients

The colors of fruits and vegetables advertise the vitamins, minerals, and antioxidants they contain. The best and easiest way to ensure you get all the vitamins, minerals, and calories you need is to create homemade juices from many different colors of fruits and vegetables, using different combinations to consume a rainbow variety of nutrients. When you use a juicing program to lose weight, you provide your body with nutritious, low-calorie, and filling beverages that facilitate healthy weight loss. After you lose the weight you desire, you can continue juicing to promote health and vitality.

ALERT

If you are concerned about diet and nutrition, juicing for weight loss is much healthier than most crash diets. But don't expect overnight results. Rather than concentrating on juicing for weight loss, focus on juicing for health. Incorporate juicing for weight loss into a healthy eating program that you can stick with for life, and you'll end up thinner *and* healthier.

The Nutrient Advantage

Juicing for weight loss gives your body micro-nutrients with specific health benefits without overburdening your system with calories or fat. Instead of starving yourself or eating a low-calorie diet that lacks essential nutrients, you'll drink a concentrated cocktail packed with the enzymes, vitamins, and minerals that are necessary for a healthy diet and nutrition program. This will enable your body to function optimally.

Suppressing Appetite and Cutting Cravings

Fresh juice also acts as a natural and safe appetite suppressant that eliminates cravings for calorie-laden sweets and junk foods. By drinking a glass of fresh juice before your meal, you'll fill yourself up, experience a rapid decrease in appetite, and naturally eat less.

FACT

Jerusalem artichoke and parsnip are age-old remedies for eliminating cravings for fatty and sugary foods, so if you feel a craving coming on, head for your juicer instead! You can pump up the effects of your juice diet by including ginger, which stimulates your body's natural heat-burning power.

Stabilizing Blood Sugar Levels

Vegetable juice helps your body stabilize blood sugar levels, a vital factor in weight loss. Wildly fluctuating blood levels can lead to depression, mood swings, and binge eating. Vegetable juice contains much less sugar and about half the calories of fruit juice, but still manages to satisfy your sweet tooth without loading you up with sugar. Carrots, which are naturally sweet, will satisfy your sweet tooth without inflicting caloric or fat damage to your waistline, and will also help elevate healthful levels of good cholesterol.

Natural Diuretics

Certain fruits and vegetables also serve as natural diuretics and detox agents that eliminate bloating and puffiness. They include alfalfa, asparagus, dandelion, cucumber, parsley, lemon, kiwi, and melon. Large doses of parsley juice can be toxic, so limit your consumption to between ½ to 1 cup daily and avoid it entirely if you're pregnant.

Naturally Lowering Cholesterol

Juicing can help you naturally lower your cholesterol by providing a low-fat, high-carbohydrate alternative to high-fat diets. Ongoing studies show that people who eat a high-fiber, low-fat, plant-based diet have lower cholesterol and bad (LDL) cholesterol levels.

Research shows that the soluble fiber found in abundance in fruits and veggies—especially in apple and pear juice—helps lower cholesterol and LDL levels. The pectin found in citrus peel is especially effective in lowering cholesterol.

ALERT

Juicing lemons and limes with the peel is an easy and delicious way to consume lots of healthy pectin. Just be careful not to do the same with orange, grapefruit, or tangerine peels. All three contain bitter-tasting oils that can cause stomachaches, diarrhea, and other digestive problems.

Perhaps the most encouraging thing about juicing for weight loss is that you'll feel and look so much better than if you attempted to lose the same weight on a crash diet that depletes your nutrient stores and energy. With juicing, you'll have sustained energy, shinier hair, stronger nails, and smoother skin.

Before you begin juicing for weight loss, consult your health practitioner to rule out pre-existing conditions or problems. This is especially true if you are pregnant, suffer from chronic conditions, or are taking medications whose effectiveness is inhibited by grapefruit juice.

Celery Carrot

» ## Good for lowering cholesterol

Baby carrots are full of flavor, but because they are not totally mature they are not as flavorful as full-grown carrots. It is important to remove carrot greens because keeping them on robs the carrot of moisture and vitamins.

INGREDIENTS | YIELD: 1 CUP

3 carrots, peeled
2 stalks celery, leaves intact

Juice carrots and celery. Stir.

Per Serving

CALORIES: **155**
FAT: **0.23g**
SODIUM: **198mg**
FIBER: **11g**
PROTEIN: **4g**
SUGARS: **19g**
CARBOHYDRATES: **40g**

Watermelon Orange

» ## Good for reducing water retention

Eating foods used as diuretics is helpful in managing water retention or bloat. Some of these foods are watermelon, garlic, cantaloupe, and dill.

INGREDIENTS | YIELD: 1¼ CUPS

1 cup watermelon
1 orange, peeled

Juice watermelon and orange. Stir.

Per Serving

CALORIES: **110**
FAT: **0.48g**
SODIUM: **1.5mg**
FIBER: **2.8g**
PROTEIN: **2.9g**
SUGARS: **22g**
CARBOHYDRATES: **28g**

Mini Melons

Watermelons are available in small individual sizes. They are about the size of a cantaloupe melon. You may want to use a melon baller, a small bowl-shaped tool, to cut rounds of melon. These can be placed on a skewer and used to decorate your juice.

Broccoli Cabbage Patch

» ## Good for reducing bloat

Cabbage juice is good for weight loss, but it's best to mix it with something else so that it does not cause as much gas in your stomach. Cabbage is a cruciferous vegetable that contains some vitamin A and a good amount of vitamin C.

INGREDIENTS | YIELD: 1½ CUPS

1 cup broccoli
¼ small head red cabbage
3 romaine lettuce leaves

Juice broccoli. Set aside. Juice cabbage and lettuce. Stir together.

Per Serving

CALORIES: **48**
FAT: **0.41g**
SODIUM: **43mg**
FIBER: **4g**
PROTEIN: **3.3g**
SUGARS: **3.4g**
CARBOHYDRATES: **9.6g**

Green Juice

» ## Good for reducing cravings for sour foods

Cravings for sour foods can come from a lack of acetic acid. Green vegetables are high in chlorophyll and help with these types of cravings.

INGREDIENTS | YIELD: 1½ CUPS

3 celery stalks, leaves intact
½ cucumber
1 red apple, cored
1 fist spinach
1 fist beet greens

Juice ingredients in the order listed. Stir together.

Per Serving

CALORIES: **111**
FAT: **0.9g**
SODIUM: **237mg**
FIBER: **8.7g**
PROTEIN: **4.7g**
SUGARS: **15g**
CARBOHYDRATES: **25g**

Carrot Beeter

» Good for lowering cholesterol

Carrot juice has been shown to help lower cholesterol, and beets provide a good source of magnesium, which can help reduce cholesterol.

INGREDIENTS | YIELD: 1¼ CUP

3 carrots, peeled
1 beet, greens cut off

Juice carrots. Set aside. Juice beet. Stir together.

Per Serving

CALORIES: **177**
FAT: **0.19g**
SODIUM: **182mg**
FIBER: **12g**
PROTEIN: **4.7g**
SUGARS: **25g**
CARBOHYDRATES: **46g**

Skinny Dip

» Good for weight loss

Citrus sometimes satisfies cravings for high fat foods. Lemon juice helps digestion, making sure that the liver rids itself of any impurities, which is essential to losing weight and keeping off excess weight.

INGREDIENTS | YIELD: 1¼ CUP

1 lemon, rind intact
1 lime, rind intact
1 cup sparkling water

Halve lemon and lime. Juice. Add sparkling water to lemon-lime juice. Stir.

Per Serving

CALORIES: **42**
FAT: **0.51g**
SODIUM: **6.9mg**
FIBER: **7.4g**
PROTEIN: **1.7g**
SUGARS: **1g**
CARBOHYDRATES: **19g**

Lemons

California is the leading producer of lemons in the United States. They are available year round. Make sure you juice a lemon immediately before you're going to use it. Lemons lose 20 percent of their vitamin C after eight hours at room temperature.

Piece of Pie

>> **Good for reducing cravings and weight loss**

This sweet combination can fill you up and satisfy your cravings.

INGREDIENTS | YIELD: 1½ CUPS

3 Granny Smith apples, cored
1 teaspoon cinnamon

Juice apples. Add cinnamon and stir.

Per Serving

CALORIES: **136**
FAT: **0.63g**
SODIUM: **3.1mg**
FIBER: **6.2g**
PROTEIN: **0.088g**
SUGARS: **27g**
CARBOHYDRATES: **37g**

Apple Yammer

>> **Good for weight loss**

This juice is high in vitamins A and C. It's a great way to add fiber to your diet and satisfy your sweet tooth while keeping it healthy.

INGREDIENTS | YIELD: 1 CUP

1 yam, cut into pieces
1 red apple, cored

Juice yam and apple. Stir.

Per Serving

CALORIES: **232**
FAT: **0.59g**
SODIUM: **14mg**
FIBER: **8.2g**
PROTEIN: **2.8g**
SUGARS: **9.5g**
CARBOHYDRATES: **51g**

Garlic Melon with Sprig of Dill

>> **Good for reducing water retention**

Garlic is an old fashioned cure for water retention and is said to provide and prolong strength. It was given to Egyptian slaves when they built the pyramids.

INGREDIENTS | YIELD: 1 CUP

¼ cantaloupe, peeled
2 whole garlic cloves
Fresh baby dill sprigs

Juice cantaloupe and garlic. Stir and garnish with dill.

Per Serving

CALORIES: **86**
FAT: **0.57g**
SODIUM: **32mg**
FIBER: **2.1g**
PROTEIN: **2.8g**
SUGARS: **14g**
CARBOHYDRATES: **24g**

Spinach Apple

>> **Good for reducing bloat**

Spinach is rich in iron and vitamins A, C, and E. It helps protect against osteoporosis. It is good for constipation and calcium absorption.

INGREDIENTS | YIELD: ¾ CUP

1 cup spinach leaves
1 red apple
¼ lemon, rind intact
1 celery stalk

Juice spinach, apple, lemon, and celery. Stir.

Per Serving

CALORIES: **84**
FAT: **0.61g**
SODIUM: **67mg**
FIBER: **5.5g**
PROTEIN: **1.7g**
SUGARS: **10g**
CARBOHYDRATES: **16g**

Asparagus Carrot

>> ## Good for easing cellulite

Asparagus is a good source of vitamin E. It is a natural diuretic that is low in calories and high in vitamins and minerals.

INGREDIENTS | YIELD: ¾ CUP

1 cup asparagus
3 carrots, peeled

Juice asparagus and carrots. Stir.

Per Serving

CALORIES: **168**
FAT: **0.15g**
SODIUM: **120mg**
FIBER: **12g**
PROTEIN: **5.7g**
SUGARS: **22g**
CARBOHYDRATES: **44g**

A Hidden Clove

>> ## Good for reducing water retention

The sweetness of the carrots will offset the strong taste of garlic, and the dill adds a touch of green.

INGREDIENTS | YIELD: 1 CUP

4 carrots, peeled
2 garlic cloves
1 sprig baby dill

Juice carrots and garlic. Stir. Garnish with baby dill.

Per Serving

CALORIES: **213**
FAT: **0.17g**
SODIUM: **159mg**
FIBER: **12g**
PROTEIN: **5g**
SUGARS: **26g**
CARBOHYDRATES: **61g**

CHAPTER 5

Juice Fasting

Proponents of juice fasting claim the antioxidant, cleansing power of freshly made juice is the most potent detoxification program for healing and recovery. They also claim that juice, which is high in vitamins and antioxidants, cleanses the immune system and helps prevent serious conditions and diseases, including cancer and diabetes. Critics of juice fasting insist the practice is unnecessary and potentially dangerous. They claim it can lead to malnutrition, dehydration, diarrhea, and a serious electrolyte imbalance.

Juice Fasting: Controversial Cleansing

A juice fast is considered an extreme form of detoxification because no solid food is consumed. More moderate detox methods, such as detox diets, include solid foods. Although they've been around for years, there's been renewed interest in detox diets in the past few years, in part because some supermodels and celebrities have used them to trim down for the runway or the red carpet.

The Pros of Juice Fasts

Proponents of juice fasting claim the process gives the body a much-needed spring cleaning, allowing it to take a break from the laborious process of digestion. They claim juice fasting assists the immune system in clearing out dead, diseased, and damaged cells. At the same time, the many natural nutrients found in fresh juice revitalizes the immune system.

ESSENTIAL

Some advocates of juice fasting claim it's the most important thing you can do for improved health. They credit juice fasts with fading age spots, lowering blood pressure and cholesterol, and making skin and hair look healthier. However, there are no studies proving these anecdotal findings.

The Case Against Juice Fasts

The American Dietitian Association and most medical doctors are not enthused by the latest juice fast diets, especially those that are ultrarestrictive and have you drinking jacked-up lemonade for weeks at a time. As juice fasts have become increasingly popular among celebrities, medical professionals have sounded the alarm over possible risks from lengthy or repeated fasts.

They claim juice fasts may result in vitamin deficiencies, muscle breakdown, blood-sugar problems, and frequent liquid bowel movements. Because juice fasts are skimpy on solid foods and fiber, those using them are urged to "move things along" by using daily enemas and laxatives and staying close to the bathroom.

Crash diets also take a toll on your body chemistry, lowering your blood sugar levels and depleting your body's supply of important miner-als necessary for maintaining normal electrolyte balances. If you're suffer-ing from a chronic disease such as diabetes, cancer, or a heart condition, you're particularly vulnerable to changes in body chemistry, so don't embark on a fast without your doctor's approval. Because of their low nutrient value and potential dangers, fasts and detox diets are not recom-mended for children, pregnant women, seniors, and those with digestive conditions.

Types of Juice Fasts

There are many detox diet guides, each with its own magic formula for helping you cleanse your body of unwanted toxins and excess weight. Some have you drinking nothing but lemonade, fruit juice, or purées, claiming this will help flush out environmental or dietary toxins. Others instruct you to eliminate entire food groups, such as dairy and meat products or even all solid foods, in an effort to purify your system. Despite their claims, most are so dangerously low in calories and nutrients that they can lead to serious imbalances in the body.

Juice Fasts Aren't Necessary

According to experts at the Mayo Clinic, your body is already well-equipped to flush out toxins via your kidneys, liver, and skin. Cleansing diets that claim to remove "bad" toxins from your system may remove or even deplete your intestines of healthy bacteria required for healthy functioning.

ALERT

Going on juice fasts or very low-calorie diets often takes a big toll on your health and may lead to lethargy, grumpiness, joint pain, and many other symptoms. Because these diets often require that you also use laxatives, enemas, and colonics to cleanse and flush out toxins, they can strand you in the bathroom and lead to chronic dehydration.

You're Not Cleansed, You're Starving

Proponents claim they feel lighter and more energetic after fasting; in fact, studies of starvation show the longer you fast, the more lethargic and less focused you become. And because most of these diets contain very little protein, it can be difficult for the body to rebuild lost muscle tissue. Also, medical experts attribute the "high" you feel not to cleansing, but to the body kicking into starvation mode.

FACT

While some people lose weight quickly on juice fasts, the vast majority regain all the weight they lose, according to the American Psychological Association. And while people may lose 5 to 10 percent of their weight in the first few months of juice fasting, two-thirds of them regain even more weight than they lost within five years.

Best Fasting Fruits

For those who want to give it a try, here's a list of the best fruits for juice fasting. Although there is no medical research proving these fruits are effective in cleansing your body, they certainly supply a lot of healthy nutrients.

Best Internal Cleansers

Juice fast proponents claim juices made from beets, cabbage, wheatgrass, sprouts, lemons, carrots, celery, green peppers, oranges, parsley, apples, and grapefruit will help your body detox. The best diuretics include watermelon, parsley, cucumber, lemon, kiwifruit, asparagus, and cantaloupe with the seeds.

Bulking agents, including psyllium husks and flaxseed, will curb your appetite and keep you near the bathroom. Herbs that juicing proponents tout as cleansers include herbal teas like dandelion and nettle, which purportedly help cleanse the liver and kidneys.

Getting Started on a Juice Fast

Juice fasting proponents claim you'll get the most from your juice fast—which typically last three to five days—by preparing yourself physically and mentally for the challenge. Before you start a juice fast, it is strongly recommended that you consult your doctor to discuss the effects the fast may have on your body. Although many chiropractors, naturopaths, natural healers, masseuses, and other alternative medicine practitioners offer nutritional counseling and supplements as part of their services, they do not have the training to replicate the advice of a medical physician.

Physical Prep for Juice Fasts

To make the transition from solid to liquid foods, about five days before your fast begin weaning off grains, breads, dairy, fish, and meat, and consume a pre-fat diet high in cooked vegetables, salads, fruits, and juices. The next day, limit your foods to raw salads, juices, and fruits, becoming progressively stricter as your fast approaches but being careful not to eliminate juice and water from your diet. Try replacing breakfast with juice and gradually work up to ingesting only juice before dinner.

FACT

Try eating nothing but grapes on one of your pre-fast days—they act as a strong detoxifying agent. Another day, eat nothing but melons or apples or citrus, which also allegedly have cleansing effects. Lettuce and sprouts are also good pre-fast foods.

Doing a Fast

If you're new to fasting, it's highly recommended you do your first fast under the supervision of fasting experts at health spas or clinics. Experts claim that three-day fasts are especially effective for breaking binges, cravings, and other bad eating habits. However, you may want to start with a one-day fast, especially if you're doing it on your own.

What to Expect

During a short fast lasting a few days, the pH balance of your stomach changes, becoming more alkaline. As your stomach contracts and the digestive tract is cleansed, you will experience the most dramatic weight loss as water, minerals, and water soluble vitamins are heavily excreted and you lose up to 75 grams of protein per day. You're also likely to experience hunger, headaches, light headedness, and copious urination.

During longer fasts lasting anywhere from four days to a week, the liver begins to eliminate chemicals and toxins in your body, which may make you feel nauseous, exhausted, nervous, and short of breath. You may develop bad breath, diarrhea, body odor, and skin eruptions.

During extended fasts lasting two weeks or longer, blood toxins are eliminated from the body as deep tissue cleansing and organ detox begins. You may experience anything from stress and irritability to a sense of euphoria and well-being, which medical science attributes not to cleansing and regeneration, but to starvation.

How to Break a Fast Safely

Although you may be tempted to eat everything in sight after coming off a fast, it's important to ease into normal eating gradually to avoid stomachaches, indigestion, diarrhea, and over-stressing vital organs like your heart, lungs, and liver. Remember that while you were fasting, your stomach was essential asleep. If you were on a longer fast, your stomach also shrank. To "wake up" your digestive system, it's important to sit down when you eat to promote digestion, eat very small meals, and eat very slowly, chewing your food thoroughly.

ALERT

Don't push yourself to return to your normal activity level or exercise regimen until you feel ready. If you feel tired, rest. Above all, listen to your body. If you experience flatulence, nausea, or diarrhea, it's probably a sign you need to consume smaller meals and slow down.

Phase 1

You can safely transition from a fast to normal eating by taking it in three easy phases. Phase 1 is the initial period after fasting, or roughly half the number of days you fasted. If you fasted for four days, Phase 1 would be the first two days after fasting. If you fasted for three days, Phase 1 would be the first day or so after fasting. During Phase 1, your main goal is to reawaken your digestion system without overloading it.

- Consume only soft foods with a high water content, including light soups, leafy greens, and juices fortified with wheat germ, spirulina, chlorella, or ground-up almonds, sesame seeds, or sunflower seeds. You may also want to consume fruit smoothies made with bananas, apples, and flaxseed.
- When you feel ready to move onto solid foods, start with juicy fruits such as watermelon, grapefruit, oranges, apples, pears, pineapples, cantaloupe, papaya, and mango.

- If you feel okay consuming juicy fruits, try incorporating heavier fruits, such as peaches, apricots, tomatoes, green peppers, and cucumbers, into some meals.
- If you crave a salad, make a salad of leafy green sprouts, such as buckwheat, turnip, cabbage, onion, radish, alfalfa, clover, and sunflower sprouts. Avoid bean sprouts in the early stages of breaking a fast; they are difficult to digest.
- Try incorporating vegetable broths into some meals, including broths made with vegetables or potatoes. To stimulate circulation, add garlic, miso paste, and cayenne pepper to your broth.
- If you feel okay consuming light broths, make broths that contain a larger amount of potatoes or rice.

Phase 2

During Phase 2, which lasts anywhere from a day after short fasts to five days after a ten-day fast, you can eat everything from Phase 1 and introduce leafy green vegetables as well as unsaturated fats, including olives, avocados, nuts, seeds, and olive oil.

- Begin with dry salads. If you feel okay, try adding homemade dressings made with olive oil and lemon, tofu, and avocado.
- Enjoy small amounts of nuts and seeds on salads or ground up in salad dressings, juices, and smoothies.
- Make thicker soups, gradually increasing the amount of vegetables, potatoes, and rice you can comfortably tolerate.
- Don't eat any cooked vegetables (aside from those in soups), grains, beans, bread, dairy, and animal products.

Phase 3

During Phase 3, you gradually return to a normal diet. This phase lasts anywhere from a day after a short fast to five days after a longer, ten-day fast.

- Begin by reintroducing rice, baked potatoes, and steamed vegetables.
- If you feel okay, try adding cereals, grains, and bread.

- Gradually reintroduce dairy and animal products. Listen to your body and back off if you experience digestive problems.
- To avoid reversing the effects of your fast, avoid fried foods, high-fat cheeses, foods with added sugar, and foods with artificial flavorings and dyes—permanently, if possible.

Juice Fasting Danger Signs

Proponents of juice fasts claim the temporary side effects, which include headaches, tiredness, hypoglycemia, constipation, acne, increased body odor, and bad breath, are simply the price you have to pay to detoxify your body.

More serious side effects associated with fasting, such as fainting, dizziness, low blood pressure, heart arrhythmia, weight loss, hunger, vomiting, and kidney problems, are a signal that something is wrong. Another dangerous side effect of juice fasts is diarrhea, which can lead to dehydration and electrolyte loss.

ALERT

Never use grapefruit juice during a juice fast if you're taking prescription drugs. Grapefruit contains a compound that can alter the way those drugs are metabolized by the body, either reducing or increasing their effects. Recent research has found that pomegranate juice may have similar results.

Do not ignore these symptoms. Discontinue the juice fast immediately and see a qualified physician.

If they are continued for a long time, juice fasts can lead to serious nutritional deficiencies. Especially dangerous are protein and calcium deficiencies that can lead to conditions like muscle wasting, brittle hair and nails, osteoporosis, and frequent bone fractures.

Cucumber Melon Pear

» **Good for juice fasting**

Melons belong to the family of gourds, just like squash and pumpkin. There are two large categories of melon, the muskmelon and the watermelon.

INGREDIENTS | YIELD: 1 CUP

1 cucumber, peeled
½ honeydew melon or cantaloupe, rind removed
1 pear

Juice cucumber, melon, and pear. Stir.

Per Serving

CALORIES: **203**
FAT: **0.77g**
SODIUM: **68mg**
FIBER: **8.7g**
PROTEIN: **4.1g**
SUGARS: **39g**
CARBOHYDRATES: **58g**

Green Apple Broccoli

» **Good for juice fasting**

Broccoli is rich in bioflavonoids. It is high in vitamins A and C, calcium, and iron. Part of the cabbage family, broccoli is available year round but is best between October and April. Keep it refrigerated for up to four days.

INGREDIENTS | YIELD: 1½ CUPS

6 broccoli spears
3 Granny Smith apples
⅛ cup Italian parsley

Juice broccoli, then apples. Add parsley to juicer. Stir and garnish with an extra sprig of parsley.

Per Serving

CALORIES: **253**
FAT: **1.4g**
SODIUM: **60mg**
FIBER: **13g**
PROTEIN: **5.1g**
SUGARS: **28g**
CARBOHYDRATES: **41g**

Peach Pineapple

>> **Good for juice fasting**

Fruit juice may be thinned out with water to make it less strong. This drink is a good source of fiber.

INGREDIENTS | YIELD: 1½ CUPS

1 cup fresh pineapple
1 peach

Juice pineapple. Juice peach. Stir.

Per Serving

CALORIES: **131**
FAT: **0.52g**
SODIUM: **1.6mg**
FIBER: **3.1g**
PROTEIN: **3.1g**
SUGARS: **28g**
CARBOHYDRATES: **35g**

Peaches
Peaches are available from May to October in the United States. Peach skin color ranges from light pinkish white to a yellow gold. Peaches bruise very easily, so try to select ones that do not have soft spots. Don't squeeze the fruit; even a gentle squeeze can bruise it.

Apple Grapefruit

>> **Good for juice fasting**

Grapefruit is a good source of vitamin C. Choose grapefruit with thin skin, which has a fine texture. Do not store at room temperature for more than one day. They will keep up to two weeks in the refrigerator if stored in a plastic bag in the vegetable drawer.

INGREDIENTS | YIELD: 1 CUP

2 red apples
½ pink grapefruit, peeled

Juice apples and grapefruit. Stir.

Per Serving

CALORIES: **167**
FAT: **0.69g**
SODIUM: **2.5mg**
FIBER: **6.2g**
PROTEIN: **1.2g**
SUGARS: **17g**
CARBOHYDRATES: **33g**

Cucumber Pepper

>> **Good for juice fasting**

Sweet bell peppers are an excellent source of vitamins A and C. Choose cucumbers with firm skin and no shriveling or soft spots.

INGREDIENTS | YIELD: 1 CUP

1 cucumber, peeled
1 celery stalk
½ green bell pepper

Juice cucumbers, celery, and pepper. Stir.

Per Serving

CALORIES: **40**
FAT: **0.21g**
SODIUM: **46mg**
FIBER: **2.9g**
PROTEIN: **2g**
SUGARS: **9g**
CARBOHYDRATES: **17g**

Cucumbers

Cucumbers are available year round. Store them unwashed in your refrigerator for up to ten days. Wash them just before using. Leftover cucumbers can be refrigerated again; just tightly wrap them in plastic and they will keep for up to five days.

Kale Apple

>> **Good for juice fasting**

This healthy body cleanser includes kale, a member of the cabbage family. It has a mild cabbage-like flavor and comes in many varieties and colors. Kale is a cruciferous vegetable that is a good source of vitamins A and C, folic acid, iron, and calcium.

INGREDIENTS | YIELD: ¾ CUP

2 Granny Smith apples, cored
1 kale leaf

Juice apples and kale. Stir.

Per Serving

CALORIES: **112**
FAT: **0.62g**
SODIUM: **14mg**
FIBER: **4.3g**
PROTEIN: **0.94g**
SUGARS: **17g**
CARBOHYDRATES: **25g**

Super Green Juice

» Good for juice fasting

Green juices are known for their cleansing capabilities. Romaine lettuce is sometimes referred to as Cos lettuce after the island in the Aegean Sea where it originated.

INGREDIENTS | YIELD: 1½ CUPS

1 red apple, cored
4 romaine lettuce leaves
1 cucumber, peeled
1 celery stalk, leaves intact
1 carrot, peeled
1 garlic clove, peeled

Juice ingredients in the order listed. Stir.

Per Serving

CALORIES: **127**
FAT: **0.41g**
SODIUM: **88mg**
FIBER: **6.9g**
PROTEIN: **3.2g**
SUGARS: **22g**
CARBOHYDRATES: **44g**

Carrot Banana

» Good for juice fasting

Bananas are satisfying treats that help you to feel full. This juice is highly nutritious and provides potassium, vitamin A, and vitamin C.

INGREDIENTS | YIELD: 1 CUP

3 carrots
1 banana

Juice carrots. Add carrot juice and banana to blender and blend well.

Per Serving

CALORIES: **274**
FAT: **0.49g**
SODIUM: **118mg**
FIBER: **13g**
PROTEIN: **4.6g**
SUGARS: **33g**
CARBOHYDRATES: **64g**

Avoid Discolored Bananas

Once bananas are peeled and exposed to the air they begin to turn brown. If you want to peel your banana ahead of time, soak it in acidulated water to keep it from turning brown. Make acidulated water by adding a few drops of lemon juice to the water.

Kiwifruit Apple

» **Good for juice fasting**

Kiwi are high in vitamin C and contain copper, potassium and dietery fiber. Kiwi can remove excess sodium from the body. The fiber also helps cleanse the body more effectively.

INGREDIENTS | YIELD: 1 CUP

2 red apples, cored and sliced
3 kiwifruit, peeled

Juice apples and kiwi. Stir.

Per Serving

CALORIES: **231**
FAT: **3g**
SODIUM: **9.4mg**
FIBER: **11g**
PROTEIN: **2.7g**
SUGARS: **42g**
CARBOHYDRATES: **64g**

Orange Carrot

» **Good for juice fasting**

If you feel hungry, try drinking this juice as a snack to satisfy your appetite.

INGREDIENTS | YIELD: 1 CUP

1 orange, cut into wedges
3 carrots, peeled

Juice carrots and orange. Stir.

Per Serving

CALORIES: **206**
FAT: **0.31g**
SODIUM: **117mg**
FIBER: **12g**
PROTEIN: **4.4g**
SUGARS: **32g**
CARBOHYDRATES: **55g**

Berry Melon

» **Good for juice fasting**

The high water content in fruit juice has long been touted as a natural cleansing agent. The water in your fruit isn't just ordinary water; it's full of vitamins, minerals, enzymes, and electrolytes.

INGREDIENTS | YIELD: 1½ CUPS

½ cantaloupe, rind removed
1 cup strawberries

Juice cantaloupe and strawberries. Stir.

Per Serving

CALORIES: **170**
FAT: **1.2g**
SODIUM: **59mg**
FIBER: **6.6g**
PROTEIN: **4.6g**
SUGARS: **25g**
CARBOHYDRATES: **32g**

Cucumber Lemonade

» **Good for juice fasting**

Lemon juice is a natural diuretic that helps eliminate excess fluids. This simple, refreshing juice is perfect for a hot summer's day or night.

INGREDIENTS | YIELD: 1 CUP

2 cucumbers, peeled
1 lemon, peeled

Juice cucumbers and lemon. Stir.

Per Serving

CALORIES: **65**
FAT: **0.2g**
SODIUM: **9.2mg**
FIBER: **3.8g**
PROTEIN: **2.6g**
SUGARS: **14g**
CARBOHYDRATES: **30g**

CHAPTER 6

Juice Detoxing and Cleansing

Advocates of juice detoxing claim it's an age-old cure that continues to work in modern times to alleviate the body of excesses. Juice detox diets revolve around juices as well as solid foods like whole fruits and vegetables, while juice fasts are liquid diets that exclude all solid foods. Proponents of juice detox diets claim they promote self-healing and rejuvenation by giving the body a rest from its job of digesting food and supplying the body with the vitamins, nutrients, and antioxidants it needs to draw out and eliminate toxins via increased urination and bowel movements.

The Cons of Juice Detox Diets

Physicians and other medial experts insist detox diets are unnecessary and ineffective quick fixes that are potentially dangerous—and can even be deadly. Severe juice detox diets can lead to fatigue, indigestion, poor skin tone, muscle pain and weakness, halitosis, and unexplained weight loss.

ALERT

Critics claim that juice detox diets are unnecessary because the body already has several systems in place to flush out toxins. They argue that the liver, kidneys, and gastrointestinal tract all do a perfectly good job of eliminating toxins from the body within hours of consumption.

Many juice detox diets rely on water and raw fruit to supply nutrients and laxatives, enemas, or colonic irrigation to speed the detox process. They result in only temporary water weight loss and are potentially dangerous. Laxative abuse can cause severe dehydration and heart or colon damage. Colonic irrigation, another fixture of some juice detox diets, carries the risk of bowel perforation or infection, both of which can cause death. Those who oppose juice detox diets claim that while eliminating large quantities of alcohol, smoke, and junk food from a person's lifestyle can certainly be beneficial, most juice detox diets are not moderate enough to be healthful.

The Reality of the Alleged Benefits

People embarking on juice detox diets often report improved energy, clearer skin, regular bowel movements, improved digestion, and increased concentration and clarity. In addition, many people report losing weight by adhering to strict regimens that typically revolve around low-calorie, low-carb foods, and liquid meals.

However, critics of detox diets claim the alleged benefits of juice fasting are actually the result of other factors: Fewer headaches can be traced to reductions in alcohol and caffeine intake, clearer skin can result from improved hydration, less bloating can result from eating less food, and the energy boost and euphoria is actually a reaction to starvation.

Side Effects of Juice Detox Diets

One of the most common side effects within the first few days of starting the juice detox diet is a headache, which is often the result of caffeine withdrawal. For this reason, many people taper off from caffeine before starting a juice detox diet.

ALERT

If you experience a worsening of symptoms or new symptoms that occur during a juice detox diet, it's time to stop and see your physician. Juice detox diets that are continued for an extended period of time may result in nutritional deficiencies, especially protein and calcium.

Other side effects range from excessive diarrhea, which can lead to dehydration and electrolyte loss, to constipation if you're consuming excess fiber without also increasing your fluid intake. Tiredness, irritability, acne, weight loss, and hunger may also occur.

Enhancing and Speeding the Effects of Juice Detox Diets

In addition to following a detox diet, you can also speed the process and its benefits in a number of ways, from massage and aerobic exercise to the use of colonics and enemas. While there are no medical studies proving these therapies actually enhance detoxing, many of them are perfectly healthy on their own.

Here are some of the more popular ways advocates recommend enhancing your juice detox diet:

- Cleanse your lungs of the pounds of pollutants you inhale each day by doing yoga, aerobic exercise, and using machines that add moisture to your environment, including vaporizers, ultrasonic humidifiers, and dehumidifiers. Drinking teas like comfrey, horehound and lobelia, which have cleansing qualities, will also purify your lungs.

- Cleanse your skin and increase circulation, which helps reduce toxins, by using a loofa. Use a natural sea-fiber brush as well as steam baths, which soften skin and stimulate circulation; hot baths with Epsom or Dead Sea salts; or stimulating herbs such as ginger, sage, or cayenne.
- Flush your kidneys by drinking distilled water, which has no mineral or nutritional content.
- Increase the flow of urine by using cleansing herbs high in vitamin C, such as juniper berries, parsley, and wild carrot, and juices made with watermelon rind, parsley, cranberry, cucumber, celery, aloe vera, wheatgrass, dandelion, strawberry, and asparagus.
- Detox your liver, your body's most important detox organ, by purging it with juices made of carrot, beet, wheatgrass, lemon, grapefruit, apple, and spinach. Or use healing herbs in teas or hot and cold compresses. Good herbs to use include black cohosh, bitterroot, goldenseal, and mandrake. You can also add a teaspoon of olive oil to juices to stimulate the release of bile from the gall bladder.
- Get a full body massage. This is one of the best ways to enhance detoxification because it mechanically stimulates the liver. Advocates claim that daily massages can make your juice detox diet twice as fast and effective.
- Drink natural laxative and bulk drinks to maintain the movement of waste through the colon. These include juices made with flaxseed and psyllium seeds. Stimulating herbs include peppermint, rhubarb root, aloe, wheatgrass, and goldenseal.
- Aerobic exercise is also important during juice detox diets because it increases respiration and sweating out of toxins. Running, jogging, walking, biking, swimming, and dancing are all good exercise options. But don't overdo it during detox diets. The point of aerobic exercise in this case is not to build strength, but to enhance detoxification.

Best Detox Fruits and Vegetables

If you've heard of super foods, you already know that many fruits and vegetables provide you with extensive health benefits. Studies show that many fruits and vegetables contain a variety of cancer-fighting substances. Super foods are rich in nutrients and phytochemicals that help cleanse the body and prevent serious diseases such as diabetes and rheumatism. Many fruits and vegetables are also high in glutathione, a powerful antioxidant that converts fat-soluble toxins to less harmful forms that you can easily excrete.

Top Ten Detox Foods

If you're thinking about cleansing your body and lowering your weight, eating clean is a great first step, according to detox diet proponents. The following ten fruits and vegetables are known for their cleansing and purifying qualities. In addition, the following foods energize cleansing enzymes in the liver, your body's own detox agent.

1. **Green leafy vegetables**. The chlorophyll helps flush out environmental toxins such as heavy metals, pesticides, and air pollution. Load up on parsley, spinach, kale, chard, mustard greens, and wheatgrass. Research shows that chlorophyll may also block genetic changes that cause the production of carcinogenic substances in cells.
2. **Lemons**. High in vitamin C, the detox vitamin, lemons help convert toxins into a water-soluble form that's easily flushed away.
3. **Watercress**. These peppery little green leaves are rich in minerals and also have a diuretic effect that helps move things through your system.
4. **Garlic**. Garlic activates liver enzymes that help filter out wastes. Research shows garlic juice may also inhibit the growth of tumors.
5. **Green tea**. Green tea is rich in antioxidants and tannins, which help reduce the growth of tumors. It also contains catechins, which speed up liver activity and help flush out toxins, and polyphenols, which inhibit the formation of some carcinogens.
6. **Broccoli**. This cruciferous veggie contains up to fifty times more cancer-fighting, enzyme-stimulating activity than any other vegetable.
7. **Beets**. Beet juice cleanses and nourishes the liver.
8. **Psyllium and sesame seeds**. High in soluble fiber, psyllium flushes toxins and cholesterol from the system. Stir powdered psyllium into juice to help cleanse your colon. Sesame seeds help protect liver cells from the damaging effects of alcohol and other chemicals. Include a tablespoon of tahini, a concentrated form of sesame seeds, into vegetable juices.

9. **Carrots**. Carrots are high in beta-carotene and are also believed to have potent anti-cancer properties. They also help flush out toxins.
10. **All fruits**. High in vitamin C, fiber, and nutritious fluids, fruits are packed with hundreds of disease-fighting phytochemicals and antioxidants. Tomatoes are good sources of lycopene, which has been shown to help prevent prostate cancer. They are also packed with phytochemicals that block the formation of carcinogenic compounds in the body.

Flushing It All Out

Juice detox diets are also helpful for flushing out internal organs important in cleansing and purifying your body, including your kidneys, gallbladder, intestines, and liver.

Cleansing Your Kidneys

The kidneys are the body's most important sites for eliminating toxins and are also instrumental in maintaining a healthy acid-alkaline balance in the body. Produce that acts as a natural diuretic strengthens the kidneys and helps promote the elimination of waste through urination.

FACT

To reduce the incidence of kidney stones, drink heavily diluted cranberry juice or nettle tea. Kidney stones, which form when several substances crystallize in the urine, can form after long periods of inactivity as well as from consuming a high-acid diet. Foods high in acid include meat, dairy, coffee, and soft drinks.

The most important fruit and vegetable juices to consume to detox your kidneys include carrot, beet, celery, asparagus, cucumber, sprouts, jicama, fresh mint, watermelon, papaya, and coconut milk.

Detoxing Your Gallbladder

Bile is made in the liver and stored in the gallbadder until it's needed by the small intestine. Bile acids are essential for keeping cholesterol soluble so it doesn't form gallstones—which are usually caused by a diet high in fat and sugar and low in fiber.

ESSENTIAL

To cleanse your gallbladder of toxins, eat only a vegan diet, avoiding all meat, poultry, fish, eggs, and dairy products, as well as fried foods and nuts. Instead, consume a diet high in fresh fruit and vegetable juices, including apples, carrots, beets, cucumbers, lemon juice, and chamomile tea.

In addition, avoid alcohol, sugary food, food that contains gluten, soft drinks, junk food, caffeine, and tobacco. Drink diluted prune juice once a week.

Intestinal Flush

As intestinal waste builds up, the motion of the intestines becomes less effective, and waste takes longer to go through the digestive tract, which can lead to constipation and parasitic infections. It can also prevent your body from absorbing nutrients and permit toxins to enter the bloodstream instead of being eliminated. To cleanse your intestines, drink high-fiber juices with added psyllium or flaxseed.

Make a "milkshake" that includes psyllium and bentonite clay (available in health food stores). This has been used for centuries to cleanse the intestine, according to nutritionist Cherie Calbom, M.S., author of the *The Juice Lady's Guide to Juicing for Health*. Advocates claim that bentonite clay is particularly effective in absorbing toxins. This filling shake will reduce your appetite as it cleanses your intestines, facilitating weight loss.

Liver Cleanser

Your liver is your largest internal organ, and it's also one of the most important when it comes to detoxifying your body, filtering blood, excreting toxins, and creating and secreting bile.

Overexposure to toxic chemicals, drugs, and alcohol can impair the liver and lead to a host of health issues, including digestive problems, dizziness, fatigue, migraines, body odor, bad breath, age spots, insomnia, loss of memory or an inability to concentrate, loss of sexual desire, anxiety, allergies, yeast infections, constipation, cellulite, hemorrhoids, and an inability to tolerate heat and cold.

FACT

The easiest way to cleanse the liver is to go on a vegan diet for a week, avoiding alcohol, tobacco, sweets, and junk food. Fruits and vegetables that help cleanse the liver include carrots, apples, lemons and limes, dandelion greens, tomatoes, radishes, string beans, romaine lettuce, Brussels sprouts, mint, and wheatgrass.

Juice Detox Dos, Don'ts and Danger Signs

Juice detox diets aren't for everyone and should not be considered until you consult a physician to rule out medical causes for fatigue, indigestion, cough, muscle pain, and poor sleep, all of which can be signs of serious diseases and illnesses.

People Who Should Not Use Juice Detox Diets

There are certain people who should never embark on juice detox diets, or should do so only under the supervision of a physician. They include pregnant or nursing women, children, and people with anemia, eating disorders, diabetes, kidney disease, thyroid disease, autoimmune disease, cancer, terminal illness, certain genetic diseases, and other chronic conditions.

ALERT

If you abuse drugs or alcohol, going on a juice detox diet will not help you kick the habit. Instead of trying to kick the habit yourself with a do-it-yourself juice detox diet, talk to your physician about going through an in-house alcohol or drug detox program that is supervised by trained professionals.

One Size Doesn't Fit All

Not all juice detox diets are created equal. Many commercial juice detox diets and books offer one-size-fits-all claims when a more individualized approach is actually required. Juice detox diets also vary in their benefits and healthfulness. Some, including water diets and those that prescribe eating only one food for several days at a time, can be quite damaging. Others lack adequate nutrients to sustain health and energy because of their highly restrictive nature.

FACT

Is your juice detox diet really eliminating toxins from your body? Experts claim no one really knows. While you can find commercial tests that allegedly measure the level of specific toxins in the body, the tests are not recognized or considered valid by the medical community, who consider them a waste of time and money.

Those who embark on juice detox diets are often at the mercy of manufacturers' claims and promises. Neither the Food and Drug Administration nor the Federal Trade Commission monitors detox diets and preparations and the health claims they promise.

Danger Signs of Juice Detox Diets

Celebrities and supermodels may sing the praises of juice detox diets, but remember that very few of them are going it alone. Most of them have help from personal physicians and full-time nutritionists, personal trainers, and/or chefs, all of whom can ensure they get the nutrients they need to avoid serious health ramifications.

Dawn Page is a dramatic example of what can happen if you follow a dangerous detox diet. After consulting with a nutritionist, the British woman went on what was touted as "the Amazing Hydration Diet," consuming large amounts of water and drastically limiting her intake of salt. After a few days, she was rushed to the hospital because of uncontrolled vomiting, and was ultimately left with permanent brain damage and diagnosed as an epileptic.

Although she sued and won $1.6 million dollars from the manufacturer of the diet, she will have to live with the consequences of this diet for the rest of her life. She now suffers seizures and memory and learning problems, is unable to drive, and has to take medication.

ALERT

Many celebrities who go on juice detox diets are young and healthy enough to sustain temporary nutritional deficiencies. This may not be the case for someone who is older, or whose health is already compromised by health issues or diseases. If you're already suffering from a disease, consult your physician before embarking on a detox diet.

Some Common Nightmares of Juice Detox Diets

Medical experts cite a host of possible medical problems associated with juice detox diets. They include loss of important nutrients in the body, which can lead to lethargy and illness, loss of skin elasticity because of rapid weight loss, and sickness.

ALERT

One particularly dire warning listed in the *Master Cleanser* diet book, a best-selling detox diet, is that you can become ill or even die if you don't go off of the diet properly. If you're convinced a detox diet is for you, but you're not the sort of person to follow directions to the letter, you may want to rule out *Master Cleanser*.

Other dangers include an increased risk of yo-yo dieting (most detox dieters regain their lost weight as soon as they go back on solid foods because they never learn how to maintain a healthy weight while eating real food), eating disorders, and embarrassing gas or bowel leakage.

Look Before You Leap

What's particularly frightening about Dawn Page's story is that she started the diet on the recommendation of a nutritionist. The moral of the story: Always talk to your doctor before you go on any sort of diet, no matter how harmless it may seem.

Citrus and Cucumber

» Good for treating kidney stones and cleansing the liver and gallbladder

This refreshing juice provides the tang of citrus and the kick of ginger. Soothing cucumber softens the flavor so you end up with a well-balanced drink.

INGREDIENTS | YIELD: ¾ CUP

1 cucumber, peeled
1 orange, peeled
¼" slice ginger root

Juice cucumber, orange, and ginger root. Stir.

Per Serving

CALORIES: **95**
FAT: **0.4g**
SODIUM: **5.1mg**
FIBER: **4g**
PROTEIN: **2.6g**
SUGARS: **19g**
CARBOHYDRATES: **29g**

Super Melon

» Good for detoxing

This recipe provides fruits that are rich in beta-carotene, vitamin C, and potassium.

INGREDIENTS | YIELD: 1½ CUPS

1 cup watermelon, rind removed
1 cup cantaloupe, rind removed
1 orange, peeled

Juice melons and orange. Stir.

Per Serving

CALORIES: **164**
FAT: **0.83g**
SODIUM: **27mg**
FIBER: **4.4g**
PROTEIN: **4.5g**
SUGARS: **36g**
CARBOHYDRATES: **43g**

Cantaloupe or Muskmelon?
Cantaloupe was named for a castle in Italy. Real cantaloupe is from Europe and is not exported. American cantaloupe is technically called muskmelon; the fruit was probably introduced to North America in the sixteenth century. Cantaloupe should have a netting appearance on a beige-colored skin when it is ripe.

Papaya Strawberry

» Good for intestinal health

Papaya is a great cleansing fruit and is also good for people with liver problems, constipation, and urinary disorders.

INGREDIENTS | **YIELD: 1¼ CUPS**

2 papayas
1 cup strawberries, hull intact

Juice papayas and strawberries. Stir.

Per Serving

CALORIES: **103**
FAT: **0.65g**
SODIUM: **5.7mg**
FIBER: **5.6g**
PROTEIN: **1.9g**
SUGARS: **19g**
CARBOHYDRATES: **32g**

What is Papain?

Papayas contain papain, a digestive enzyme that is used in meat tenderizers to break down tough meat fibers. South Americans have used papain to tenderize meat for centuries, and it is now available in powdered meat tenderizers all over the world. Papaya is a very good source of vitamins A and C.

Blueberry Banana

» Good for curing bladder infections

Berries are blood purifiers. They contain antioxidants, which protect your body from heart disease and cancer, and help prevent bladder infections, high blood pressure, fatigue, colds, and bad breath.

INGREDIENTS | **YIELD: 1½ CUPS**

2 cups blueberries
1 banana, peeled

Juice blueberries. Add banana and blend well. Stir.

Per Serving

CALORIES: **241**
FAT: **1.2g**
SODIUM: **3.7mg**
FIBER: **8g**
PROTEIN: **3.8g**
SUGARS: **38g**
CARBOHYDRATES: **59g**

Blueberries

Blueberries are extremely low in calories—½ cup has just 40 calories—but they're also high in antioxidants. These sweet yet tart fruits pack a nutritious punch. Blueberries also protect against short-term memory loss, lower cholesterol, and enhance memory. Blueberries are readily available, but you can also pick your own. Find a farm near you at *www.pickyourown.org*.

Apple Beeter

» Good for liver health

Beet juice can detoxify your liver. Beets encourage liver function and health and are good for treating alcoholism.

INGREDIENTS | YIELD: 1 CUP

1 beet, greens removed
2 red apples, cored

Juice beet and apples. Stir.

Per Serving

CALORIES: **101**
FAT: **0.46g**
SODIUM: **66mg**
FIBER: **5g**
PROTEIN: **1.7g**
SUGARS: **23g**
CARBOHYDRATES: **32g**

Bitter Remedy
If any of your juices are too bitter for your taste, apples are a perfect sweetener. You can add one or two apples to a juice until it reaches your desired level of sweetness. Beets can be a bitter-tasting vegetable, so this recipe is a good one to try extra apples in.

Watermelon Straight Up

» Good for detox

Watermelon is a good treat after a workout or whenever you feel dehydrated. It is very high in electrolytes and vitamin C.

INGREDIENTS | YIELD: 1 CUP

1 cup watermelon, rind removed
1 lime, peeled

Juice watermelon and lime. Stir.

Per Serving

CALORIES: **65**
FAT: **0.32g**
SODIUM: **2.8mg**
FIBER: **2g**
PROTEIN: **2.2g**
SUGARS: **11g**
CARBOHYDRATES: **20g**

Watermelon
Watermelon is native to Africa. The most popular in the United States is the long oval shaped variety or striped two-tone green. They average fifteen to thirty-five pounds. Watermelon is available May through September. In Japan, farmers figured out a way to grow square watermelons to save space. However, they cost a premium.

Zucchini Juice

» **Good for liver health**

Zucchini is a good source of vitamin C, lutein, and sodium, which are healthy nutrients for your liver. In addition, lutein promotes good eye health.

INGREDIENTS | YIELD: 1 CUP

1 green zucchini
3 carrots, peeled
2 red apples, cored

Juice zucchini, carrots, and apples. Stir.

Per Serving

CALORIES: **226**
FAT: **1g**
SODIUM: **131mg**
FIBER: **13g**
PROTEIN: **5g**
SUGARS: **37g**
CARBOHYDRATES: **64g**

Zucchini

Zucchini is available year round. Choose smaller zucchini because they tend to be younger and more tender. Zucchini is one of the most versatile vegetables. It can be enjoyed on its own or shredded and used to bake bread or complement the flavors of other dishes.

Super Gallbladder Assister

» **Good for gallbladder health**

Dark green leafy vegetables can help with gallbladder problems. They are also excellent detoxifiers.

INGREDIENTS | YIELD 1 QUART

1 bunch spinach
1 cucumber, peeled
½ bunch celery, leaves intact
1 bunch parsley
½" piece fresh ginger root
2 apples, cored
½ lime, peeled
½ lemon, peeled

Juice ingredients in order. Stir.

Per Serving

CALORIES: **225**
FAT: **2.6g**
SODIUM: **461mg**
FIBER: **17g**
PROTEIN: **14g**
SUGARS: **28g**
CARBOHYDRATES: **48g**

The Benefits of Green Juice

Green juice provides enzymes that the body needs to digest food as well as substantial amounts of chlorophyll, which increases the flow of oxygen in our bodies.

Orange Beet

>> ## Good for liver health and detoxing

Beet juice must be mixed with other juices. This is a great combination and perfect way to get your beets.

INGREDIENTS | YIELD: ¾ CUP

2 oranges, peeled
1 beet, greens removed

Juice oranges and beet. Stir.

Per Serving

CALORIES: **165**
FAT: **0.81g**
SODIUM: **65mg**
FIBER: **8.1g**
PROTEIN: **4.5g**
SUGARS: **31g**
CARBOHYDRATES: **42g**

Beets
Beets are root vegetables. The leaves and the root are edible; the root is a bulb with reddish flesh. Greens should be removed from beets immediately since they remove moisture from the beet. Beets may be stored for up to three weeks in the refrigerator in a plastic bag.

Carrot Cucumber Beet

>> ## Good for liver health

This is a great drink for detoxing the liver. The carrots give it sweetness, making it easy to enjoy.

INGREDIENTS | YIELD: 1¼ CUPS

3 carrots, peeled
1 cucumber, peeled
1 beet, greens removed

Juice carrots, cucumber, and beet. Stir.

Per Serving

CALORIES: **201**
FAT: **0.41g**
SODIUM: **186mg**
FIBER: **13g**
PROTEIN: **6.7g**
SUGARS: **31g**
CARBOHYDRATES: **59g**

Beet Colors
Beets come in many colors, from deep red to orange. They also can be white. The Chioggia beet is called a candy cane beet because it has red and white rings. Small or medium beets are more tender than larger ones. Beets can be enjoyed on their own or flavored with some butter, salt, and pepper for a simple side dish.

Green Apple Broccoli

» **Good for curing bladder infections**

Broccoli is rich in vitamins A, B, C, and K; fiber; zinc; folic acid; magnesium; iron; and beta-carotene.

INGREDIENTS | **YIELD: 1½ CUPS**

2 Granny Smith apples, cored
1 orange, peeled
⅛ cup Italian parsley
1 cup broccoli

Juice apples and orange. Juice broccoli and Italian parsley. Stir.

Per Serving

CALORIES: **161**
FAT: **0.89g**
SODIUM: **31mg**
FIBER: **8g**
PROTEIN: **4.1g**
SUGARS: **32g**
CARBOHYDRATES: **47g**

Italian Parsley

Italian parsley is also known as flat leaf parsley. It has more nutrients and flavor than curly parsley and is easy to grow in an herb garden or window box. Choose parsley with no signs of wilting and bright green leaves. You can juice it with apples and bananas for a sweet, slightly tangy drink.

Mango Tea

» **Good for detox**

The fresh juice of mango mixed with an herbal tea of your choice provides a really great tasting tea.

INGREDIENTS | **YIELD: 2 CUPS**

½ mango, pit removed
1 herbal tea bag, brewed with hot water

Juice mango. Brew tea. Add ¼ cup mango juice to tea. Stir.

Per Serving

CALORIES: **70**
FAT: **0.23g**
SODIUM: **4.5mg**
FIBER: **2.1g**
PROTEIN: **1g**
SUGARS: **15g**
CARBOHYDRATES: **18g**

Herbal Teas

Herbal teas have been around for many years and have been used to treat a variety of health problems. They are also known for their earthy taste and soothing effect. There is a wide variety of herbal teas available in the market, some especially recommended for the detoxification process. As well as being delicious and nutritious, herbal teas are often caffeine-free.

CHAPTER 7

Juicing for Increased Happiness and Mental Stability

You are what you eat. Fortunately, the vitamins, minerals, antioxidants, and phytochemicals in fruits and vegetables are natural mood stabilizers that have been shown to alleviate a host of emotional and mental problems, including depression, panic attacks, stress, migraines, attention deficit disorder, and tinnitus—even Alzheimer's disease. Nutritional deficiencies can set off or exacerbate existing conditions. Juicing is a delicious, natural way to alleviate stress and anxiety, providing a condensed form of essential nutrients needed for mental and emotional health.

Nutrients that Enhance Mental Health and Wellness

Feeling down, depressed, or anxious? Before deciding to treat the problem with antidepressants or other powerful mood lifters, you may want to give the friendly produce in your refrigerator bin a chance. New studies show that fresh fruits and vegetables contain powerful mood elevators that promote mental and emotional health without the side effects of medication.

ALERT

A new study from the American College of Obstetricians and Gynecologists finds that the dangers of antidepressant use in pregnant women outweigh the advantages. Women using antidepressants during pregnancy had a higher risk of miscarriage, low birth weight, and preterm delivery. There was also an increased risk of congenital heart defects in the baby.

The side effects of antidepressants include weight gain or loss, intense restlessness, insomnia, fatigue, sexual dysfunction, panic attacks, and anxiety. Other studies show an increased risk of bleeding disorders, such as gastro-intestinal bleeding, bruising, and nosebleeds. Antidepressants also carry a high potential for drug interactions and have been linked with worsening depression and suicide, especially in teenagers.

Those Wonderful Vitamin Bs

Fortunately, you can avoid those dangerous and unpleasant side effects by substituting nature's own mood elevators—B-complex vitamins. Vitamin B deficiencies have been linked to depression and anxiety. Vitamin B also helps metabolize neurotoxins that may be linked to anxiety problems and can help with severe forms of depression.

Here's a rundown of the many types of vitamin B that can help combat anxiety:

- **Thiamine, or B1**, reduces feelings of irritability and mental confusion. A deficiency of B-1 can lead to fatigue, irritability, depression, anxiety, and loss of appetite, insomnia, and memory impairment. Thiamin also helps to temporarily correct some complications of metabolic disorders associated with genetic diseases.

- **B12** is important in the formation of red blood cells. Deficiencies of B12 vitamin can cause mood swings, paranoia, irritability, confusion, and hallucinations. The vitamin is most active against depression. Because the human body stores several years' worth of vitamin B12, nutritional deficiency is extremely rare, although inability to absorb vitamin B12 from the intestinal tract can be caused by pernicious anemia. In addition, strict vegetarians or vegans who are not taking in proper amounts of B12 may be prone to deficiency.

- **Inositol** is a compound found in vitamin B that has been proven to alleviate panic attacks.

- **Pantothenic acid** helps reduce stress by building the body's resistance to it.

- **Niacin (vitamin B3)** has been shown to help reduce anxiety, depression, and insomnia, and has a chemical composition similar to Valium, a benzodiazepine tranquilizer.

- **Vitamin B5** helps the body manufacture anti-stress hormones.

- **Pyridoxine, or vitamin B6**, is another vitamin that helps diminish anxiety, especially in women.

- **Folic acid** is a B vitamin that is instrumental in keeping your blood healthy. A deficiency in folic acid causes a decrease in healthy red blood cells, which carry oxygen throughout your body. The result is lethargy and headaches, which may cause irritability and anxiety.

ALERT

Alcohol, nicotine, sugar, and caffeine destroy B vitamins, so it's essential to consume an adequate amount of B-complex vitamins every day. Juicing is an easy and delicious way to consume a variety of B vitamins in one glass.

The Wonders of Vitamin C

Vitamin C is useful for regulating cortisol secretion in the body. Cortisol is necessary for the fight or flight response to stressful situations, but too much of it can be unhealthy. Cortisol is released by the adrenal glands and sends stress signals throughout the body and mind.

FACT

The daily recommended dosage for vitamin C is 60 milligrams, but you may need to take a much higher dose to reduce stress. In a study published in the *International Journal of Sports Medicine*, vitamin C was found to be most effective in regulating adrenal stress hormones at 1,500 milligrams per day in athletes.

Vitamin E to the Rescue

Psychological stress can result in oxidative stress; that's when free radicals accumulate in the body and result in cell damage. Vitamin E can help combat oxidative stress by working with vitamins B and C to repair and protect the nervous system. Vitamin E also supports a healthy immune system, which helps prevent mood swings. A deficiency of vitamin E in the body can make stress quickly turn into more serious problems like depression. Oxidative stress can also lead to neuron damage and cancer, but vitamin E protects the body against this type of damage as well.

The Wonders of Vitamin D

Research published in *Medical Hypotheses* found that a deficiency of vitamin D increased anxiety and altered emotional behavior in mice. Another study found that a deficiency of vitamin D was also associated with depression and poor moods.

Happy Minerals

Minerals help relieve anxiety and mineral deficiencies that are sometimes indirect causes of anxiety.

- **Magnesium:** Too little causes confusion, agitation, anxiety, and hallucinations.
- **Iron:** Transports life-sustaining nutrients throughout the body along with oxygen while removing carbon dioxide. Iron ensures a healthy immune system and creates energy. A deficiency in iron can cause a variety of health problems including fatigue, irritability, and headaches.
- **Taurine:** A little-known amino acid that plays an essential role in metabolism and mental functioning. Studies also link taurine to the regulation of insulin in the body. In addition, taurine stimulates the body's immune system. Taurine has also been suggested as a potential treatment for epilepsy, cardiovascular disease, diabetes, alcoholism, cystic fibrosis, and Alzheimer's. Many vegetarians are deficient in this amino acid and should take a supplement to ensure mental health.
- **Potassium:** Necessary for proper functioning of cells, nerves, and muscle cells. Deficiencies in potassium can cause weakness, fatigue, depression, and anxiety.
- **Chromium:** Helps stabilize blood sugar levels, which in turn helps prevent mood swings and depression.
- **Manganese:** Too little results in low levels of neurotransmitters serotonin and epinephrine, which can result in depression and anxiety.
- **Zinc:** A zinc deficiency may cause depression, anxiety, and lethargy.
- **Calcium:** Deficiencies in calcium affect the nerve fibers, leading to nervousness and irritability.
- **Selenium:** Deficiencies can result in anxiety, confusion, and depression.
- **Omega-3 fatty acids:** Found in flaxseed and fish, they help alleviate stress and depression.

Comfort Carbs

Carbohydrates have the ability to increase tryptophan in the brain. Tryptophan is an amino acid needed to produce serotonin, the "happy" neurotransmitter that can help stave off the effects of stress. Fruits, vegetables, and whole grains are all high in carbohydrates.

Herbs that Help

Several herbs also help combat the blues, including lemon balm, ginger, ginkgo biloba, licorice root, oat straw, peppermint, Siberian ginseng, kava kava, and St. John's Wort.

The Nutritional Dangers of Chronic Stress

Stress is the number one cause of a host of ailments that plague society today. Along with exercise, adequate sleep, and a healthy social circle, a diet rich in vitamins and minerals is the best way to fight everyday stress.

ESSENTIAL

Stress releases a number of hormones that rob the body of certain nutrients, including potassium, zinc, and B-complex vitamins. If stress continues for a prolonged period of time, it can put you at risk for heart disease, sleep disorders, obesity, diabetes, memory impairment, and anxiety and depression.

Many people reach for salty, sugary, or greasy snacks and caffeine or alcohol when they are stressed. These are called food stressors because they actually intensify stress inside the body, while foods dubbed as food supporters, including water, vegetables, fruit, and omega-3 rich oils from flaxseed and fish, can help the body fight stress.

By consuming foods that are less than nutritious during stressful times, you deplete your stores of B vitamins, vitamin C, vitamin A, and magnesium, thereby increasing your stress level and upsetting your nervous system, tensing your muscles, and raising your blood pressure.

Best Fruits and Vegetables for Mental Stability and Happiness

Fruits and vegetables are packed with all of the above vitamins and minerals, making them a logical choice when you need a mental boost.

Produce High in B vitamins

From B1 to B12, the B vitamins contain many nutrients you need to maintain well-being and fight depression. B1 or thiamine is found in beef, legumes (beans, lentils), milk, nuts, oats, oranges, pork, rice, seeds, wheat, whole grain cereals, and yeast, including brewer's yeast. In industrialized countries, foods made with white rice or white flour are often fortified with thiamin (because most of the naturally occurring thiamin is lost during the refinement process).

Foods high in inositol include oranges, grapefruit, cantaloupe, peaches, watermelon, strawberries, and tomatoes.

To get Pantothenic Acid, reach for cauliflower, broccoli, and kale. Foods rich in vitamin B3 include peanuts, wheat bran, and brewer's yeast and you can also find small amounts in mushrooms and asparagus. You can find lots of B5 in peanuts, mushrooms, split peas, soy beans and soy flour, and B6 in kale, spinach, turnip greens, bell peppers, and prunes. Foods rich in B12 vitamins include tofu and tempeh. Foods high in folic acid include fava, roman, soy and white beans; lima beans, chickpeas, lentils, spinach and cooked asparagus. It is also present in peanuts, sunflower seeds, romaine lettuce, and orange and pineapple juices, according to Cherie Calbom, author of *The Juice Lady's Guide to Juicing for Health.*

Where to Find Vitamin C

Many fruits and vegetables are high in vitamin C, including citrus fruit, and parsley, which has three times the amount of vitamin C found in oranges. Other great sources of vitamin C include kale, broccoli, Brussels sprouts, watercress, cauliflower, cabbage, strawberries, papaya, spinach, turnips, mangos, asparagus, and cantaloupe.

FACT

To boost the effectiveness of vitamin C, enjoy it with produce that's also high in beta-carotene. Beta-carotene is found in fruits and vegetables with orange skin, such as carrots and mangos, as well as many leafy greens.

Getting Vitamins E and D

Produce rich in vitamin E includes spinach, watercress, asparagus, carrots, and tomatoes.

To get lots of vitamin D, reach for sunflower seeds, sunflower sprouts, and mushrooms, and be sure to get lots of daily sunlight.

Studies show that not getting enough sun prevents the body from producing vitamin D3, the hormonal form of vitamin D. People who live in temperate latitudes with long, cold, and gray winters, may be more prone to multiple sclerosis because of a lack of vitamin D.

Produce that Supplies Carbs and Carotene

Most fruits and vegetables provide carbohydrates, but you'll find an abundance of them in starchy vegetables like potatoes, corn, and rice.

Carotenes are plant pigments that help prevent free-radical damage to the body and help boost the immune system. Find them in carrots, kale, spinach, chard, beet greens, watercress, mangos, cantaloupe, apricots, broccoli, and romaine lettuce.

Mineral-Rich Produce

Here's what to juice to consume a wide array of minerals:

✓ Foods rich in magnesium include beet greens and beets, spinach, parsley, dandelion greens, garlic, blackberries, broccoli, cauliflower, carrots, and celery.

✓ Find iron in parsley, dandelion greens, broccoli, cauliflower, strawberries, asparagus, chard, blackberries, cabbage, beets with greens, carrots, and pineapple.

✓ Foods rich in potassium include parsley, chard, spinach, garlic, carrots, celery, radishes, cauliflower, watercress, asparagus, and cabbage.

- ✓ You'll find plenty of manganese in spinach, beet greens and beets, carrots, broccoli, cabbage, peaches, tangerines, apples, oranges, and pears.
- ✓ Foods rich in zinc include ginger root, turnips, parsley, garlic, carrots, grapes, spinach, cabbage, cucumber, and tangerines.
- ✓ Calcium-rich produce includes kale, parsley, dandelion greens, watercress, beet greens, broccoli, spinach, romaine, string beans, oranges, celery, and carrots.
- ✓ Find selenium in chard, turnips, garlic, oranges, radishes, grapes, carrots, and cabbage.
- ✓ Find omega-3 acids in flaxseed and hemp oil.

How Juicing Helps with Happiness and Mental Stability

It would be difficult to consume all of the fruits and vegetables that contribute to happiness in a single week. But one of the many benefits of juicing is that it allows you to mix and match a wide variety of fruits and vegetables and enjoy myriad nutritional benefits.

The Mix and Match Game

All the recipes in this chapter contain a variety of fruits and vegetables that help fight stress and anxiety by providing a highly condensed version of vitamins, minerals, phytochemicals, and antioxidants.

FACT

By creating a juice that contains a teaspoon of flaxseed (omega-3), cantaloupe (carotene), bananas (carbohydrates), citrus fruit (vitamins B, C, magnesium, and many minerals) and berries (antioxidants), you can cover many of your nutritional needs in one glass of juice. The different combinations of fruits and veggies you can combine in juice are as endless as your imagination!

The Stress Connection

Juicing makes it easy and convenient to consume a diet that is low in fat and sugars and high in fiber. In addition, the carbohydrates found in produce and juice help increase serotonin levels in the brain, producing a feeling of calm.

The natural sugars in juice stave off lethargy and help maintain steady blood sugar levels, which can prevent wildly fluctuating highs, lows, and sugar crashes, while the essential fatty acids in produce may also play a role in alleviating depression. Studies show that people with deficiencies are more prone to anxiety.

How Juicing Helps Other Mental Disorders

The nutrients in juice can help alleviate serious conditions that are associated with stress, such as panic attacks, migraine headaches, and tinnitus, or ringing in the ears.

Juicing for Panic Attacks

Panic attacks are sudden and overwhelming feelings of fear for no reason. They have been linked with everything from food allergies to vitamin and mineral deficiencies. Because low blood sugar, or hypoglycemia, may play a role in triggering panic attacks, drinking juice high in natural sugar and fiber can help alleviate them. In particular, fruits and vegetables high in the B vitamins and the mineral magnesium can help ward off panic attacks.

Juicing for Migraines

Migraines are debilitating headaches that cause throbbing pain, nausea, vomiting, sensitivity to light, ringing in the ears, chills, sweating, and many other symptoms. Although medical science has yet to discover exactly what causes migraines, researchers suspect they may be triggered in part by an excess of serotonin in the brain.

The following nutrients may help ease those pounding headaches:

- **Omega-3s.** Important for brain function, they also have anti-inflammatory and nerve-protecting actions.
- **Ginger.** It has an anti-histamine and anti-inflammatory effect and inhibits blood vessels from swelling at the onset of a headache and nerves, instantly relieving nerves of pressure.
- **Vitamin B2/riboflavin.** Some studies show they reduce the frequency of migraines, though not their duration or severity.
- **Magnesium.** It helps relax blood vessels and maintain normal nerve function. It is found in wheat germ, beans, soy products and dark green leafy vegetables.
- **Caffeine.** It may relieve migraines by constricting blood vessels in your head. Migraines are caused in part by blood vessels that dilate and trigger pain in nerves located in blood vessel walls.

FACT

Toxemia, a condition caused by abnormal levels of toxins in the blood, can irritate the blood vessels and nerves in the head and neck, leading to headaches or migraines. To reduce the incidence of migraines, some experts recommend lowering the level of toxins in your body through meditation, yoga, and a diet of uncooked foods and juices.

Certain foods may also trigger migraines by causing the blood vessels in your head to dilate quickly. The most common culprits are caffeine, MSG, artificial sweeteners, pork, hard aged cheese, red wine, spinach, shellfish, alcohol, strawberries, nitrates, and peanuts. Eliminating these foods from your diet can help prevent migraines.

Getting Rid of the Ringing

A highly annoying condition in which you hear ringing in one ear or both, tinnitus is another condition whose cause is uncertain. However, scientists know it can sometimes be triggered by medications, especially aspirin, as well as by toxins, underlying nutritional deficiencies, and temporomandibular joint syndrome (TMJ), or medical conditions related to the jaw.

To prevent or alleviate tinnitus, eat plenty of vegetables and fruits. Vitamins A, B, and E; proteins; and zinc all are important to prevent tinnitus. Avoid saturated foods, coffee, tea, refined alcohol, and overly sugary and salty food. Vegetables with a high sodium content include celery and asparagus.

FACT

Tinnitis may be caused or exacerbated by vitamin deficiencies, including a lack of chromium (found in brewer's yeast, green pepper, and apples), manganese (found in spinach, turnip greens and beet greens), and choline (found in green beans). Consuming adequate amounts of vitamin B12 (from a vitamin pill) and folic acid (found in spinach, turnip greens, and sweet peppers) may help alleviate symptoms.

Juicing for ADHD

A complicated disease marked by inattention, lack of focus, and hyperactivity, attention deficit hyperactivity disorder (ADHD) is believed to have genetic components and affects millions of children and adults. Scientists have discovered that ADHD may be exacerbated by consuming too much simple sugar, which can disrupt normal blood sugar levels and lead to depression, aggression, hostility, and wild mood swings. In addition, ADHD may be exacerbated by environmental toxins, including heavy metals, and underlying nutritional deficiencies.

Produce that Can Alleviate ADHD Symptoms

Although there's no cure for ADHD, you may be able to ease symptoms by consuming a diet that's low in refined sugars and high in fresh fruits and vegetables, which provide nutrients required for focus and concentration. In addition, it may help to consume juice high in antioxidants and health-producing enzymes, which help reduce toxins in the brain by fighting free radicals. Choose produce high in vitamins E and C, which help fight free radicals, and beta-carotene and selenium, which are both potent antioxidants.

Eliminate Foods that Exacerbate Symptoms

ADHD experts recommend eliminating caffeine, sugar and other sweets, processed food, MSG, aspartame (Nutrasweet) and other sugar substitutes, and any foods that contain preservatives, food dyes, or other chemicals. This includes food found at fast food restaurants, which use MSG and preservatives. Doctors also suggest replacing soda and milk with homemade vegetable and fruit juice.

Juicing for Alzheimer's Disease

Alzheimer's disease is characterized by a buildup of protein in the brain. Although scientists have not been able to measure it in living victims, autopsies have shown the buildup leads to the atrophy of tissue in the frontal and temporal parts of the brain and results in loss of mental capacity.

FACT

Studies show that more than half of people older than age eighty-five suffer from some sort of dementia, the majority of which is caused by Alzheimer's disease. Symptoms range from hallucinations and delusions to aggression, wandering, depression, incontinence, eating disorders, and overt sexuality.

According to the Alzheimer's Association, scientists are still studying how plaque in the brain (which is composed of protein), and "tangles," or twisted fibers of protein that form within dying brain cells in the brain, are related to Alzheimer's disease.

Some experts believe the disease can be prevented by reducing free radical damage in the brain caused by exposure to toxins. Aluminum is one suspected cause of this damage; much-higher-than-normal deposits of aluminum have been found in the brains of those with Alzheimer's.

How Juicing Can Help

Although juicing certainly can't cure Alzheimer's, recent studies show that consuming a diet high in fruits and vegetables, both of which are high in antioxidants, may help prevent cell damage by fighting free radicals in the brain. Fruits contain protective antioxidants called polyphenols that protect the cells from oxidative stress.

According to research presented in the *Journal of Food Science*, neuronal cells treated with extracts from everyday fruits, including apples, bananas, and oranges, protected the cells from oxidative stress. The cells treated with apple extract were most protected, but bananas and oranges showed excellent results. Grapes, cherries, and plums were found to have high antioxidant activity similar to apples.

ESSENTIAL

Because antioxidants gobble up free radicals that damage brain tissue, consuming fruits and vegetables high in antioxidants, beta-carotene, vitamins C and E, and selenium are a good place to start if you have Alzheimer's in the family. Omega-3 fatty acids, zinc, and vitamin B12 may also help ward off the disease.

In another study, blueberries were shown to contain flavanols and anthocyanins, antioxidants that seem to improve memory. Researchers believe these substances help improve memory by strengthening existing neuronal connections, which in turn helps stimulate the regeneration of cells.

Beware of Aluminum

Studies conducted in Norway indicate that people exposed to high levels of aluminum have an increased incidence of Alzheimer's disease and dementia.

FACT

Supplements do not offer the same protective effects against Alzheimer's as fresh juice, which provides the maximum benefits of antioxidants. With the exception of vitamin B12, which is difficult to find in abundance in fruits and vegetables, you can get all the preventive nutrients you need to ward off Alzheimer's by juicing a variety of fresh fruits and vegetables.

The best way to prevent Alzheimer's may be to consume a varied selection of fresh produce in juice that offers high antioxidant activity similar to what was found in apples, grapes, cherries, and plums. Recent studies showed that elderly people who drink fruit or vegetable juice three times per week reduce their risk of Alzheimer's compared to people who drink juice less than once per week.

Garden Delight

» **Good for stress relief and depression**

Do not juice stems or leaves of tomatoes. They can add a bitter flavor to your juice.

INGREDIENTS | YIELD: 1 CUP

1 Roma tomato
1 fist parsley
2 celery stalks, leaves intact
1 bell pepper
2 beet green leaves

Juice ingredients in order listed. Stir.

Per Serving

CALORIES: **70**
FAT: **0.94g**
SODIUM: **236mg**
FIBER: **8.2g**
PROTEIN: **4.4g**
SUGARS: **3g**
CARBOHYDRATES: **20g**

Cherry Plum

» **Good for reducing Alzheimer's disease**

Cherry juice can help prevent premature aging and stop migraine headaches.

INGREDIENTS | YIELD: 1 CUP

1½ cups cherries, pitted
2 black plums, pitted

Juice cherries and plums. Stir.

Per Serving

CALORIES: **99**
FAT: **0.6g**
SODIUM: **2.3mg**
FIBER: **3.1g**
PROTEIN: **1.7g**
SUGARS: **33g**
CARBOHYDRATES: **43g**

Spicy Melon

» ## Good for reducing migraines

Drink a juice made with fresh ginger as soon as you start to feel the symptoms of a migraine.

INGREDIENTS | YIELD: ¾ CUP

½ cantaloupe, peeled
¼" slice fresh ginger root
½ lemon, peeled

Juice cantaloupe, ginger root and lemon. Stir.

Per Serving

CALORIES: **137**
FAT: **0.98g**
SODIUM: **59mg**
FIBER: **4.6g**
PROTEIN: **4g**
SUGARS: **15g**
CARBOHYDRATES: **17g**

A Honey Orange Dew

» ## Good for reducing migraines and stress

This juice is a great source of vitamin C. Honeydew melons are available year round. When they are perfectly ripe, the skin is wrinkled.

INGREDIENTS | YIELD: 1½ CUPS

½ honeydew melon, peeled
½ orange, peeled
½ cup watermelon, peeled

Juice melons and orange. Stir.

Per Serving

CALORIES: **183**
FAT: **0.13g**
SODIUM: **64 mg**
FIBER: **4.2g**
PROTEIN: **3.4g**
SUGARS: **25g**
CARBOHYDRATES: **31g**

Vitamins to the Rescue

Research shows that many antioxidants interact with and protect each other. Vitamin C, for instance, can react with a damaged vitamin E molecule and convert it back to its antioxidant form, while the antioxidant glutathione can return vitamin C to its original form. Studies also show that vitamin C enhances the protective effects of vitamin E.

Fruit Punch

» Good for reducing Alzheimer's disease

Making this fruit punch is much healthier than buying commercial fruit punches, which are loaded with sugar, dyes, and other additives.

INGREDIENTS | YIELD: 1 CUP

1 cup red grapes
1 red apple, cored
5 cherries, pitted
½ lemon, peeled

Juice ingredients in order listed. Stir.

Per Serving

CALORIES: **144**
FAT: **0.8g**
SODIUM: **5.6mg**
FIBER: **4.4g**
PROTEIN: **2.1g**
SUGARS: **32g**
CARBOHYDRATES: **41g**

What is Fruit Punch?

The word punch actually goes back to the year 1632! Many punches are made with wine or rum. Many fruit punches on the market are dyed red and have only a small portion of actual fruit in them. They are filled with corn syrup, citric acid, and artificial flavors. Juice your own to truly reap the nutritional benefits.

Mango Carrot

» Good for reducing ADHD

These ingredients are helpful for ADHD because they are high in selenium and beta-carotene. Carrots can be stored refrigerated in a plastic bag for 3–4 weeks. If your carrots are limp, crisp them up in a bowl of ice water.

INGREDIENTS | YIELD: 1 CUP

3 carrots, peeled
1 mango, peeled and pitted

Juice carrots and mango. Stir.

Per Serving

CALORIES: **276**
FAT: **0.46g**
SODIUM: **121mg**
FIBER: **13g**
PROTEIN: **5.1g**
SUGARS: **50g**
CARBOHYDRATES: **74g**

Popeye's Secret Blend

» Good for reducing migraines

This juice is high in magnesium, which is a natural muscle relaxant. Spinach is very rich in iron and a great source of vitamins A and C. The leaves tend to be gritty, so rinse them thoroughly.

INGREDIENTS | YIELD: 1 CUP

1 cup spinach leaves
1 cucumber, peeled
2 carrots, peeled

Juice spinach, cucumber, and carrots. Stir.

Per Serving

CALORIES: **125**
FAT: **0.13g**
SODIUM: **106mg**
FIBER: **7.6g**
PROTEIN: **3.9g**
SUGARS: **19g**
CARBOHYDRATES: **39g**

Melon Treat

» Good for reducing ADHD

Vanilla extract is made by macerating vanilla beans in a solution of alcohol and water. This mixture is aged for several months. Pure vanilla extract must contain 13.35 ounces of vanilla beans per gallon and 35 percent alcohol. Vanilla extract is brown, clear, and very fragrant.

INGREDIENTS | YIELD: 1 CUP

½ cantaloupe, rind removed
1 lime, peeled
1 tablespoon honey
1 teaspoon pure vanilla extract

Juice cantaloupe and lime. Stir in honey and vanilla extract.

Per Serving

CALORIES: **218**
FAT: **0.94g**
SODIUM: **60mg**
FIBER: **5.6g**
PROTEIN: **4.3g**
SUGARS: **34g**
CARBOHYDRATES: **40g**

Pepper Apple

» ## Good for reducing tinnitus

Bell peppers were named for their shape. Sweet peppers come in many different colors, including yellow, red, orange, green, and even purple. They have a mild and sweet flavor. They are excellent sources of vitamins C and A.

INGREDIENTS | YIELD: 1 CUP

2 red apples, cored
1 bell pepper

Juice apples and pepper. Stir.

Per Serving

CALORIES: **97**
FAT: **0.28g**
SODIUM: **3.3mg**
FIBER: **4.6g**
PROTEIN: **1g**
SUGARS: **17g**
CARBOHYDRATES: **32g**

Carrot Bean

» ## Good for reducing tinnitus

The chlorine found in green beans helps combat tinnitus. Chlorine protects the liver from accumulating fat, is essential for brain development in fetuses, and may help with memory loss associated with aging.

INGREDIENTS | YIELD: 1 CUP

3 carrots, peeled
1 cup French green beans

Juice carrots and beans. Stir.

Per Serving

CALORIES: **185**
FAT: **0.1g**
SODIUM: **121mg**
FIBER: **13g**
PROTEIN: **5g**
SUGARS: **21g**
CARBOHYDRATES: **46g**

Depression Zapper

» **Good for reducing depression**

Dark green vegetables pack a wallop of nutrients, especially folate, which plays a role in the production of serotonin in the brain. Great juicing sources of folate include spinach, kale, Swiss chard, and peas.

INGREDIENTS | YIELD: 1¼ CUPS

4 broccoli spears
½ cup spinach leaves
3 Swiss chard leaves
½ bell pepper

Juice broccoli, spinach, and chard. Juice bell pepper. Stir together.

Per Serving

CALORIES: **76**
FAT: **0.64g**
SODIUM: **348mg**
FIBER: **6.2g**
PROTEIN: **6.1g**
SUGARS: **1.6g**
CARBOHYDRATES: **12g**

Friendly Folate

Men who consumed high levels of folate from green leafy vegetables enjoyed a reduced risk of lung cancer, and women who consumed more leafy greens were 44 percent less likely to get breast cancer, according to the Iowa Women's Health Study.

CHAPTER 8

Juicing for Anti-Aging and Longevity

Forget about Ponce de Leon. The new Fountain of Youth is your juicer, where you can combine all the essential vitamins, minerals, amino acids, essential fatty acids, enzymes, and herbs found in fruits and vegetables into a power-packed anti-aging and life-promoting drink. Scientists now know that antioxidants, the substances that neutralize free radicals, are found in abundance in fresh fruits and vegetables.

Nutrients that Delay Aging

As you age, your body's ability to process nutrients decreases, which means you need to increase your intake of certain vitamins and minerals to stay strong and healthy, and to delay the signs of aging.

While you can get your vitamins and minerals in supplements, your best sources are fresh fruits and vegetables. They provide these nutrients to your body in a more potent form, and your body absorbs more than it would from supplements. Because juice offers a fresh, concentrated version of nutrients, juicing is one of the best ways to fight aging.

FACT

Contrary to common knowledge, the action of free radicals isn't all unhealthy. Most of it is generated by many normal, life-sustaining biochemical reactions that are usually quickly neutralized by the body's built-in free radical scavenging compounds. Only when they multiply out of control do free radicals pose a threat to health and longevity.

Fortunately, by consuming an adequate amount of antioxidants in fresh fruit and vegetable juice, you can ward off the free radical damage that causes chronic degenerative diseases and premature aging. The best known antioxidants for fighting free radicals include vitamins A, C, and E; alpha lipoic acid; and carotenoids.

Those Amazing Carotenoids

Many fruits and vegetables get their vibrant yellow, orange, and red hues from nutrients called carotenoids, the nutrients in plants that are responsible for their color. They include carotenes, which are found in yellow and orange vegetables, and zanthophylls, which are found in green ones. Although they are also found in abundance in leafy greens, the large amount of chlorophyll in these vegetables drowns out the bright colors.

Studies show that carotenoids help strengthen the immune system and may also help prevent heart disease, stroke, certain cancers, and some vision problems, including cataracts and age-related macular degeneration.

Alpha Lipoic Acid to the Rescue

Alpha lipoic acid is a potent antioxidant that plays a metabolic role in the body's conversion of food into energy. In addition, it enhances the healthy effects of glutathione and vitamins C and E. Foods rich in alpha lipoic acid include red meat and brewer's yeast. If you're a vegetarian, you can find alpha lipoic acid supplements that are free of animal products in your local health food store.

Twenty to fifty times more potent than vitamin C and E, proanthocyana-dins (PCOs) are powerhouse antioxidants found in plants and vegetables that may reduce levels of bad cholesterol (LDL) and help prevent hardening of the arteries.

Amazing Vitamin C

Vitamin C is an essential nutrient and a powerful antioxidant that can help reduce the incidence of Parkinson's disease. It may also reduce cardio-vascular disease by raising the level of good cholesterol (HDL) and reduce oxidation of bad cholesterol.

Studies show that vitamin C also helps prevent cataracts, lowers blood pressure in borderline hypertension, and helps prevent many types of cancer. Vitamin C is also a top antiviral agent that helps fight infections, colds, influenza, mononucleosis, hepatitis, and chicken pox.

The Importance of Bs

Although the entire vitamin B family helps reduce aging, chlorine is one of the most essential B vitamins for preventing premature mental aging. Chlorine is an essential part of a neurotransmitter in the brain that's responsible for normal brain functioning.

Anti-Aging Minerals, Herbs, and Other Nutrients

The trace mineral selenium is essential for anti-aging and longevity because it protects the body from dysfunctions of the immune system and helps prevent certain cancers.

Perhaps the biggest super herb for youthfulness is ginkgo biloba. This powerful antioxidant stimulates blood circulation to the brain and the extremities. It also increases the brain's tolerance for oxygen deficiency, wards off oxygen deprivation to the heart, and prevents nerve damage from toxic chemicals.

Vitamin K, a fat-soluble vitamin, is beneficial in preventing bone-related disorders like osteoporosis. It also reduces disorders of the heart and blood vessels, helps prevent stroke and Alzheimer's disease, and reduces the incidence of arteriosclerosis.

The Thirty-Three Best Anti-Aging Fruits and Vegetables

The North Carolina Research Campus, encompassing eight universities working together for the benefit of health and longevity, has put together a list of the best foods to consume for health, longevity, and anti-aging.

The Best Fruits for Anti-Aging and Longevity

Here are the best fruits to consume to boost energy and ward off the signs of aging, according to the study compiled by the North Carolina Research Campus (NCRC):

- **Pineapple** promotes joint health and reduces asthma inflammation. Pineapple is high in vitamin C and also contains bromelain, an enzyme that promotes digestion, reduces arthritis, prevents swelling after trauma, relieves sinusitis, reduces angina, and suppresses appetite.
- **Blueberries** restore antioxidant levels and reverse age-related brain decline. They also prevent urinary tract infections. Blueberries are rich in compounds that strengthen collagen structure. Their distinctive blue color comes from anthocyanins, powerful antioxidants that are so prevalent in blueberries that they push blueberries right to the top of the antioxidant champion food tree. There are at least five types of anthocyanins in blueberries, and blueberries contain more antioxidants than other super foods.
- **Tomatoes** reduce inflammation and lower the risk of developing cardiovascular disease and esophageal, stomach, colorectal, lung, and pancreatic cancer. Packed with the antioxidant lycopene, which helps prevent degenerative diseases and reduce the risk of certain cancers, tomatoes also help fight inflammation.
- **Apples** support immunity, fight lung and prostate cancer, and lower Alzheimer's risk. Apples provide a wide range of phytonutrients such as catechin, quercetin, phloridzin, and chlorogenic acid, which act as antioxidants to fight disease. Apples also contain fiber and flavonoids.

- **Avocados** reduce liver damage, lower the risk of oral cancer, and help reduce high cholesterol.
- **Blackberries** build bone density, suppress appetite, and enhance fat burning. Blackberries are rich in bioflavonoids.
- **Cantaloupe** enhances the immune system, protects against sunburn and swelling, and acts as a natural diuretic. It contains a compound called adenosine, which thins the blood and relieves angina.
- **Cherries** help reduce the pain of arthritis and gout, lower high cholesterol, and decrease inflammation. Cherries contain high amounts of the compound keracyanin, the agent responsible for healing gout, as well as high levels of bioflavonoids.
- **Cranberries** help ease prostate pain and protect against lung, colon, and leukemia cancer cells. Cranberry juice is also effective in preventing urinary tract infections. Cranberries are high in vitamin C.
- **Kiwifruit** helps fight wrinkles, lowers the risk of blood clots, decreases blood lipids, and relieves constipation. One kiwifruit has nearly twice the vitamin C of an orange and can help reduce inflammation.
- **Mango** enhances the immune system, lowers cholesterol, and helps protect the arteries. Mangos are rich in bromelain, an enzyme that aids digestion.
- **Oranges** lower bad cholesterol, help reduce the risk of certain cancers, and fight childhood leukemia. The pectin in oranges is a natural appetite suppressant, and oranges are loaded with vitamin C.
- **Papaya** contains bromelain, an enzyme that aids digestion, lowers the incidence of lung cancer, and helps burn fat.
- **Plums** and **prunes** are packed with fiber, which alleviates constipation, and antioxidants, which protect against bone loss in menopause.
- **Pomegranates** contain enzymes that help protect against sunburn, fight bad cholesterol, and help lower the risk of prostate cancer. Pomegranates are loaded with some of the most potent known antioxidants.
- **Pumpkin** helps protect joints from certain types of arthritis, reduce the risk of certain cancers, and decrease inflammation. Pumpkin contains vitamin C and lots of fiber.
- **Raspberries** help fight the growth of certain cancers, and their high levels of antioxidants help decrease high cholesterol levels.

Raspberries are also a traditional remedy for high blood pressure and are loaded with vitamin C.

- **Strawberries** help reduce the incidence of Alzheimer's disease, lower bad cholesterol, and inhibit the growth of colon, prostate, and oral cancers. Strawberries are packed with B vitamins, vitamin C, and ellagic acid, an anti-cancer compound.
- **Watermelon** protects the skin from sunburn, offers nutritional support for male fertility, and helps decrease the risk of certain cancers, including prostate, ovarian, cervical, oral and pharyngeal cancers. Watermelon is rich in electrolytes.
- **Bananas** help decrease symptoms associated with asthma, boost fat burning, and decrease the risk of certain cancers. Bananas are rich in potassium, vitamin B6, vitamin C, and dietary fiber—all important for heart health.

Super Vegetables for Anti-Aging and Longevity

Here are the best vegetables to include in your juices to stay younger and healthier longer, according to the NCRC:

- **Spinach** helps with mental alertness and reduces the risk of certain cancers, including cancer of the liver, ovaries, colon, and prostate. Spinach is also packed with vitamins A, B, C, D, and K.
- **Red bell peppers** help prevent sunburn, build cardiovascular health, and decrease the risk of certain cancers, including lung, prostate, ovarian, and cervical cancer. Peppers are a good source of vitamin C.
- **Broccoli** decreases the risk of certain cancers, including prostate, bladder, colon, pancreatic, gastric, and breast cancer; helps decrease damage associated with diabetes; and helps protect against brain injuries. Broccoli is packed with antioxidants and vitamins B6, C, and E.
- **Carrots** protect DNA, battle cataracts, and offer protection against certain cancers. Carrots are high in beta-carotene, a potent healer. Carrots provide vitamins A, B, and C as well as calcium, potassium, and sodium.

- **Cauliflower** helps inhibit the growth of breast cancer cells, protects against prostate cancer, and stimulates the body's detox systems. Cauliflower contains the compound allicin, which helps reduce the risk of stroke and improves heart health. Allicin also helps detoxify the blood and liver. Cauliflower is high in vitamin C.
- **Artichokes** aid blood clotting and reduce bad cholesterol. Artichokes are high in vitamin C and fiber.
- **Arugula** enhances the health of the eyes, lowers the risk of birth defects, and reduces the risk of fracture. High in beta-carotene, the antioxidant that fights heart disease, arugula is also high in vitamin C, folic acid, potassium, and fiber.
- **Asparagus** helps promote healthy bacteria in the digestive system, guards against birth defects, and builds a healthy heart. Asparagus is rich in vitamins A and B1.
- **Green cabbage** helps with blood clotting and reduces the risk of certain cancers, including prostate, colon, breast, and ovarian cancer. Green cabbage also aids detoxification. Cabbage is also a great source of vitamin C, calcium, and fiber and contains the nitrogenous compound indoles, which helps lower blood pressure. Cabbage has more nutrients that protect against cancer than any other vegetable. Fresh cabbage juice has been shown to completely restore the gastrointestinal tract and heal ulcers in seven days, according to research conducted at Stanford University.
- **Kale** helps regulate estrogen levels, prevent sun damage to the eyes, and build bone density. Kale contains vitamins A, B, and C.
- **Sweet potatoes** reduce the risk of stroke and cancer and offer protection against blindness. Sweet potatoes are rich in carotene, vitamin C, calcium, and potassium.
- **Mushrooms** help decrease the risk of certain cancers, including colon and prostate. They also lower blood pressure and enhance the body's natural detox systems.
- **Butternut squash** helps fight wrinkles, promote good night vision, and build a healthy heart. Butternut squash provides vitamins A and C, potassium, and niacin.

Why Juicing Helps Anti-Aging and Longevity

According to the American Dietetic Association, drinking juice made wholly from fruits and vegetables is an ideal way to get the greatest nutritional benefit. Look at the color of your juice. The more vibrant the color, the more powerful the juice. Flavonoids, the plant pigments responsible for the colors in fruits and vegetables, also have anti-inflammatory, anti-allergic, anti-viral, and anti-carcinogenic properties.

According to research compiled by the North Carolina Research Campus, the American Dietetic Association, the American Cancer Foundation, and the American Diabetes Association, there are almost as many reasons to juice for longevity and anti-aging as there are fruits and vegetables to juice with:

✓ Fresh juice contains proteins, carbohydrates, essential fatty acids, vitamins, and minerals in a form your body can easily absorb.

✓ Fresh fruit and vegetable juice is rich in potassium and low in sodium, which helps promote cardiovascular health and prevent cancer.

✓ The enzymes in juice are essential for digestion and the absorption of nutrients in your food.

✓ Juice is loaded with powerful antioxidants called carotenes, found in dark leafy green vegetables and red, purple, and yellow-orange fruit and vegetables, all of which neutralize cancer-causing free radicals and promote longevity.

✓ Apple-celery juice reduces inflammation, promotes calm, and restores restful sleep.

✓ Juice from alkaline vegetables including carrots, tomatoes, parsley, spinach, kale, and celery helps detoxify the liver, kidneys, blood, and muscle tissue of toxins that have been accumulating for years.

✓ Cucumber juice is rich in silica, which strengthens connective tissue of muscles, tendons, ligaments, cartilage, and bone. Cucumber juice also promotes strong, lustrous hair, glowing skin, and strong nails.

✓ The nutrients in fresh fruit and vegetable juice are also responsible for reducing or eliminating acne, anemia, high cholesterol, bladder infections, bronchitis, canker sores, carpal tunnel, constipation, gallstones, glaucoma, headaches, hypertension, indigestion, insomnia, kidney stones, macular degeneration, menopause, morning sickness, osteoporosis, prostate enlargement, psoriasis, ulcers, varicose veins, and water retention.

Juicing for Menopause

Fruits and vegetables contain a plethora of substances that help alleviate the symptoms of menopause, including thinning skin and hair, depression, weight gain, insomnia, irritability, and hot flashes.

Natural Phytoestrogens

Plants have chemicals called phytoestrogens that help protect your body's health. Similar in structure to estrogen, they act as weak estrogen in your body and may trick it into thinking it has more estrogen than it really does, thus diminishing some of the signs and discomforts of lower estrogen levels in menopause.

ALERT

It's still not clear if plant estrogens like soy may increase the growth of cancer cells. However, if you have a type of cancer that is dependent on estrogen, such as estrogen-positive breast cancer, it's probably best to avoid consuming soy and other plants high in phytoestrogens on a daily basis.

Benefits of Boron

Boron is a very useful mineral that helps your body hold on to estrogen and reduce calcium secretion, which in turn helps promote strong bones. Boron is found in many fruits and vegetables, including plums, prunes, strawberries, apples, tomatoes, pears, grapefruit, raspberries, oranges, turnips, carrots, cauliflower, lettuce, onions, soybeans, sweet potatoes, and cucumbers.

Full of Beans

Beans help curb your appetite by slowing the absorption of glucose into the bloodstream, and they are packed with fiber to keep you full and regular. In addition, they are good sources of calcium, folic acid, vitamin B6, and a low-fat source of protein.

Drink Your Juice

Try easing menopausal symptoms by drinking juice instead of tea, coffee, and soft drinks. Most citrus fruit contains more than 100 phytochemicals. Orange juice provides calcium, folic acid, and vitamin C, while carrot juice provides three essential phytochemicals, including phenolic acids, terpenes, and carotenoids. Purple grape juice packs some of the same powerful antioxidants found in red wine—and you don't need a designated driver to enjoy it!

Importance of Calcium

Menopausal women need 1,000 to 1,500 milligrams of calcium per day. Good veggie sources include juice made from broccoli and leafy green vegetables.

Juicing for Memory

It's a fact of life that as you age, you lose brain cells. However, if you're careful to eat the right foods and take care of yourself, you can actually improve your memory with age. A wide variety of fruits and vegetables contain compounds that protect and even improve your brain cells, according to the USDA Human Nutrition Center. Vitamins B and E help maintain the chemical balance of nutrients in your brain, correct nutrient deficiencies, and repair the damage caused by environmental toxins.

Consuming lots of essential fatty acids can improve brain function in adults. In fact, a decrease in essential fatty acids in the brain can actually cause age-related cognitive decline, dementia, and Alzheimer's disease.

Polyphenol, found in the skin of red grapes, helps protect against cognitive disorders. The antioxidant alpha lipoic acid (ALA), found in flaxseed and hemp oil, can prevent neurodegenerative diseases by elevating antioxidants in various brain regions responsible for improving memory.

Medical research conducted on people between the ages of twenty and ninety-two showed that B vitamins folate, B12 and B6 improved brain function and memory. In addition, several other minerals and nutrients have been shown to improve recall, including acetyl L-carnitine, omega-3 fatty acids, phosphatidyl choline serine, CO Q10, L-glutamine, and gingko biloba.

The Best Produce for Memory

Omega-3 oils found in flaxseed and nuts can help reduce the cell inflammation that triggers cell damage and memory loss. If you're looking for a super veggie for memory, look no further than spinach.

A recent study showed that when elderly people ate spinach, it prevented memory loss and even reversed it. Researchers attributed the results to the high level of folate, or folic acid, in spinach, a nutrient that has been proven to help fight Alzheimer's disease as well as other age-related memory losses. By using 2/3 cup of fresh spinach in your juice, you can fulfill your RDA for folic acid.

Onions are also great for memory. They contain fisetin, a naturally occurring flavonoid that stimulates pathways that improve long-term memory. Red onions contain anthocyanin and quercetin and are even better for memory than yellow and white onions, which also contain significant amounts of quercetin. Tomatoes, oranges, apples, peaches, kiwi, persimmons, and grapes are other great sources of fisetin.

Don't Forget Your Berries

Blueberries contain the memory-boosting phytochemical anthocyanins, which promotes brain function. They also offer protection against diabetes, heart disease, and cancer. Strawberries contain fisetin, a compound that stimulates pathways that improve long-term memory.

FACT

Research at the USDA Human Nutrition Center shows that drinking blueberry juice can help improve memory. Mice that were fed blueberries on a daily basis showed improvements in the memory and exploratory areas of their brains when compared with control mice that were not fed blueberries.

Juicing for Hypertension

Your blood pressure is a measure of how much pressure your blood puts on your arteries as it flows through them. If you have high blood pressure, it means your blood is putting too much pressure on your arteries. Also called hypertension, high blood pressure in adults is expressed as anything over 120/80mm Hg.

FACT

Fruits and vegetables are an essential part of a diet for managing hypertension. They provide a range of nutrients, such as vitamins, minerals, and antioxidants that help in lowering blood pressure. Antioxidants are also essential for heart health, protecting the cardiovascular system, and maintaining steady blood pressure during pregnancy.

Your blood pressure is affected by many different things in your life, including your activity level, diet, stress response, age, reactions to different medications, and even the time of day. Your blood pressure tends to be highest in the morning and lowest when you're asleep.

You can promote healthy blood pressure by consuming foods high in certain antioxidants that work together to relax your arteries and reduce free radical damage.

How to Lower Blood Pressure

Diet and exercise play a role in lowering blood pressure. It's also important to stop smoking; cigarette smoke causes damage to blood vessel walls.

ALERT

Although all fruits and vegetables seem to contribute to lowering the risk of heart attacks, the most beneficial include green leafy vegetables such as lettuce, spinach, Swiss chard, and mustard greens; cruciferous vegetables such as broccoli, cauliflower, cabbage, Brussels sprouts, bok choy, and kale; and citrus fruits such as oranges, lemons, limes, and grapefruit (and their juices).

Consider the following studies when deciding how to make juice that can lower your blood pressure:

- Studies show that some types of casein peptide helps lower blood pressure by causing blood vessels to open, or dilate.
- Scientists at the University of California, Davis, conducted studies on adults who were pre-hypertensive and found that grape seed extract helped reduce their blood pressure.
- A study by the Lipid Research Laboratory in Haifa, Israel, showed that antioxidant compounds in pomegranates may play a role in reducing blood pressure by decreasing the effects of damaging free radical damage.
- Research conducted as part of the Harvard-based Nurses' Health Study and Health Professionals Follow-up Study, which included almost 110,000 men and women whose health and dietary habits were followed for fourteen years, found that the higher the average daily intake of fruits and vegetables, the lower the risk of developing cardiovascular disease. People who consumed eight or more servings of fresh fruits and vegetables daily were 30 percent less likely to

have a heart attack or stroke than those who consumed just one and a half servings.

When researchers combined findings from the Harvard studies with several other long-term studies in the United States and Europe and looked at coronary heart disease and stroke separately, they discovered a similar protective effect: Individuals who ate more than five servings of fruits and vegetables per day had roughly a 20 percent lower risk of coronary heart disease and stroke, compared with individuals who ate less than three servings per day.

ESSENTIAL

Fiber, which is abundant in fruits and vegetables, can help keep blood pressure down, while most of the minerals found in vegetables also help prevent heart attacks and strokes. A potassium deficiency may cause high blood pressure and can be corrected by consuming fruits and vegetables rich in the mineral.

Best Vegetables for Lowering High Blood Pressure

You can juice your way to lower blood pressure by combining some of the following foods into fresh, delicious juice:

- **Swiss chard.** High in vitamins A, K, C and E, and fiber, it also contains heart-healthy minerals like magnesium, manganese, potassium, iron, copper, and calcium.
- **Broccoli.** Rich in vitamins A and C, it's also high in calcium and a low-fat alternative to dairy products. Broccoli is also packed with fiber and folic acid.
- **Cabbage.** A great source of vitamin C and fiber, cabbage also contains the nitrogenous compound indoles, which helps lower blood pressure.
- **Cauliflower.** It contains the compound allicin, which helps reduce the risk of stroke and also improves heart health. Allicin also helps detoxify the blood and liver.

- **Spinach.** It is high in choline and inositol, chemicals that help prevent heart diseases like arteriosclerosis.
- **Lettuce.** Rich in beta-carotene, the antioxidant that fights heart diseases, lettuce also contains vitamin C, folic acid, potassium, and fiber.

Best Fruits for Healthy Blood Pressure

Fruits are packed with vitamin C and also are proven to help lower blood pressure.

- **Citrus fruits.** This family of fruit is the most efficient in lowering high blood pressure and is a rich source of vitamin C, carbohydrates, potassium, folate, and phytochemicals, which help prevent heart disease.
- **Bananas.** Bananas are rich in potassium, the antioxidant vitamin B6, vitamin C, and dietary fiber—all important for heart health.
- **Apples.** Apples provide a wide range of phytonutrients such as catechin, quercetin, phloridzin, and chlorogenic acid, which act as antioxidants to fight disease. Apples also contain fiber and flavonoids.

Juicing for Common Aches and Pains of Aging

Bursitis, tendonitis, arthritis, and most of the other aches and pains that are characteristic of aging stem from a common problem: inflammation. Inflammation is actually just part of the body's defense against infections, toxins, and irritation, but it can cause pain and discomfort.

The Antioxidant Connection

Nearly one out of three Americans—66 million adults—has arthritis. According to the Arthritis Foundation, 43 million have been diagnosed with arthritis and another 23 million live with undiagnosed chronic joint symptoms.

New research shows that relief is as close as your grocery store and juicer. According to a study published in the *American Journal of Clinical Nutrition*, antioxidants called carotenoids help reduce the risk of developing arthritis and other inflammatory disorders.

The culprit behind oxidation is free radicals, which play a role in damaging joints. By combating free radicals, antioxidants also help eliminate the inflammation that accompanies it.

ALERT

Arthritis and other problems caused by inflammation, including tendonitis and bursitis, are among leading causes of disability among Americans over the age of fifty, and costs related to inflammation cost the U.S. economy more than $86 billion a year. Unfortunately, half of those who have these conditions don't believe anything can be done to help.

Two crucial antioxidants for combating inflammatory diseases are beta-cryptoxanthin and zeaxanthin. People who develop inflammatory diseases typically consume 40 percent less cryptoxanthin and 20 percent less zeaxanthin than those who don't. In addition, consuming adequate vitamin A helps curtail arthritis and other diseases associated with inflammation.

Fruits and Veggies that Ease Inflammation

According to the *American Journal of Clinical Nutrition*, increasing your intake of key fruits and vegetables can help prevent arthritis and other inflammatory diseases. Produce contains high levels of antioxidants and phytochemicals, both of which play a role in reducing inflammation.

ALERT

Free radical damage contributes to inflammation. Vitamin C is a key antioxidant that has anti-inflammatory properties. You can find it in citrus fruit, berries, and dark leafy greens. To get the most antioxidant power from your juice, follow the rainbow principle. Because the color of a fruit signifies its antioxidant content, create juices from fruits that represents all colors of the rainbow.

According to the Arthritis Foundation, the following fifteen fruits and vegetables are powerhouses of antioxidants and phytochemicals, so mix and match them for juices that help relieve the aches and pains:

- ✓ **Oranges.** Consuming one glass of freshly squeezed orange juice per day can help reduce inflammatory disorders such as rheumatoid arthritis.
- ✓ **Berries.** Berries are loaded with antioxidants and vitamin C. Blueberries have more antioxidant concentrations than other berries, but cranberries, blackberries, strawberries, and raspberries are all rich sources of antioxidants.
- ✓ **Kiwi.** One kiwifruit has nearly twice the vitamin C of an orange and can help reduce inflammation.
- ✓ **Apples.** According to research conducted at Cornell University, apples contain antioxidants that fight inflammation, allergies, cancer, and viruses.
- ✓ **Cherries.** Research shows that drinking four ounces of cherry juice a day helps relieve inflammation even when you stop drinking the juice, so be sure to include it in your favorites.
- ✓ **Parsley.** Rich in beta-carotene, parsley also helps relieve inflammation.
- ✓ **Prunes.** Prunes are rich in antioxidants, and research at the Center on Aging at Tufts University found they contain more than twice the antioxidant power of other produce.
- ✓ **Carrots.** They are high in antioxidants, vitamin A, and carotenoids.
- ✓ **Broccoli.** Rich in beta-carotene, broccoli is also high in vitamin C, which helps reduce inflammation.
- ✓ **Pineapple.** Loaded with the enzyme bromelain, a powerful and natural anti-inflammatory agent, pineapple is a potent de-inflammatory.
- ✓ **Beans.** Protein-rich beans reduce inflammation by replacing the body protein broken down by inflammation.
- ✓ **Red grapes.** Packed with antioxidants, red grapes help lower inflammation and also help prevent heart disease and cancer.
- ✓ **Tomatoes.** Loaded with the antioxidant lycopene, which helps prevent degenerative diseases and reduces the risk of prostate and other cancers, tomatoes also help fight inflammation.

✓ **Sweet potatoes.** Sweet potatoes are rich in antioxidant vitamins A, C, and E. Just ½ cup provides twice the RDA for vitamin E.

✓ **Papayas.** This tropical fruit is high in the enzyme papain, which has potent anti-inflammatory properties.

Juicing for Muscle Cramps

Muscle cramps are common, affecting about half the general population. These painful spasmodic contractions of muscles can affect any muscle group of the body but most often attack the muscles of the calves, legs, and feet, which bear the most strain. Muscle cramps are caused by a variety of factors, including dietary deficiencies, oxygen deficiency in the tissue, hormonal imbalances, menopause, and aging.

ALERT

Low levels of minerals known as electrolytes—which include potassium, sodium, calcium, and magnesium—can contribute to muscle cramps. You can find potassium in bananas, oranges, cantaloupe, lettuce, and leafy greens; magnesium in nuts and beans; and calcium in broccoli.

Vitamins that Alleviate Cramps

To eliminate cramps, eat fruits and vegetables high in the previously mentioned minerals as well as vitamins D and B6, found in leafy greens, broccoli, apples, and bananas. In addition, eat produce high in vitamin C, which helps assimilate calcium in the body and prevents it from accumulating in the joints, where it can cause cramping. Good sources of vitamin C include broccoli, cabbage, citrus, spinach, and asparagus.

Vitamin E helps prevent nocturnal leg cramps by improving blood flow through the arteries. Find it in tomatoes, watercress, carrots, asparagus, and spinach.

Muscle cramps are also often caused by dehydration, so if you're getting frequent cramps, drink more juice to hydrate yourself and fortify it with the key nutrients that combat cramping.

Juicing for Backaches

Backache, as the name suggests, is simply pain in the back, and it is among the most common ailments. Backache can affect a person at any age, but it is commonly seen in people older than fifty. Backaches can be caused by slipped disks, osteoarthritis, and osteoporosis. More rarely, they are caused by deformation of natural spine curvature (scoliosis), tumors, and infections in the spine. Backaches are very common in women, who most often suffer them during their menstrual periods.

Nutrients that Ease Backaches

Minerals needed to diminish and prevent backache include calcium and magnesium. Magnesium is found in all fresh green vegetables, apples, figs, wheat germ, and all seeds and nuts, especially almonds.

FACT

Simple home remedies for getting rid of backache include making a juice that contains glucose or honey in warm water and drinking it early in the morning on an empty stomach, and drinking the juice of one lemon mixed with common salt twice a day for about a week.

Healing Herbs

A wide variety of herbs can also help alleviate backache. They include the following:

- **Ginger** limits the creation of prostaglandins and leukotrienes that cause aches and swelling
- **Saw palmetto** is an anti-inflammatory
- **Chamomile** relaxes muscles
- **Feverfew** and **burdock** provide pain relief
- **Yarrow** strengthens muscles
- **Stinging nettle** reduces pain
- **Cayenne pepper** offers topical pain relief
- **Willow bark** alleviates pain
- **Rosemary** is an anti-inflammatory

- **Devil's claw** is helpful for pain relief and arthritis
- **Angelica** is useful for pain relief and is also an anti-inflammatory and antispasmodic
- **Mustard seed extract** is good for easing pain
- **Valeria, cat's claw,** and **licorice** offer anti-inflammatory results
- **Horsetail** speeds healing and reduces pain
- **Rapeseed** extract reduces inflammation and increases circulation
- **Mint** offers pain relief
- **Coriander** reduces pain
- **Bilberry** increases circulation
- **Celery seed** is a muscle relaxant
- **Kava root** is a pain reliever and anesthetic
- **Wheatgrass** contains nutrients that strengthen muscle and keep the spine flexible
- **Comfrey** contains many nutrients that help prevent backache

The Role of Exercise

If you suffer from chronic back pain, consult your physician. She can recommend exercises that may ease your pain. If necessary, she may be able to refer you to a physical therapist.

Cucumber Tomato

❱❱ Good for reducing muscle cramps

Tomatoes are high in vitamin C, and they also contain plenty of vitamins A and B, potassium, iron, and phosphorous. They have as much fiber as one slice of whole wheat bread and are low in calories.

INGREDIENTS | YIELD: 1 CUP

1 cucumber, peeled
1 Roma tomato

Juice cucumber and tomato. Stir.

Per Serving

CALORIES: **36**
FAT: **0.31g**
SODIUM: **9mgg**
FIBER: **1.6g**
PROTEIN: **1.6g**
SUGARS: **6g**
CARBOHYDRATES: **16g**

What Makes a Cucumber Bitter?

As a cucumber gets older on the vine, its seeds become larger and more bitter. If you are using an old cucumber, cut it in half and scoop out the seeds with a spoon to eliminate the bitter taste. According to an old wives' tale, the more bitter the vegetable, the better it is for you. But you'll still get the nutritional benefits cucumbers have to offer without the bitter seeds.

Grape Citrus Apple

❱❱ Good for reducing bursitis

Red grapes and lemon juice have been shown to help with joint pain caused by bursitis.

INGREDIENTS | YIELD: 1¼ CUPS

1 cup red grapes
1 apple, cored
½ lemon, peeled

Juice grapes, apple, and lemon. Stir.

Per Serving

CALORIES: **102**
FAT: **0.54g**
SODIUM: **3mg**
FIBER: **3g**
PROTEIN: **1.2g**
SUGARS: **39g**
CARBOHYDRATES: **48g**

How to Choose Grapes

Buy grapes that are plumped and have good color. They should still be attached to their stems. Dark grapes should have a deep color with no green. Green grapes should have a light yellow color, which indicates that they are ripe.

Back Pain Solvent

» **Good for reducing back pain**

Vitamin K appears to help back pain. It can provide your bones with iron and calcium.

INGREDIENTS | **YIELD: 1¼ CUPS**

2 romaine lettuce leaves
1 fist of spinach
4 broccoli spears
1 carrot
1 clove garlic
¼" slice ginger root

Juice ingredients in order listed. Stir well.

Per Serving

CALORIES: **186**
FAT: **2.1g**
SODIUM: **352mg**
FIBER: **14g**
PROTEIN: **16g**
SUGARS: **2.6g**
CARBOHYDRATES: **37g**

Food Sources of Copper

Increasing copper in the body can also help with back pain. Iron and copper in the diet form red blood cells in the body. This helps keep blood vessels and nerves healthy. A lack of copper has been shown to be a factor in osteoporosis. Good sources of copper in the diet include carrots, garlic, and ginger root.

Carrot Beets a Cantaloupe

» **Good for reducing high blood pressure**

Studies show that beets can be vital in managing blood pressure. This yummy juice should do the trick.

INGREDIENTS | **YIELD: 1½ CUPS**

½ cantaloupe, rind removed
2 carrots, peeled
1 beet, greens removed

Juice cantaloupe, carrots, and beet. Stir.

Per Serving

CALORIES: **251**
FAT: **0.98g**
SODIUM: **200mg**
FIBER: **12g**
PROTEIN: **7.2g**
SUGARS: **33g**
CARBOHYDRATES: **48g**

Cantaloupe Vitamins

Cantaloupes are excellent sources of vitamins A and C and potassium. They also contain myo-inositol, a lipid that helps prevent hardening of the arteries. Cantaloupe can absorb other food odors from your refrigerator, so wrap it well in plastic after cutting to avoid this.

Memory Enhancer

» **Good for improving memory**

Zinc has been shown by numerous studies to improve memory. The cauliflower in this juice provides zinc, and the vitamin E found in the tomatoes protects your cell membranes.

INGREDIENTS | YIELD: 1 CUP

1 tomato
3 red lettuce leaves
½ cup cauliflower

Juice tomato, lettuce, and cauliflower. Stir well.

Per Serving

CALORIES: **59**
FAT: **1.2g**
SODIUM: **44mg**
FIBER: **4g**
PROTEIN: **3.7g**
SUGARS: **1.4g**
CARBOHYDRATES: **7.8g**

How to Wash Lettuce
Wash and drain lettuce very well. You should blot the lettuce with a towel to ensure that you have removed all of the excess moisture. Do not soak lettuce. This will make the leaves soft. Even if you buy organic lettuce, it is important to rinse it before eating it.

Fountain of Youth Cocktail

» **Good for anti-aging**

This refreshing juice is packed with vitamins and antioxidants. Start your morning with all the nutritious benefits this juice has to offer.

INGREDIENTS | YIELD: ¾ CUP

1 pint blackberries
1 pint raspberries
½ lemon, peeled
¼" slice ginger root

Juice berries, ginger, and lemon. Stir.

Per Serving

CALORIES: **268**
FAT: **3.1g**
SODIUM: **7mg**
FIBER: **32g**
PROTEIN: **6.3g**
SUGARS: **27g**
CARBOHYDRATES: **63g**

What are Antioxidants?
Antioxidants are nutrients that can prevent or slow the oxidative damage to our bodies. When our body cells use oxygen, they naturally produce free radicals that can cause damage. Antioxidants work as scavengers, gobbling up the free radicals and preventing and repairing the damage they cause.

Taste of the Isles

>> ## Good for reducing bursitis

Bromelain, which is found in pineapple, is a natural anti-inflammatory that reduces swelling.

INGREDIENTS | YIELD: 1½ CUPS

1 cup strawberries, hulls intact
1 cup pineapple
1 papaya, seeded

Juice ingredients in order listed. Stir.

Per Serving

CALORIES: **151**
FAT: **0.76g**
SODIUM: **5.2mg**
FIBER: **6g**
PROTEIN: **3.8g**
SUGARS: **29g**
CARBOHYDRATES: **44g** '

Bromelain

When Christopher Columbus visited Guadeloupe in 1493, the natives gave him pineapple. In 1891, bromelain was discovered to have therapeutic uses in treating arthritis. It has been shown to help reduce the swelling caused by joint pain. It occurs in all parts of the pineapple, but is most concentrated in the stem.

Carrot Turnip

>> ## Good for reducing muscle cramps

Vitamin C helps improve circulation. Vitamin E helps control night time cramps in muscles. Cramps are frequently a result of dehydration.

INGREDIENTS | YIELD: 1¼ CUPS

1 Granny Smith apple, cored
1 turnip, peeled
3 carrots, peeled

Juice apple, carrots, and turnip. Stir.

Per Serving

CALORIES: **224**
FAT: **0.34g**
SODIUM: **239mg**
FIBER: **14g**
PROTEIN: **4.8g**
SUGARS: **39g**
CARBOHYDRATES: **67g**

Turnips

Fresh turnips are a root vegetable and are available year round. They have a strong flavor, so it helps to juice them in relatively small quantities with other fruits and vegetables. They provide a good source of vitamin C and can be used to treat scurvy, which is caused by vitamin C deficiency.

Pear Grape

» ## Good for reducing menopause symptoms

This juice provides you with good sources of boron, which is very useful for those with osteoporosis.

INGREDIENTS | **YIELD: 1 CUP**

2 Anjou pears
1 cup red grapes

Juice pears and grapes. Stir.

Per Serving

CALORIES: **163**
FAT: **0.85g**
SODIUM: **1.8mg**
FIBER: **11g**
PROTEIN: **3.3g**
SUGARS: **42g**
CARBOHYDRATES: **55g**

Anjou Pears

These are large pears that are greenish yellow in color. The skin sometimes has a hint of red and they have a very sweet taste. They are among the most popular varieties of pears. Store them at room temperature to keep them from going bad.

Heart Health in a Glass

» ## Good for reducing oxidative damage

Oxidative damage contributes to heart disease and other heart problems. A recent study conducted by researchers in London found that eating five daily servings of fruits and vegetables reduces the risk of stroke by 25 percent.

INGREDIENTS | **YIELD: 1¼ CUPS**

1 celery stalk, leaves intact
1 cup wheatgrass
1 fist spinach leaves
½ lemon, peeled
2 kale leaves

Juice ingredients in order. Stir.

Per Serving

CALORIES: **72**
FAT: **1g**
SODIUM:**100mg**
FIBER: **4g**
PROTEIN: **3g**
SUGARS: **2g**
CARBOHYDRATES: **8g**

Wheatgrass

Wheatgrass does not affect people who are allergic to grains. It is said to increase red blood cell count and lower blood pressure. Wheatgrass has a high concentration of vitamins and enzymes, and it is also a good source of chlorophyll.

Blackberry Banana

» Good for reducing muscle cramps

Potassium is essential for helping muscles contract properly during exercise and reduce cramping up. The banana in this drink provides the potassium you need.

INGREDIENTS | YIELD: 1 CUP

2 pints blackberries
½ lemon, peeled
1 banana

Juice blackberries and lemon. Add banana and blend until smooth.

Per Serving

CALORIES: **333**
FAT: **3g**
SODIUM: **7.2mg**
FIBER: **32g**
PROTEIN: **6.9g**
SUGARS:
CARBOHYDRATES:

Blackberries

Blackberries grow on bushes with thorns. They are purple-black in color and are usually available in the summer. If the hulls are still attached, the berries were picked too soon and they will be very tart. Blackberries contain salicylate, the substance found in aspirin, and are among the top ten antioxidant foods.

CHAPTER 9

Juicing for Beautiful Skin, Hair, and Nails

If you're dropping a small fortune on dream creams for your skin, pricy hair products, and weekly manicures, you're missing out on the most effective and least expensive way to feed your skin, hair, and nails—juicing! Beauty and health begin on the inside with a healthy diet of fresh fruits and vegetables that provide your skin, hair, and nails with the nutrients they need to be strong and lustrous. Without the right nutrients, your skin, hair, and nails will look bland no matter what else you do.

Caring for Your Outer Layer

Your skin is one of the most powerful indicators of your health. Wrinkles and dry or oily skin, acne, inflammation, psoriasis, and many other skin conditions are your body's way of telling you you're not getting the nutrients you need for optimum health. If you're turning to topical cosmetics such as lotions, soaps, scrubs, toners, and creams to get rid of outer blemishes, beware that expensive, chemical-laden beauty products don't address the root cause of the problem: nutritional deficiencies and exposure to toxins in your environment and personal care products.

Best Nutrients for Skin

Your skin can tell you what's going on inside your body. Every skin condition, whether it's acne or aging, is the manifestation of your body's internal needs, including its nutritional requirements. If you feed your skin from the inside out, you'll start to notice big differences right away.

FACT

New studies indicate that antioxidants and specific nutrients can help keep your skin looking vibrantly healthy and years younger when combined with a good diet. The skin reacts particularly well to certain vitamins, minerals, and antioxidants that nourish the skin and give it a youthful glow.

How to Eat for Your Skin

Here are some of the most important nutrients for beautiful, glowing skin:

- **Selenium** plays a key role in skin cancer prevention and protects skin from sun damage. If you're a sun worshipper, selenium could help reduce your chance of burning.
- **Silica** is a trace mineral that strengthens the body's connective tissues. Too little can result in reduced skin elasticity and slower healing of wounds.

- **Zinc** controls the production of oil in the skin and may also help control some of the hormones that create acne. It clears skin by taming oil production and controlling the formation of acne lesions.
- **Essential fatty acids**, also called omega acids, moisturize and maintain the skin's flexibility. Without enough of them, the skin produces a more irritating form of sebum, or oil, which dries the skin and clogs pores, causing acne and inflammation.
- **Vitamin C** reduces damage caused by free radicals, a harmful byproduct of sunlight, smoke, and pollution that destroys collagen and elastin (fibers that support your skin structure) and results in wrinkles and other signs of aging.
- **Vitamin E** helps reduce sun damage, wrinkles, and uneven textures caused by sun damage.
- **Vitamin B complex**, especially biotin, is the nutrient that forms the basis of skin, nail, and hair cells. Without enough, dermatitis (an itchy, scaly skin reaction) and hair loss can occur.
- **Vitamin A** is necessary for the maintenance and repair of skin tissue.

FACT

Research shows that skin cancer patients who took 200 micrograms of selenium per day had 37 percent fewer malignancies, a 50 percent reduced risk of death from skin cancer, and a 17 percent decrease in overall mortality. Another study indicated that taking oral selenium and copper helped reduce the formation of sunburn cells in human skin.

The Best Fruits and Vegetables for Skin Health

Fortunately, you don't need to swallow a zillion pills a day to consume the nutrients you need to take care of your skin. Fruits and vegetables are loaded with nutrients that nourish the skin. Combine them in juice and you'll get the benefits of each fruit or vegetable's unique antioxidants, phytochemicals, vitamins, and minerals.

Here is a list of the best dietary sources of the nutrients you need:

selenium	whole-grain cereals, seafood, garlic, eggs
zinc	fresh oysters, pumpkin seeds, ginger, pecans, Brazil nuts, oats, eggs, lean meat, poultry
silica	leeks, green beans, garbanzo beans, strawberries, cucumber, mango, celery, asparagus, rhubarb
omega-3 fatty acids	salmon, halibut, sardines, albacore, trout, herring, walnut, flaxseed oil, canola oil, shrimp, clams, light chunk tuna, catfish, cod, spinach

ESSENTIAL

The typical American diet is overabundant in omega-6 fatty acids found in baked goods and grains, and lacking in omega-3s. Balancing your intake of omega-3s with omega-6s will result in smoother, younger-looking skin. If you're finding it difficult to get enough, fish oil capsules or evening primrose oil supplements can help keep your skin smoother and younger-looking.

The Power of Vitamin C

Getting enough vitamin C is easy because it's found in an abundance of foods, including citrus fruits, bell peppers, broccoli, cauliflower, and leafy greens. You can also take vitamin C supplements, up to 500 to 1,000 milligrams per day, according to the American Academy of Dermatology.

Getting Enough E

Vitamin E is found in scores of foods, including vegetable oils, nuts, seeds, olives, spinach, and asparagus. You can also take a supplement, but beware that doses over 400 International Units per day be can toxic.

In addition to consuming these vitamins in juices, it's important to wear a sunscreen with an SPF of at least 25 and limit your sun exposure.

Getting Enough Vitamin A

Many fruits and vegetables are loaded with vitamin A, including sweet potatoes, carrots, beetroot, broccoli, spinach, winter squash, kale, peas, red peppers, oats, tomato juice, apricots, peaches, apples, and lemons.

ESSENTIAL

People who drink excessive amounts of caffeine and alcohol are at a higher risk of having excessive iron in their systems, which may deplete their body's stores of vitamin A. Consuming too much vitamin A from animal sources or supplements may be toxic, so be careful to steer a safe middle ground.

Although you can't drink it, topical vitamin A can also make a significant difference in your skin. Studies show people who used creams with topical A enjoyed a reduction in lines, wrinkles, and acne, as well as relief from psoriasis.

Getting Your Vitamin Bs

Vitamin B is water-soluble, which means you need to replenish your body's supply every day. Luckily, it's found in many of your favorite foods, including bananas, potatoes, tempeh, lentils, other whole grains, chili peppers, green vegetables, eggs, dairy products, turkey, tuna, and liver. Biotin, the crucial B-vitamin for skin, is found in bananas, eggs, oatmeal, and rice, and your body also makes some biotin on its own.

ALERT

Brewer's yeast, which is used to make bread and beer, is also an excellent source of vitamin B. But too much of a good thing can hurt you! Drinking alcohol in excess interferes with your body's absorption of vitamin B1, so be careful not to defeat your own purpose.

Vegans should take note that vitamin B12 is extremely difficult to get in sufficient amounts from plants. If you do not eat meat, dairy, or eggs, consider taking supplements or vitamin B-fortified foods.

Dealing with Specific Skin Problems

As well as giving you beautiful skin, a balanced diet can also help alleviate some of the most common skin problems, including age spots, acne, eczema, psoriasis, canker sores, and varicose veins. Studies show that the vast majority of skin problems respond to "healing" fruits and vegetables that are easy to juice. They include apples, apricots, berries, cantaloupe, grapes, mangos, papaya, pears, carrots, cucumber, leafy greens, beets and beet greens, pumpkin, squash, and watercress.

Crash-dieting can trigger acne, so don't overdo it! Extreme changes in food intake such as almost total avoidance of fat or inclusion of fat as the sole source of food greatly destabilizes the amount of secretions from the pores, which has been found to be a major cause of acne.

In addition, consuming a sufficient amount of essential fatty acids (found in nuts, olive oil, and oily fish) can help ward off the dryness that can trigger acne. Other healing foods that tackle skin problems include soy products, edible seeds (pumpkin, sesame, sunflower, and flax), lentils, oats, seaweed, spirulina, whole grains, and yogurt. Drinking eight glasses of water daily, which can include the water in your juice, can help flush out toxins that create skin problems.

Alleviating Acne

The age old adage that we are what we eat holds particularly true in the case of skin ailments like acne. Studies conducted on Inuit children after World War II indicated that eating a balanced diet with lower-glycemic carbohydrates and fats such as fresh vegetables and juice helped prevent acne. The more saturated fats and junk food the children in the study consumed, the more likely they were to develop acne.

Chronic acne may also signal you're not getting enough essential vitamins, including beta-carotene (found in kale, parsley, and carrots); vitamin E (found in spinach, asparagus, and carrots); folic acid (found in spinach, kale, and beet greens); selenium (found in turnips, oranges, and red Swiss chard); chromium (found in apples, green peppers, and potatoes); zinc (found in ginger root, carrots, and parsley) and essential fatty acids (found in green juices). On the flip side, foods high in trans-fatty acids, including milk products, butter, margarine, shortening, and hydrogenated vegetable oils, can exacerbate acne.

ALERT

If you have acne, it may be time to cut back on the burgers and fries. That's because fast food is a leading culprit in acne—and not just because of the fat and carb overload. Fast food is also packed with iodine, which can result in skin flare-ups when consumed in excess.

Food allergies can also trigger acne or skin problems. When you eat a food you're allergic to, your body creates toxic substances to fight the allergic reactions. The body expels the toxins, and zits and blemishes pop up. Common food allergies include soft drinks, chocolate, tomatoes, milk, and junk foods made with refined carbohydrates. If you break out every time you eat a certain food, you may want to see a dermatologist or allergist, who can administer blood tests that help isolate the culprit.

ALERT

Sluggish digestion can also cause acne. When your body doesn't eliminate toxins and allergens from your kidneys and bowels quickly enough, the results can show up as acne. If you're prone to regular or chronic breakouts, consider putting your skin on a cleansing or detox diet.

Juicing for Acne

Fortunately, many fruits and vegetables naturally help clear up break-outs, so juicing is an ideal way to prevent or clear up stubborn cases of acne. Beta-carotene, which is abundant in fresh fruits and vegetables, is a natural way to reduce sebum production, while vitamin B6 can help prevent acne breakouts associated with menstrual cycles. Zinc helps reduce inflammation and facilitates healing and tissue regeneration, and chromium can help improve insulin sensitivity and glucose tolerance levels.

Alleviating Age Spots

Age spots, often called liver spots because of their unattractive brown color, can crop up on your face, hands, arms, or legs, and make you look and feel years older. Age spots are actually caused by free radicals—toxins that accumulate in your body and trigger everything from acne to cancer—as well as dietary imbalances and deficiencies.

To alleviate age spots, use juicing to fill in the nutritional gaps. Nutrients that eliminate age spots include beta-carotene (found in kale, parsley, carrots, and spinach); vitamin C (found in spinach, green peppers, kale, parsley, and citrus fruit such as oranges, lemons, grapes, cherries, and grapefruit); and vitamin E (found in carrots, asparagus, and spinach). In addition, you might want to put your skin on a cleansing diet that eliminates caffeine, alcohol, fast food, junk food, and foods with a high sugar content.

Easing Psoriasis

Psoriasis is a medical condition that occurs when skin cells grow too quickly. Faulty signals in the immune system cause new skin cells to form in days rather than weeks, causing a pile-up of itchy silvery scales and thick, scaly skin called plaques that typically develop on the elbows, knees, lower back, and scalp. About half of people with psoriasis also have dull nails with pits and ridges.

Nutrients that Help Ease Psoriasis

Scientists believe psoriasis may also be triggered by a poor diet or allergies and that specific nutrients can help alleviate or prevent it. Excessive shedding of skin can lead to a zinc deficiency, which is detrimental to skin health because zinc is necessary for absorbing linoleic acid, a fatty acid that promotes healthy skin. Pumpkin seeds, which are high in both zinc and linoleic acid, can alleviate deficiencies, as can parsley and carrots, which are high in zinc. Selenium (found in chard, ginger, and red Swiss chard) helps decrease inflammation associated with psoriasis, while beta-carotene (found in carrots, kale, and cantaloupe) helps combat substances responsible for triggering accelerated skin growth. People with psoriasis should avoid nuts, citrus fruit, and tomatoes, which can aggravate the condition.

FACT

Studies show that psoriasis is often triggered by stress, a skin injury, or strep throat, although triggers are not universal, and what triggers psoriasis in one person may not cause it to develop in another. The disease is also believed to have a hereditary component, making some people more susceptible to it than others.

Other fruits and vegetables that help ease symptoms of psoriasis include ginger, which reduces inflammation; beets, which have natural detoxifying agents; pineapples and papayas, which have enzymes that promote digestion and help decrease accelerated skin growth; and spinach, kale, and beet greens, which are high in folic acid.

ALERT

Consuming a high-fiber diet that contains a lot of raw food can help alleviate psoriasis because the fiber helps bind toxins in your bowel and reduces the rate of skin cell growth. You can also reduce the incidence of psoriasis by eliminating alcohol from your diet, and by going on a cleansing or detoxification diet (see Chapter 6).

Quieting Canker Sores

Canker sores are shallow painful sores in the mouth. They can occur anywhere in the mouth—on the inside of your lips, the insides of your cheeks, the base of your gums, or under your tongue. Canker sores are different from fever blisters or cold sores, which are usually on the outside of your lips or on the corners of your mouth.

Anyone can get canker sores, but women and people in their teens and twenties get them most often. While canker sores often run in families, they aren't contagious. It isn't clear what causes canker sores, although researchers suspect they may be triggered by stress, menstrual periods, food allergies, and poor nutrition, especially deficiencies in iron, vitamin B12, and folic acid.

Nutritional Help for Canker Sores

Cultured milk products, including yogurt, cottage cheese, and buttermilk, as well as garlic and onions, can help relieve pain and heal cankers. Other nutrients that help ease and heal canker sores include iron (abundant in beet greens, broccoli, parsley, and spinach); zinc (found in carrots, ginger, parsley, and garlic); folic acid (found in cabbage, beet greens, spinach, and kale); and beta-carotene (found in carrots, kale, parsley, and spinach).

Avoid coffee, alcohol, animal protein, and foods high in sugar and citrus, which produce excess acid in the body that contributes to canker sores.

Vanishing Varicose Veins

Varicose veins usually occur in older or pregnant women and are caused by a restriction of blood flow from the legs toward the heart. Blood pools in the veins, giving them an unsightly purplish tone and making them appear to bulge from the skin. Varicose veins are also caused by high blood pressure, which causes blockages; a lack of blood flow resulting from overly tight clothing; obesity; and lack of exercise.

FACT

Hemorrhoids are actually varicose veins of the anus or rectum. To alleviate hemorrhoids, eat a high-fiber diet containing lots of fruits and vegetables, which will help prevent constipation and eliminate unnecessary straining during bowel movements.

Dietary Intervention

Foods high in vitamin E (wheat germ, legumes, nuts and seeds, leafy greens, herbs, and soy) help improve circulation and reduce the incidence of varicose veins. Vitamin C (found in citrus fruit, peppers, berries, and leafy greens) helps strengthen blood vessels, while garlic and onions help break down the fibrin surrounding varicose veins and also contain anti-clotting agents. Dark-colored berries, including cherries, blueberries, and blackberries, help strengthen the walls of the veins and increase their tone.

More Beautiful and Bountiful Hair

If you're stressed out, burned out, or totally fried, there's a good chance your hair looks the same. Research shows that bad hair days proliferate when you don't get enough of the right vitamins or protein.

Nutrients that help hair can be found in beans, whole grains, eggs, salmon, raw nuts, flax and pumpkin seeds, berries, and dark leafy greens. As a fringe benefit, salmon and greens also provide calcium for your teeth, so you're helping your hair and teeth. Berries are high in cancer-preventing antioxidants, and dark greens also contain lutein, which halts blindness and cataracts. By eating all of these nutritious fruits and vegetables, you'll have hair that looks like it came out of a commercial and you'll feel like you spent a week at a swank health spa.

FACT

Multivitamins that contain vitamins B, D, and E are great for strengthening your hair, skin, and nails in a pinch. But read the labels first. Overdosing on vitamin D can lead to excessive calcium that your body can't process and cause your hair and nails to become dull and even break off.

Ten Super foods for Hair

According to leading hair expert Nicholas Perricone, M.D., author of *The Perricone Promise,* you can promote thicker, healthier hair by consuming adequate amounts of what he calls the ten super foods for hair.

1. **Acai berries**, which contain powerful antioxidants.
2. **Allium foods**, including onions, garlic, leeks, and shallots, which contain powerful bioflavonoids.
3. **Barley**, which is high in niacin, a nutrient that helps hair growth.
4. **Wheatgrass**, which cleanses hair of toxins and has essential fatty acids that build hair protein.
5. **Buckwheat**, which has more vitamins, flavonoids, and minerals than other grains except barley.
6. **Hot peppers**, which contain capsaicin, a powerful antioxidant.
7. **Nuts** and **seeds**, which contain essential proteins, phytochemicals, and fatty acids to build healthy tresses and reduce breakage and damage.
8. **Sprouts**, which are packed with nutrients to give your hair body and lift.
9. **Yogurt** and **kefir**, which promote longevity and health.
10. **Spirulina** and **algae**, which provide essential fatty acids to build hair protein and cleanse hair of toxins.

Don't expect your hair to perk up right away when you start ingesting these super foods. Hair grows and mends slowly, and your locks will need at least three months to show real improvement, so be patient! Meanwhile, you can jazz up your beauty regimen with daily juicing—an easy way to get all those essential vitamins and minerals. Maintaining a better diet will also help color-treated hair maintain its hue and bounce.

And don't forget to hydrate your hair from the inside out. Drink at least eight glasses of water a day. Water hydrates your body and maintains a healthy moisture balance in your hair, which prevents frizzing, drying, and breakage. Drinking enough water for your hair is especially crucial if you regularly use hair dryers and/or hot rollers, color or bleach your hair, or if your hair is regularly subjected to harsh, drying chemicals, such as chlorine in swimming pools and hot tubs.

Tips for Hair Loss

If you're following a good regimen for your hair but are still losing hair or excessively shedding, or if you have hair that never seems to grow, you may be suffering from a medical condition called alopecia, or medical hair loss.

Alopecia often signals an underlying medical problem, such as an overactive or underactive thyroid gland, chronic stress, malnutrition, crash dieting, hormonal imbalances, anemia, and cancer. If you're losing hair, see a physician to rule out underlying medical causes.

ESSENTIAL

Losing your hair? Try eating more vitamins to maintain a magnificent mane. High levels of DHT, a form of testosterone linked to hair loss, can be blocked by consuming adequate amounts of omega-3s (found in fish) as well as lecithin, B vitamins, lutein, sulfur, iron, and minerals.

Nutrients that Slow Hair Loss

If your hair loss is because of nutritional deficiencies, you can ward it off by consuming these hair-healthy nutrients and foods.

✓ **Vitamin A** (found in mangos, oranges, carrots, sweet potatoes, and squash) produces sebum and promotes hair growth. Too little vitamin A causes dry hair, dandruff, and a thick scalp, which eventually causes hair loss.

✓ **Vitamin B** (found in potatoes, cereals, bananas, chicken, and beef) and in particular folic acid (found in lentils, collard greens, chickpeas, papayas, and asparagus) provides the scalp with oxygen for healthy hair growth.

✓ **Silica** (found in oats, millet, barley, whole wheat, and algae) is the most important trace mineral for healthy hair growth because your hair is made of silica. Getting enough silica also helps your body use several other essential nutrients, including boron, copper, manganese, fluorine, phosphorous, zinc, and strontium.

✓ **Iodine** (found in kelp, yogurt, milk, eggs, strawberries, and mozzarella cheese) helps prevent hair loss, although taking too much iodine in supplements may actually cause hair loss.

Building More Beautiful Nails

Your nails are made of keratin, a type of protein, as well as minerals. As you might expect, feeding your nails from the inside out means getting enough protein, iodine, calcium, zinc, iron, and vitamins B and A. If you're short on any one of these nutrients, the results are likely to show up in your nails.

What Your Nails Tell You

Dark, pale, or very thin nails signal an iron deficiency, while nails that break or split evenly or grow slowly indicate a lack of vitamin A, calcium, and protein. Too little vitamin B creates fragile nails with horizontal or vertical ridges, while vertical ridges signal anemia or iron deficiency. Frequent hangnails may be caused by inadequate vitamin C, folic acid, and protein, while moon-shaped or white tops on nails may be caused by an iron and zinc deficiency.

Nailing Deficiencies

For stronger nails that grow faster, eat plenty of calcium (found in dairy produce, fruits, and vegetables); iron, a trace element that enriches red blood cells and increases oxygenation of tissue, especially in nails that break easily (found in red meat and shellfish) and sulphur, which helps strengthen nails (found in seafood, asparagus, onion, garlic, and cabbage).

Tropical Cucumber

» ### Good for skin

This drink provides skin benefits. Cucumber contains silica, a trace mineral that helps provide strength to the connective tissues of the skin. Cucumbers help with swelling of the eyes and water retention. They are high in vitamins A and C and folic acid.

INGREDIENTS | **YIELD: 2 CUPS**

1 cup pineapple, peeled and cut into chunks
1 mango, pitted
1 cucumber, peeled
½ lemon, rind intact

Juice pineapple first, then mango and cucumber. Cut lemon into thin slices and juice it last. Stir well before serving.

Per Serving

CALORIES: **163**
FAT: **0.53g**
SODIUM: **8.8mg**
FIBER: **6.9g**
PROTEIN: **3.9g**
SUGARS: **33g**
CARBOHYDRATES: **52g**

Apple Grape

» ### Good for skin

Apple seeds may not be juiced because they contain cyanide, which is poisonous. Make sure you remove the seeds from the apple before placing it through the juicer.

INGREDIENTS | **YIELD 1 CUP**

2 red gala apples, cored
1 cup green seedless grapes

Juice apples first, then juice grapes. Stir well before serving.

Per Serving

CALORIES: **126**
FAT: **0.58g**
SODIUM: **3.1mg**
FIBER: **3.4g**
PROTEIN: **0.91g**
SUGARS: **43g**
CARBOHYDRATES: **53g**

Apple Lemonade

» Good for nails

Apples are available year round, but are best September through November. Select firm apples with good color. Skins should be smooth and have no blemishes.

INGREDIENTS | YIELD: 1 CUP

2 red gala apples, cored
2 Granny Smith apples, cored
¼ lemon, rind intact

Juice apples first. Cut lemon into thin slices and then juice it. Stir.

<u>Per Serving</u>

CALORIES: **135**
FAT: **0.65g**
SODIUM: **3.3mg**
FIBER: **6.3g**
PROTEIN: **0.27g**
SUGARS: **25g**
CARBOHYDRATES: **38g**

Apple Celery

» Good for skin

Store apples in a cool, dark place. They may also be stored in plastic bags in your refrigerator.

INGREDIENTS | YIELDS: 1¼ CUPS

1 Granny Smith apple, cored
2 celery stalks

Juice apples and celery. Stir well.

<u>Per Serving</u>

CALORIES: **47**
FAT: **0.36g**
SODIUM: **82mg**
FIBER: **3.3g**
PROTEIN: **1g**
SUGARS: **8.3g**
CARBOHYDRATES: **12g**

Apple Banana

>> **Good for hair**

You can lighten your hair naturally by washing it with a rinse made with 1 tablespoon lemon juice and 1 gallon warm water. Rinse your hair with the mixture 15 times, letting it sit for 15 minutes after the last application before rinsing with pure water.

INGREDIENTS | YIELD: 1 CUP

3 Granny Smith apples, cored
1 lemon, peeled
1 banana, peeled

Juice apples and lemon. Add banana and blend until smooth.

Per Serving

CALORIES: **190**
FAT: **0.9g**
SODIUM: **3.9mg**
FIBER: **8.1g**
PROTEIN: **1.4g**
SUGARS: **31g**
CARBOHYDRATES: **51g**

Berry Cherry

>> **Good for hair**

Cherries are named after the Turkish town of Cerasus. There are two main types of cherries: sweet and sour.

INGREDIENTS | YIELD: 1 CUP

1 cup cherries, pitted
1½ cups strawberries
1 pint raspberries

Juice cherries, strawberries, and raspberries.

Per Serving

CALORIES: **279**
FAT: **2.9g**
SODIUM: **9.4mg**
FIBER: **24g**
PROTEIN: **6.8g**
SUGARS: **34g**
CARBOHYDRATES: **67g**

Kale Apple Spinach

» ## Good for skin

This drink will help keep your skin clear of acne. Reducing junk foods and drinking healthy juice will be a step in the right direction, too.

INGREDIENTS | YIELD: 1¼ CUPS

2 red apples, cored
2 carrots, peeled
4 large kale leaves
1 fist spinach

Juice apple, carrots, kale, and spinach. Stir.

Per Serving

CALORIES: **295**
FAT: **2.9g**
SODIUM: **400mg**
FIBER: **18g**
PROTEIN: **16g**
SUGARS: **30g**
CARBOHYDRATES: **57g**

Let's Take Some E

According to *The Journal of Investigative Dermatology*, people who consumed vitamins C and E saw a reduction in sunburns caused by exposure to UVB radiation, as well as a reduction of factors linked to DNA damage within skin cells. Scientists believe these two antioxidant vitamins may help protect against DNA damage.

Ginger Carrot Beet

» ## Good for skin and reducing canker sores

The beta-carotene from the carrots will help heal the mucous membranes in your mouth. Beets are a good source of folic acid, vitamin C, and potassium. Red beets provide vitamins A and C, calcium, iron, and fiber.

INGREDIENTS | YIELD: 1 CUP

4 carrots, peeled
¼" slice ginger root
1 beet, rinsed

Juice carrots, ginger, and beet. Stir.

Per Serving

CALORIES: **231**
FAT: **0.27g**
SODIUM: **222mg**
FIBER: **15g**
PROTEIN: **5.8g**
SUGARS: **31g**
CARBOHYDRATES: **60g**

Gimme a C!

If your skin needs a vitamin C boost, you might want to supplement juicing with a topical C cream, which encourages collagen production. The cream should contain L-ascorbic acid, the only type of vitamin C that penetrates your skin layers and can be absorbed by your body.

Sunshine in a Glass

» ## Good for nails

Vary the variety of the apples to change the flavor of this sweet drink. Strawberries are among the hardiest of berries, but don't wash them until you're ready to juice them.

INGREDIENTS | YIELD: 1½ CUPS

2 red gala apples, cored
1½ cups strawberries, hull intact
¼ lime, rind intact

Cut apples into thin slices. Juice apples first and then strawberries. Cut lime into thin slices and juice. Stir well.

Per Serving

CALORIES: **143**
FAT: **1.1g**
SODIUM: **3.9mg**
FIBER: **7.5g**
PROTEIN: **2.4g**
SUGARS: **34g**
CARBOHYDRATES: **52g**

Cherry Cucumber

» ## Good for nails

Most varieties of sweet cherries are dark purple. Black bing, Lambert, and Royal Ann are popular cherry varieties. Maraschino cherries are made from Royal Ann cherries.

INGREDIENTS | YIELD: 1½ CUPS

1 cucumber, peeled
2 cups red sweet cherries, pitted
2 celery stalks, leaves intact

Juice cucumber, cherries, and celery. Stir.

Per Serving

CALORIES: **143**
FAT: **1.1g**
SODIUM: **3.9mg**
FIBER: **7.5g**
PROTEIN: **2.4g**
SUGARS: **38g**
CARBOHYDRATES: **53g**

Papaya Delight

» **Good for healthy skin and nails**

Pineapple is known to be great for the skin. This combination is fun, easy, and yummy!

INGREDIENTS | YIELD: 1½ CUPS

1 cup pineapple, peeled
7 large strawberries, hull intact
½ papaya, seeds removed

Juice pineapple, strawberries, and papaya.

Per Serving

CALORIES: **166**
FAT: **0.91g**
SODIUM: **5.7mg**
FIBER: **6.9g**
PROTEIN: **4.3g**
SUGARS: **24g**
CARBOHYDRATES: **36g**

Papaya

Papayas are native to North America. The tree grows from a seed to twenty feet in less than eighteen months. At that time it is already producing fruit. Papaya range in size from one to two pounds. They are most often grown in Hawaii and Florida.

Peach Strawberry

» **Good for hair**

Peaches bruise very easily. Look for intensely fragrant fruit that is soft. Avoid peaches that have green on them.

INGREDIENTS | YIELD: 1¼ CUPS

1 large peach, pitted
7 large strawberries, hulls intact

Juice peach and then strawberries. Stir.

Per Serving

CALORIES: **124**
FAT: **1g**
SODIUM: **2mg**
FIBER: **7.1g**
PROTEIN: **3.5g**
SUGARS: **21g**
CARBOHYDRATES: **28g**

Dilly of a Cucumber

>> **Good for skin**

Cucumbers are known to help the skin from becoming overly dry. Cucumbers contain silica, which helps improve the complexion.

INGREDIENTS | **YIELD: 1¼ CUPS**

½ large cucumber, peeled
1 celery stalk, leaves intact
2 sprigs fresh baby dill

Juice cucumber and then celery. Stir well. Add fresh sprigs of dill to the top of the drink for garnish.

Per Serving

CALORIES: **31**
FAT: **0.12g**
SODIUM: **45mg**
FIBER: **2g**
PROTEIN: **1.5g**
SUGARS: **4g**
CARBOHYDRATES: **8g**

Fresh Dill

Dill is a tasty herb and a nice addition to this drink. Dill does not juice through your juicer, so the best thing to do is serve your cucumber drink with a fresh sprig of it. If you want more dill flavor, add chopped dill to the drink.

CHAPTER 10

Juicing for Stronger Bones

Although dairy products were once considered the most important sources of calcium, new research shows that consuming a diet high in fresh fruits and vegetables is your best defense against degenerative diseases like osteopenia and osteoporosis. Studies show the high acid content of traditional calcium sources like milk and cheese actually contribute to the degeneration of bone. Consuming lots of low-acid, calcium-rich fruits and vegetables builds strong bones and prevents bone diseases by maintaining the body's healthy acid-alkaline balance.

Nutrients that Build Stronger Bones

The best way to build strong bones is to eat foods that enhance bone health. A recent study published in the *Journal of Clinical Endocrinology and Metabolism* suggests that increasing the alkalinity of your diet by eating more fruits and vegetables can improve bone health by reducing the excretion of calcium from the body.

The Dangers of High-Acid Diets

When it comes to dietary concerns regarding bone health, calcium and vitamin D have received the most attention, but there is increasing evidence that the acid-base balance of the diet is also important, according to researchers. According to a study conducted at Tufts University and Northeastern University, a diet containing a lot of protein and cereal grain causes excess acid in the body, which in turn may increase calcium excretion and lead to thinning bones.

ALERT

The high-protein, high-acid diet consumed by most Americans may be contributing to an epidemic of diseases and degenerative conditions of the joints and bones, including osteoporosis. High levels of acid in the diet suppress the production of new bone and stimulate the cells responsible for bone absorption.

The Scientific Rationale for Bone Loss

As a person ages, his or her body becomes less able to eliminate the acid produced during metabolic processes. As the levels of acid in the body rise, the body must find a way to neutralize this imbalance, so it resorts to a process called bone resorption, where bones are broken down and minerals like calcium, phosphates, and alkaline salts are released into the blood.

Fruits and Vegetables that Help Build Bone

In general, most fruits and vegetables are alkalizing, while animal flesh and food products, soda, and most junk and processed foods are highly acidifying. Based on the acid-alkali theory of bone health, consuming a diet high in fresh and raw produce and reducing your intake of high-acid foods can help you achieve a healthy degree of alkalinity in the body and thus preserve your bones. The following nutrients are essential for strong bones:

- **Calcium.** The most abundant mineral in bone, calcium builds strong bones and also helps prevent fractures and degeneration.
- **Magnesium.** Another major component in bones, magnesium helps prevent bone loss.
- **Boron.** A trace mineral essential for bone health, boron activates certain hormones that regulate bone growth and health.
- **Vitamin K.** This vitamin helps osteocalcin, the protein found in bone tissue, hang onto calcium.
- **Vitamin D.** This vitamin helps maintain the mineral balance in bone and enhances the absorption of calcium. High levels of vitamin D have been linked to substantial reductions in hip fractures in post-menopausal women.
- **Anthocyanins and proanthocyanidins.** These two compounds found in cells help build collagen and stabilize bone structure.

Fruits and Vegetables that Boost Bone Health

When fruits and vegetables are added to the diet, it creates an alkaline environment that offsets the acidity of meats and dairy products and helps preserve the structure of the bone. This positive effect on bones is even greater if you eat vegetables high in calcium, such as broccoli, kale, and turnip greens. Turnip greens especially are a calcium powerhouse, supplying 200 milligrams of calcium in a single serving.

Best Sources of Calcium, Magnesium, and Boron

Although milk is high in calcium, you will also find it in abundance in kale, collard greens, broccoli, parsley, and turnip greens, which provide calcium without the acidic fat of dairy products. Collard greens, parsley, and blackberries are packed with magnesium, another essential mineral for bone health. You can find plenty of boron in kale, collard greens, and turnip greens.

Best Sources of Vitamins for Bone Health

Excellent sources of vitamin K include kale, collard and turnip greens, broccoli, parsley, lettuce, cabbage, spinach, watercress, asparagus, and string beans. In addition, vitamin D plays a critical role in the preservation of bone health and most Americans don't get enough. Although the best source of vitamin D is through exposure to direct sunlight for ten to fifteen minutes each day, you may not be able to do this in the dead of winter. To ensure you get enough, consider taking a supplement and eating lots of fatty fish, including salmon, tuna, sardines, catfish, shrimp, and cod. Good produce sources include sunflower seeds, sunflower sprouts, and mushrooms. In addition, some brands of soy milk and orange juice are fortified with vitamin D. Red grapes and blueberries are high in anthocyanins and proanthocyanins, which are also essential for bone health.

How Does Juicing Help Bones?

Juicing is an easy way to consume high concentrates of all the vitamins, minerals, and compounds necessary to build bone health and also helps balance the body's acid-alkaline balance. Unlike meats and dairy products, which create an acidic environment in the body that has been shown to reduce the incidence of fractures, fruits and vegetables used in juicing are low in acids and high in alkaline ingredients.

Juicing for Osteopenia and Osteoporosis

Osteoporosis is a weakening of the bones. Osteopenia is the precursor to osteoporosis; the bones are beginning to lose density, and osteoporosis will develop if proper precautions are not taken. The lower your bone density, the higher your risk for broken bones. Although it's natural for bones to lose density after age thirty, certain conditions increase your risk of brittle bones. Genetics play a role, but so does lifestyle. If you don't consume sufficient amounts of bone-building nutrients, such as calcium and phosphorous, you may be more likely to develop osteoporosis or osteopenia. Certain medicines, such as steroids and excessive amounts of thyroid medications, thin bones.

Because the female hormone estrogen helps regulate calcium absorption in the bone, osteopenia and osteoporosis are very common among post-menopausal women because of their naturally declining estrogen levels. They affect millions of people in the United States, especially women over the age of fifty.

ESSENTIAL

Although medications have traditionally been used to halt or reverse the progression of osteopenia and osteoporosis, they come with side effects. Some people who prefer not to deal with these have turned to nutritional "cures," including consuming a low-acid diet high in fruits and vegetables that build bone.

The Benefit of Low-Acid Diets

Several recent studies show that consuming a diet low in acids found in meats and dairy, and high in the vitamins and minerals found in produce, can dramatically improve bone health and prevent osteopenia and osteoporosis.

In a study of more than 3,000 women in Scotland, researchers found that bone mineral density was 2 percent higher in women who consumed the lowest acid diets compared with those who ate the highest acid diets. Among pre-menopausal women, hip bone mineral density was 8 percent higher and lumbar spine density 6 percent higher in those who consumed the most potassium. The study concluded that women who consume low acid diets are 30 percent less likely to suffer risk fractures in old age.

Nutrients that Help Osteoporosis

In addition to calcium and other previously mentioned nutrients, there are still more vitamins and minerals that may help reduce or prevent osteoporosis, according to *Bone Health and Osteoporosis: A Report of the Surgeon General* from the National Institutes of Health Osteoporosis and Related Bone Diseases National Resource Center. The following nutrients are essential for bone health, according to the report:

- **Copper** assists in the regulation of certain enzymes that promote strong bone strength. Consuming too little copper can result in brittle bones.
- **Fluoride** plays a role in stimulating the growth of new bone and promotes the healthy development of bones and teeth.
- **Silicon** promotes strong bones and teeth.
- **Iron** promotes the healthy functioning of certain enzymes that play a role in bone strength.
- **Magnesium** helps calcium move in and out of bones and enhances bone strength. Consuming too little magnesium can also prevent the body from using estrogen properly. Studies suggest that not getting magnesium may interfere with our ability to process calcium. Sixty percent of the magnesium in the body is found in the bones in combination with calcium and phosphorous.
- **Manganese** helps build connective tissues, especially cartilage.
- **Phosphorous** is a component of every cell in the body and supports building bone and other tissue during growth.
- **Potassium** helps stabilize electrolytes in the body, which in turn leads to healthy bones.
- **Protein** is the body's building block for building tissue during growth and repairing and replacing tissue throughout life. It is also needed to help heal fractures and to make sure the immune system is functioning properly.
- **Zinc** helps stimulate protein synthesis in bone.

Foods that Interfere with Calcium Absorption

According to the Office of the Surgeon General, caffeine studies suggest that caffeine may interfere with calcium absorption. However, this effect can be neutralized in the presence of adequate dietary calcium.

In addition, when oxalates and calcium are found in the same food, oxalates combine with the calcium, preventing you from absorbing the calcium. Foods that are high in calcium as well as oxalates include beets, rhubarb, and spinach.

ALERT

Phosphorous is necessary for healthy bones, but some studies suggest that excess amounts of phosphorous may interfere with calcium absorption. The good news is that you can offset the loss by getting adequate amounts of calcium in your diet. The RDA is 700 mg for men and women over age thirty. You should not take in more than 4,000 mg if you are under age seventy or more than 3,000 mg if you are older than seventy.

Too much protein in your diet may convert the extra protein into calories for energy, producing a chemical called sulfate in the process. Sulfate causes loss of calcium.

Sodium also affects the balance of calcium in the body by increasing the amount you excrete in urine and perspiration. Vitamin A also plays an important role in bone growth, but excessive amounts of the retinol form of vitamin A may increase the breakdown of bones and interfere with vitamin D, which is needed to absorb calcium. The beta-carotene form of vitamin A does not appear to cause these problems. Ipriflavone, a synthetic isoflavone, has been linked to a reduction in lymphocytes, a type of white blood cell that fights infection.

Fruits and Vegetables that Help Prevent Osteoporosis and Bone Disease

You can find all of the nutrients you need for increased bone health in fresh fruits and vegetables that are suitable for juicing, according to the National Institutes for Health.

✓ **Copper** is found in nuts, seeds, wheat bran, cereals, whole grain products, and cocoa products.

✓ **Boron** is found avocado, nuts, and prune juice.

✓ **Fluoride** is found in fluoridated water and teas.

✓ **Iron** is found in parsley, cruciferous veggies, carrots, beets with greens, pineapple, and blackberries.

✓ **Silicon** is found in root veggies, cucumbers, and bell peppers.

✓ **Isoflavones** are found primarily in soybeans and soy products, chickpeas, and other legumes.

✓ **Magnesium** is found in leafy vegetables such as spinach, potatoes, nuts, seeds, whole grains including bran, wheat, oats, and chocolate. Smaller amounts are found in bananas, broccoli, raisins, and shrimp.

✓ **Manganese** is found in cruciferous veggies, spinach, beets, apples, tangerines, pears, and oranges.

✓ **Phosphorous** is found in milk, yogurt, ice cream, cheese, peas, meat, and eggs.

✓ **Potassium** is found in milk, yogurt, chicken, turkey, fish, bananas, raisins, cantaloupe, celery, carrots, potatoes, and tomatoes.

✓ **Vitamin C** is found in citrus fruit, tomatoes and tomato juice, potatoes, Brussels sprouts, cauliflower, broccoli, strawberries, cabbage, and spinach.

✓ **Protein** is found in legumes, grains, nuts, seeds, and vegetables.

✓ **Vitamin K** is found in collards, spinach, salad greens, broccoli, Brussels sprouts, cabbage, plant oils, and margarine. Patients on anticoagulant medication should work with their physicians to monitor their vitamin K intake to ensure they consume the right amount. Consuming too much or too little vitamin K can interfere with blood clotting.

✓ **Zinc** is found in whole grains, dry beans, and nuts. Nutritionists recommend that vegetarians double the RDA, as zinc is harder to absorb on a vegetarian diet. Calcium supplementation may reduce the absorption of zinc.

✓ **Calcium** is found in cruciferous veggies, string beans, oranges, celery, carrots, lettuce, watercress, beet greens, kale, parsley, and broccoli.

✓ **Vitamin D** is found in sunflower seeds, sunflower sprouts, and mushrooms.

Juicing for Osteoarthritis and Rheumatoid Arthritis

Millions of people suffer from osteoarthritis and rheumatoid arthritis. Osteoarthritis, the most common type of arthritis, most often affects women over the age of forty-five. It causes the cartilage lining the joints to degenerate and results in early morning stiffness, joint pain that gets worse over time, and loss of joint functions, according to the National Institute of Arthritis and Musculoskeletal and Skin Diseases. As the disease progresses, you may lose mobility in your joints.

Rheumatoid arthritis, a far more serious form of the disease, is chronic inflammation that affects the joints and entire body and results in extreme fatigue, stiffness, bone degeneration, and deformities that limit range of motion and mobility. Women are more likely than men to suffer from this condition.

As in osteoporosis, medication is typically the first line of defense against osteoarthritis and rheumatoid arthritis. Adverse side effects have led many to replace or supplement medications with fresh fruit and vegetable juices, which contain antioxidants that can battle toxins that lead to inflammation and disease, according to the National Institutes of Health. Juicing is an excellent way to increase your fruit and vegetable intake and get the nutrients your body needs.

Boning Up

» **Good for strong bones**

Broccoli is a good source of vitamins A and C. It also contains riboflavin, calcium, and iron.

INGREDIENTS | YIELD: 1¼ CUPS

2 carrots, peeled
1 red delicious apple, cored
1 cup broccoli

Juice carrots, apple, and then broccoli. Stir.

Per Serving

CALORIES: **157**
FAT: **0.44g**
SODIUM: **109mg**
FIBER: **10g**
PROTEIN: **4.7g**
SUGARS: **23g**
CARBOHYDRATES: **44g**

Cherry Greets Blueberry

» **Good for strong bones**

Two healthy berries combine to make this purple juice very good as well as good for you.

INGREDIENTS | YIELD: 1¼ CUPS

1 cup sweet cherries, pitted
2 cups blueberries

Juice cherries and blueberries. Stir.

Per Serving

CALORIES: **257**
FAT: **1.3g**
SODIUM: **2.9mg**
FIBER: **8.8g**
PROTEIN: **4.4g**
SUGARS: **44g**
CARBOHYDRATES: **61g**

Super Blueberries

There are about sixteen varieties of blueberry. They have more antioxidants than any other fruit or vegetable, and they're also high in fiber, potassium, and vitamins A and C.

Lettuce Patch

» Good for strong bones

The addition of carrot makes this dark green healthy juice a bit sweeter.

INGREDIENTS | **YIELD: 1½ CUPS**

1 cup romaine lettuce
1 parsnip
½ cup spinach
1 carrot, peeled

Juice ingredients in order listed. Stir well before serving.

<u>Per Serving</u>

CALORIES: **165**
FAT: **0.65g**
SODIUM: **69mg**
FIBER: **11g**
PROTEIN: **3.6g**
SUGARS: **13g**
CARBOHYDRATES: **39g**

Parsnips

Parsnips came to America in the early seventeenth century, but their popularity didn't take off immediately. They are a white root vegetable that is available year round. Refrigerate for up to 2 weeks in a plastic bag. They contain vitamin C and iron.

Many Greens

» Good for strong bones

High in vitamin C and fiber, Savoy cabbage is a cruciferous vegetable. It originated in the Savoy region, which straddles the border of Italy and France. It has a mild and slightly sweet flavor.

INGREDIENTS | **YIELD: ¾ CUP**

1 cup broccoli
3 red lettuce leaves
¼ head Savoy cabbage

Juice ingredients in order listed. Stir well before serving.

<u>Per Serving</u>

CALORIES: **77**
FAT: **0.55g**
SODIUM: **82mg**
FIBER: **7.5g**
PROTEIN: **6.2g**
SUGARS: **3.6g**
CARBOHYDRATES: **12g**

Carrot Kale

» Good for reducing osteoarthritis

Ginger is said to ease the symptoms of arthritis, but scientific studies have so far been mixed.

INGREDIENTS | YIELD: 1 CUP

2 carrots, peeled
¼" slice ginger root
1 red apple, cored
2 kale leaves
¼ cup parsley

Juice carrots, ginger, and apple. Juice kale and parsley. Stir together.

Per Serving

CALORIES: **162**
FAT: **0.73g**
SODIUM: **111mg**
FIBER: **8.4g**
PROTEIN: **3.7g**
SUGARS: **21g**
CARBOHYDRATES: **40g**

It's a Snap

» Good for strong bones

Snap peas belong to the green bean family. They were named for the sound they make when you break them in half.

INGREDIENTS | YIELD: ¾ CUP

1 cup snap peas
2 carrots, peeled
2 celery stalks

Juice snap peas, carrots, and celery. Stir.

Per Serving

CALORIES: **142**
FAT: **0.35g**
SODIUM: **166mg**
FIBER: **11g**
PROTEIN: **5.2g**
SUGARS: **15g**
CARBOHYDRATES: **39g**

Pick a Pepper

» Good for reducing osteoarthritis and rheumatoid arthritis

Bell peppers and celery often test positive for pesticide residue. Buy organic versions of these vegetables or make sure you scrub them thoroughly before you juice them.

INGREDIENTS | YIELD: 1½ CUPS

½ green bell pepper
½ red bell pepper
½ yellow bell pepper
1 celery stalk
½ cucumber
1 teaspoon turmeric

Juice peppers, celery, and cucumber. Stir in turmeric.

Per Serving

CALORIES: **86**
FAT: **0.5g**
SODIUM: **47mg**
FIBER: **6.1g**
PROTEIN: **3.7g**
SUGARS: **7g**
CARBOHYDRATES: **27g**

Salad in a Glass

» Good for strong bones

You can vary this recipe by switching the lettuce to romaine lettuce or red leaf lettuce.

INGREDIENTS | YIELD: 1 CUP

1 cup broccoli
3 butterhead lettuce leaves
1 carrot
2 red radishes
1 green onion

Juice ingredients in order listed. Stir. Garnish glass with green onion tops.

Per Serving

CALORIES: **95**
FAT: **0.52g**
SODIUM: **81mg**
FIBER: **7.5g**
PROTEIN: **5.3g**
SUGARS: **9g**
CARBOHYDRATES: **21g**

Butterhead Lettuce

Butterhead lettuce is small and round. Its leaves have a soft buttery texture. The flavor is sweet. Gentle washing is required for this type of lettuce because it is delicate. It's a tasty way to juice for strong, healthy bones.

Pineapple Plum Punch

» **Good for strong bones**

This juice is packed with magnesium to help build strong bones.

INGREDIENTS | YIELD: 1½ CUPS

2 black plums
1 cup pineapple

Juice plums and pineapple. Stir well before serving.

Per Serving

CALORIES: **136**
FAT: **0.62g**
SODIUM: **1.6mg**
FIBER: **2.9g**
PROTEIN: **2.9g**
SUGARS: **27g**
CARBOHYDRATES: **35g**

How to Choose a Pineapple

Choose a pineapple that is a bit soft to the touch. It should not show signs of green. The leaves should be green with no brown spots. If a pineapple is over ripe it will have soft areas on the skin. If you purchase a pineapple that is under ripe you may keep it at room temperature for a few days. Pineapple is available fresh or canned. If you cannot get fresh pineapple, choose a canned variety packed in its own juice.

Strawberry Patch

» **Good for strong bones**

Strawberries provide a great source of vitamin C as well as some iron and potassium. If you cannot get fresh berries, you may substitute frozen strawberries for your juice.

INGREDIENTS | YIELD: 1 CUP

1 apple, cored
1 cup strawberries, hulls intact

Juice apple and then strawberries. Stir well before serving.

Per Serving

CALORIES: **81**
FAT: **0.64g**
SODIUM: **2.1mg**
FIBER: **4.3g**
PROTEIN: **1.5g**
SUGARS: **19g**
CARBOHYDRATES: **30g**

Purple Cow

» **Good for strong bones**

Calcium is a mineral essential for building and maintaining bones. It is found in dairy products as well as spinach, turnip greens, and broccoli.

INGREDIENTS | **YIELD: 1½ CUPS**

1 cup blueberries
1 pint blackberries
½ cup skim milk

Juice berries. Stir in milk.

Per Serving

CALORIES: **250**
FAT: **2g**
SODIUM: **68mg**
FIBER: **17g**
PROTEIN: **8.5g**
SUGARS: **35g**
CARBOHYDRATES: **55g**

Strawberry Pineapple Grape

» **Good for strong bones**

Fresh berries are available during the peak season of April through June. If you cannot get fresh strawberries, substitute frozen berries for your juice.

INGREDIENTS | **YIELD: 1½ CUPS**

1 cup pineapple
1 cup red grapes
1 cup strawberries, hulls intact

Juice pineapple, grapes, and strawberries. Stir before serving.

Per Serving

CALORIES: **184**
FAT: **0.98g**
SODIUM: **4.9mg**
FIBER: **5.5g**
PROTEIN: **4g**
SUGARS:**50g**
CARBOHYDRATES: **66g**

Cantaloupe Straight Up

>> **Good for strong bones**

One cup of cantaloupe contains your daily requirement for antioxidants. Cantaloupe is also a good source of potassium, vitamin B6, dietary fiber, and niacin (vitamin B3).

INGREDIENTS | **YIELD: 1 CUP**

½ cantaloupe, rind removed

Juice cantaloupe.

Per Serving

CALORIES: **121**
FAT: **0.79g**
SODIUM: **57mg**
FIBER: **3.6g**
PROTEIN: **3.6g**
SUGARS: **14g**
CARBOHYDRATES: **14g**

Watermelon-Lime-Cherry

>> **Good for reducing osteoarthritis**

Use a melon baller to scoop out watermelon or cantaloupe balls, then thread the balls onto wooden skewers. Place on parchment paper lined baking sheet and freeze. Use to garnish juices.

INGREDIENTS | **YIELD: 1 CUP**

1 cup watermelon, rind removed
1 cup cherries, pitted
½ lime

Juice watermelon, cherries, and lime. Stir. Garnish with melon skewer.

Per Serving

CALORIES: **134**
FAT: **0.77g**
SODIUM: **6.9mg**
FIBER: **4.1g**
PROTEIN: **3.4g**
SUGARS: **23g**
CARBOHYDRATES: **35g**

CHAPTER 11

Juicing for Energy and Stamina

Fruits and vegetables can provide the energy and stamina you need for physical exertion as well as mental focus and concentration. If you're looking for the ultimate fast food, juicing combines the best nutrients from a variety of fruits and vegetables for maximum energy and stamina. Fruits are packed with simple and complex sugars, carbohydrates, vitamin C, and B vitamins, all of which provide instant and/or sustained energy, as well as iron and copper, power nutrients that promote stamina and endurance.

Best Nutrients for Energy and Stamina

If you're chronically tired, you could be running low on the fuel your body needs to keep you running. Whether you need to power your workout or increase your energy level for work, you'll find all the necessary nutrients in a glass of delicious juice.

Where to Find Nutrients for Energy

Here's a look at some of the most important vitamins and nutrients for maintaining high energy and stamina.

- **Vitamin B complex** refuels cells with energy that can be depleted by a variety of factors, including stress, insomnia, and overworking. Several medical conditions, including iron-deficiency anemia and hypothyroidism, can also cause tiredness and fatigue. Before assuming your fatigue is because of a lack of vitamin B, see your doctor. A simple blood test can rule out medical reasons.

  - **Vitamin B12** is especially crucial for energy and stamina. A lack of vitamin B12, or pernicious anemia, can cause weight loss, lack of muscle control, and yellow-blue color blindness. This deficiency is often triggered by gastrointestinal problems such as bacterial or parasitic infections.
  - **Folic acid (vitamin B9)** is essential for energy and stamina. A lack of folic acid in the diet may lead to folic acid-deficiency anemia, which can cause insomnia, sleep disorders, and a sore, red tongue.
  - **Biotin (vitamin B7)** promotes energy production as well as growth and development. Biotin deficiency can result in dermatitis.
  - **Niacin (vitamin B3)** is required by all cells in the body for energy production and promoting healthy skin, nerves, and proper digestive system functioning.
  - **Riboflavin (vitamin B2)** is important for growth, nerve function, red blood cell production, healthy skin, and the release of energy from foods.

- **Thiamin (Vitamin B1)** is necessary for energy production, especially from carbohydrates. It is also important for normal functioning of the heart, nervous system, and muscles.

- **Iron** deficiencies can cause general anemia, with symptoms that may include tiredness, fatigue, headaches, dizziness, inflammation of the lips, a red tongue, and spoon-like indentations in the fingernails. Overdosing on iron can cause constipation and prevent other minerals from being absorbed. Consume between 18-45 milligrams daily. A quick way to determine if you're iron deficient is to pull down your lower eyelid. If the color of the inner rim is pale pink or whitish, you may be anemic. If it's dark pink, you're not anemic.
- **Vitamin C** provides energy and boosts the absorption of iron.
- **Pantothenic acid** helps the body sidestep stress and promotes energy.
- **Vitamin E** is an antioxidant that can help prevent a chemical reaction called oxidation, which results in free radicals that contribute to aging, cancer, and many other diseases. Vitamin E is also essential for the proper functioning of nerves and muscles.

Special Iron Needs for Women

Most women lose around 35 milliliters of blood (about 2 tablespoons) during a four- to six-day menstrual cycle, which isn't enough to lead to fatigue or anemia. But if you start losing more than 80 milliliters, you could be at an increased risk for anemia, especially if you're a vegetarian who rarely or never eats meat, which is an excellent source of iron. If this sounds like you, talk to your physician. He can administer a blood test to determine if and how much you should supplement. In the meantime, eat more iron-rich foods, including nutrient-dense juice comprised of dark, leafy green vegetables.

Fruits and Vegetables that Provide Energy and Stamina

You can find all the vitamins and minerals to promote energy and stamina in a variety of fresh fruits and vegetables, so mix and match the following produce in your juices for an energy boost.

- ✓ **Vitamin B complex** is found in leafy greens, broccoli, and bananas.
- ✓ **Vitamin B12** is found naturally only in animal products, but you can also find it in small amounts in tofu and tempeh.
- ✓ **Folic acid (vitamin B9)** is abundant in asparagus, spinach, kale, cabbage, and blackberries.
- ✓ **Biotin** is found in chard, romaine lettuce, carrots, and tomatoes.
- ✓ **Niacin (vitamin B3)** is abundant in brewer's yeast, rice and wheat bran, and peanuts.
- ✓ **Riboflavin (vitamin B2)** is found in collard greens, kale, parsley, broccoli, beet greens, and prunes.
- ✓ **Thiamin (vitamin B1)** is abundant in seeds, nuts, split peas, buckwheat sprouts, sunflower seeds, and garlic.
- ✓ **Iron** is abundant in beets with greens, carrots, apples, blackberries, parsley, broccoli, cauliflower, strawberries, asparagus, chard, cabbage, and pineapple.
- ✓ **Vitamin C** is provided by kale, parsley, broccoli, Brussels sprouts, watercress, cauliflower, citrus fruit, mangos, papayas, asparagus, and strawberries.
- ✓ **Pantothenic acid** is found in broccoli, cauliflower, and kale.
- ✓ **Vitamin E** is found in tomatoes, carrots, asparagus, watercress, and spinach.

Juicing for Chronic Fatigue Syndrome

According to research conducted by the Centers for Disease Control (CDC), between 1 and 4 million Americans suffer from chronic fatigue syndrome (CFS). Many are seriously impaired, and at least a quarter are unemployed or on disability because of CFS. Yet only about half have consulted a physician for their illness.

According to the CDC, the earlier a person with CFS receives medical treatment, the greater the likelihood that the illness will resolve. About 40 percent of people in the general population who report symptoms of CFS have a serious, treatable, and previously unrecognized medical or psychiatric condition, such as diabetes, thyroid disease, or substance abuse.

CFS symptoms might last for months or even years, and they may come and go sporadically. Unfortunately, many family doctors are not familiar with CFS. The best place to get an accurate diagnosis is with a rheumatologist. There is no one test for CFS. Instead, your specialist will first rule out other possible causes of symptoms, including systemic lupus and influenza, before arriving at a diagnosis of CFS.

Research shows that CFS is caused by an energy crisis in your body. Studies show that more than 90 percent of people can improve symptoms or even recover from CFS by consuming lots of fresh fruits and vegetables, getting adequate sleep and exercise, avoiding dehydrating substances such as caffeine and alcohol, and consuming more water.

The Role of Vitamin D

Recent studies at the University of Wisconsin and at the State University of New York at Buffalo have linked low levels of vitamin D to a host of chronic conditions, including CFS. Researchers agree that the present recommended daily requirement of vitamin D is much lower than the amount needed to fight disease and ensure optimum health. People with CFS need to take a vitamin D supplement every day.

Nutrients that Help Fight CFS

Some people with CFS have benefited from taking supplements of magnesium, a mineral that is involved in the cells' energy production. One British study found that people with CFS had below-normal blood levels of magnesium. After receiving injections of magnesium, 80 percent reported improvement in their symptoms.

In addition, B-complex vitamins help support the adrenal glands, which are among the major organs in the body connected with stress. B vitamins also support the nervous system and promote energy, which is essential for those with CFS.

Juicing for CFS

Juicing lets you combine mega-doses of essential nutrients into one delicious glass of juice, so mix and match the following vitamins and minerals into juice that help fight CFS and recharge your energy, concentration, and stamina.

- **Magnesium:** Celery, cauliflower, spinach, beets and beet greens, dandelion greens, garlic, romaine lettuce, parsley, and carrots are rich sources of this mineral.
- **Vitamin D:** Found mostly in cold water fish, you can add a little vitamin D to your juice via sunflower seeds and sprouts and mushrooms.
- **B vitamins:** Good sources include leafy greens, nuts, beans, asparagus, kale, broccoli, cabbage, and spinach.
- **Vitamin A and beta-carotene:** Find these nutrients in carrots, kale, parsley, chard, beet greens, watercress, broccoli, and romaine lettuce.
- **Carnitine:** Many people with CFS have low levels of this amino acid. The best sources of carnitine are avocado, fish, red meat, tempeh, and wheat. Carnitine is not found in abundance in most other fruits and vegetables.
- **Vitamin C:** This antioxidant helps fight free radicals and boosts immunity. Produce that contains abundant amounts of vitamin C include citrus fruit, kale, parsley, broccoli, Brussels sprouts, watercress, cauliflower, cabbage, spinach, turnips, and asparagus.
- **Zinc:** This mineral boosts the immune system and helps fight infections. Find it in ginger root, turnips, carrots, cabbage, lettuce, cucumbers, and garlic.
- **Coenzyme Q10:** This little-known nutrient is similar to that of vitamins E and K and can be found in soybeans, vegetable oils, and many meats. Like vitamins C and E and beta-carotene, coenzyme Q10 is also a member of the antioxidant family, a group of nutrients that protect your body's tissues from everyday wear and tear by disarming destructive free radicals. Coenzyme Q10 also promotes energy by helping cells convert protein, fat, and carbohydrates into energy. Coenzyme Q10 is not found in fruits and vegetables.

ALERT

If you have CFS, be sure to get enough sun. Studies show that short periods of sun exposure help regulate circadian rhythms, the body's internal "clock" that tells you when to be awake and when to be active. Because sleep problems are a major concern for CFS sufferers, mild sun exposure may promote healthy sleep patterns.

Other Dietary Interventions

When it comes to battling chronic fatigue syndrome (CFS), medical experts agree that the overall quality of your diet makes a big difference in how you feel. Here are a few other dietary changes that might prove helpful.

- Go easy on the sugar. Eating too much refined sugar weakens the immune system and may inhibit the ability of white blood cells to stay active. Fruit is high in sugar, so limit fruit juice consumption if you have CFS and stick to homemade vegetable juices.
- Cut the fat. Fatty foods are difficult to digest and can cause a general sluggish feeling, which can aggravate the fatigue associated with CFS needs. Limit your consumption of veggies that are high in fat, including avocados, nuts, and seeds.
- Avoid processed foods, which are often full of additives, preservatives and artificial colorings and flavorings. Fortunately, homemade juice contains no preservatives, and is an excellent source of nutrients for those with CFS.

Juicing for Fibromyalgia

Fibromyalgia causes widespread pain, disturbed sleep, and exhaustion. In fact, the word itself means pain in the muscles, ligaments, and tendons—the soft fibrous tissues of the body. Although the muscles hurt everywhere, they are not the only cause of the pain. Malfunctions in the way the nervous system processes pain magnify the whole-body symptoms.

Recent research in Sweden revealed that half of the fibromyalgia patients in a study found it impossible or difficult to climb stairs and a majority of patients could not run. Just standing for five minutes was extremely taxing to one-fourth of the patients. Fibromyalgia is estimated to affect 5 million Americans. Women between the ages of twenty and sixty are the most affected group.

While fibromyalgia is chronic and can be debilitating, it's not progressive or life-threatening and there are many treatments, including nutritional ones, that can help you manage your condition and live an active life.

FACT

The antioxidants vitamin C, vitamin E, and beta-carotene, and the mineral selenium are a SWAT team against free radicals, according to new research that indicates the disease is generated by free radicals.

Nutritional Intervention for Fibromyalgia

Many people suffering from fibromyalgia also have hypoglycemia, or low blood sugar, which means they are unable to tolerate carbohydrates. Because fruit is loaded with carbohydrates and natural sugars, people who have fibromyagia should reduce their intake of fruit juice to a glass or two a day and avoid caffeine and alcohol.

ALERT

According to researchers at Johns Hopkins University, it's not unusual for some patients to see as many as ten doctors before finally discovering the cause of their pain. Most sufferers wait an average of five years after onset to get an accurate diagnosis and start receiving appropriate treatment.

Nutrients that benefit fibromyalgia include magnesium, which is often deficient in fibromyalgia sufferers, and vitamin B1. Magnesium can be found in celery, cauliflower, spinach, beets and beet greens, dandelion greens, garlic, romaine lettuce, parsley, and carrots.

Good sources of vitamin B1 include seeds, nuts, split peas, buckwheat, whole wheat, millet, oatmeal, wild rice, cornmeal, sunflower and buckwheat sprouts, and garlic. It is not found in fruits and vegetables.

FACT

Regional muscle pain not related to arthritis or the nervous system often occurs in people with fibromyalgia, who describe the feeling as firm knots in their muscles that often cause restrictions in movement and radiating pain. These muscle nodules are called myofascial trigger points and may overlap with tender points used to diagnose fibromyalgia.

Juicing for Insomnia and Jet Lag

Nothing ruins your day like too little sleep. When sleep problems become chronic, the condition is called insomnia.

Insomnia induced by jet lag frequently occurs when you cross several times zones. Symptoms include sleepiness, fatigue, and hunger. You can alleviate jet lag and induce sleep by following the same nutritional advice for insomnia.

Nutritional Causes of Insomnia

Common stimulants associated with poor sleep include caffeine and nicotine. If you're tossing and turning at night, consider restricting your intake of caffeine after lunch and limiting your total daily intake.

Foods high in tyramine, an amino acid that stimulates the brain, should also be avoided if you have trouble sleeping. Produce that contains this amino acid include spinach, eggplant, tomatoes, and potatoes.

In addition, consuming too much sugar right before bedtime can create a rise in blood sugar that can stimulate you and keep you awake, so avoid drinking a lot of fruit juice right before bed if you've been having trouble sleeping.

Juicing for a Good Night's Sleep

Fruits and vegetables that are high in calming carbohydrates increase levels of the feel-good hormone serotonin in your brain and often induce sleep. The best choices for nightcap juices include complex carbs found in lentils, split peas, mushrooms, and mulberries. Other nutrients that enhance sleep include:

- **Calcium**, especially when contained in food, has a sedative effect on the body. Calcium deficiency causes restlessness and wakefulness. Make juice from calcium-rich fruits and vegetables like kale, parsley, watercress, beet greens, broccoli, romaine lettuce, string beans, oranges, celery, and carrots.
- **Vitamin B1** helps increase your body's utilization of serotonin and may help you sleep. While not widely available in produce, you can find it in sunflower seeds, buckwheat sprouts, and garlic.
- **Vitamin B6** can also help prevent insomnia. Stir a tablespoon or two of nutritional yeast into a glass of juice to promote sleep, or make a veggie juice containing kale and bell peppers. Prune juice is also high in B6 and helps facilitate sleep.
- **Vitamin B12** is another important supplement for treating insomnia. Find it in sunflower seeds.
- **Pantothenic acid (vitamin B5)** is good for relieving stress. Wheat germ, walnuts, peanuts, bananas, sunflower seeds, cauliflower, and kale are good sources.
- A lack of **folic acid** can also disrupt sleep. Good sources include cruciferous veggies and blackberries.
- **Magnesium** deficiency can result in nervousness that prevents sleep. Magnesium-rich foods include kelp, wheat bran, almonds, cashews, garlic, brewer's yeast, cruciferous veggies, and blackberries. In addition, a lack of calcium and magnesium can cause leg cramps during the night, which can keep you tossing and turning.
- **Inositol**, a B vitamin, enhances REM sleep. Good sources include citrus fruits, strawberries, and cantaloupe.
- **Chromium** helps those with blood sugar problems relax and fall asleep. Brewer's yeast is a good source of chromium.

Juicing for Better Circulation

Your fingernails naturally grow faster than your toenails—and it's all because of proximity to your heart. Your arms are much closer to the pumping action of your heart than your legs are, which means your arms enjoy better circulation than your legs, which results in faster nail growth and quicker healing.

FACT

To improve blood circulation, increase your intake of vegetables and fresh fruits, especially berries, eat plenty of foods rich in vitamins A, C, and E, and add ingredients to your daily diet that "kick up" circulation, including fennel, ginger, beetroot, cayenne, and watercress.

How to Get Your Blood Moving Through Diet

Good circulation supplies the body with the oxygen it needs and rids the body of waste. Without good circulation, you're likely to feel sluggish and heal very slowly. Fortunately, you can juice your way to healthy circulation by incorporating the following foods into your homemade juices:

- **Ginkgo biloba** is a potent herb that stimulates blood circulation, so include it in your favorite juices.
- **Pumpkin seeds** are an excellent source of vitamin E. Research shows that vitamin E can help lessen the stickiness of blood and can prevent blood clots forming, which reduces the risk of stroke and heart attack.
- **Oranges** contain bioflavonoids and vitamin C that help blood flow by strengthening capillary walls. Vitamin C is also a powerful antioxidant, which helps fight free radicals.
- **Nuts** contain a substance called niacin, or vitamin B3, that gives your blood a boost and assists circulation.

- **Watermelon** contains lycopene, which helps prevent the buildup of plaque in blood vessels that can interfere with or block blood circulation. Watermelon also promotes healthy arteries and blood circulation.
- **Garlic** helps thin blood and will prevent the buildup of plaque in blood vessels and even arteries.

You can give your circulation a jump through regular exercise, which gets your blood moving. Massage, acupressure, and acupuncture have also been shown to improve circulation and enhance relaxation.

Nighty-Nite Nightcap

» Good for reducing insomnia

Lettuce has a sedative effect that helps promote sleep. High calcium levels help your muscles relax, allowing you to sleep better.

INGREDIENTS | YIELD: 1 CUP

2 carrots, peeled
2 celery stalks
2 romaine lettuce leaves

Juice carrots, celery, and lettuce. Stir.

Per Serving

CALORIES: **110**
FAT: **0.26g**
SODIUM: **160mg**
FIBER: **8.3g**
PROTEIN: **3.1g**
SUGARS: **15g**
CARBOHYDRATES: **29g**

Jet Lag Buster

» Good for reducing jet lag symptoms

Parsley is a good source of calcium and magnesium, both known to promote sleep.

INGREDIENTS | YIELD: 1 CUP

4 carrots, peeled
2 celery stalks
2 romaine lettuce leaves
⅛ cup parsley

Juice carrots, celery, and romaine. Stir. Garnish with parsley.

Per Serving

CALORIES: **207**
FAT: **0.26g**
SODIUM: **242mg**
FIBER: **14g**
PROTEIN: **5.1g**
SUGARS: **28g**
CARBOHYDRATES: **55g**

Jet Lag Zapper

» **Good for reducing jet lag symptoms**

The 1897 Sears Catalog offered a nerve tonic made from celery. Celery is high in calcium and is widely recognized for its calming effect.

INGREDIENTS | YIELD: 1¼ CUPS

4 romaine lettuce leaves
3 carrots, peeled
½ cup cauliflower
½ lemon, peeled

Juice ingredients in order listed. Stir.

Per Serving

CALORIES: **166**
FAT: **0.18g**
SODIUM: **134mg**
FIBER: **12g**
PROTEIN: **4.5g**
SUGARS: **24g**
CARBOHYDRATES: **51g**

Ultimate "C" Energizer

» **Good for reducing anemia, chronic fatigue syndrome, and fibromyalgia**

This citrus delight is full of the mighty vitamin C, which helps your body absorb iron better.

INGREDIENTS | YIELD: 1½ CUPS

2 oranges, peeled
½ pink grapefruit, peeled
½ lemon, peeled

Juice orange and grapefruit. Juice lemon. Stir.

Per Serving

CALORIES: **189**
FAT: **0.86g**
SODIUM: **0.59mg**
FIBER: **9g**
PROTEIN: **4.3g**
SUGARS: **38g**
CARBOHYDRATES: **50g**

Popeye Picker Upper

>> **Good for reducing anemia**

Watercress is a member of the mustard family and is often recommended as a vegetable that can help those who are anemic.

INGREDIENTS | YIELD: ¾ CUP

1 apple, cored
1 cup spinach leaves
1 handful watercress

Juice apple, spinach, and watercress. Stir.

Per Serving

CALORIES: **39**
FAT: **0.27g**
SODIUM: **25mg**
FIBER: **1.9g**
PROTEIN: **0.91g**
SUGARS: **8.5g**
CARBOHYDRATES: **13g**

Orange Lemonade Lift-off

>> **Good for improved energy and stamina and for chronic fatigue syndrome and fibromyalgia**

The fake sugars in diet soft drinks and other products can actually trigger or worsen CFS and fibromyalgia, so get your energy from this all-natural, vitamin C-rich juice!

INGREDIENTS | YIELD: ¾ CUP

3 oranges, peeled
1 lemon, peeled

Juice oranges and lemon. Stir.

Per Serving

CALORIES: **211**
FAT: **1.1g**
SODIUM: **1.2mg**
FIBER: **10g**
PROTEIN: **4.8g**
SUGARS: **40g**
CARBOHYDRATES: **56g**

Sugar and CFS

Research suggests that people with CFS are deficient in an enzyme needed to metabolize sugar. The result is a buildup of lactic acid in the bloodstream, which can lead to muscle pain, vascular headaches, and neuropsychiatric disorders such as panic attacks, all of which are associated with CFS.

Apple Banana High

» **Good for reducing anemia**

The vitamin C found in the lemon and banana helps your body absorb all the iron in this drink.

INGREDIENTS | YIELD 1¼ CUPS

2 Granny Smith apples
1 pint blackberries
1 lemon
1 banana

Juice apples, blackberries, and lemon. Add banana to juice and blend. Stir well before serving.

Per Serving

CALORIES: **287**
FAT: **2.2g**
SODIUM: **8.2mg**
FIBER: **25g**
PROTEIN: **4.8g**
SUGARS: **40g**
CARBOHYDRATES: **80g**

Razzle Dazzle Berry

» **Good for improving circulation**

Try this mix of strawberries and raspberries for a really rich drink that is easy to make.

INGREDIENTS | YIELD: 1 CUP

2 cups strawberries, hulls intact
1 pint raspberries

Juice berries. Stir before serving.

Per Serving

CALORIES: **222**
FAT: **2.3g**
SODIUM: **5.9mg**
FIBER: **21g**
PROTEIN: **5.9g**
SUGARS: **36g**
CARBOHYDRATES: **63g**

Pineapple Tangerine

» **Good for easing chronic fatigue syndrome and fibromyalgia**

Pineapples and tangerines are both good sources of iron and vitamin C. Vitamin C can prove stamina and circulation.

INGREDIENTS | YIELD: 1 CUP

1 cup pineapple, peeled
1 tangerine, peeled

Juice pineapple and tangerine. Stir.

Per Serving

CALORIES: **127**
FAT: **0.038g**
SODIUM: **3.5mg**
FIBER: **3.3g**
PROTEIN: **2.4g**
SUGARS: **25g**
CARBOHYDRATES: **33g**

Pineapple Cucumber

» **Good for energy and stamina**

This refreshing combination has great health benefits. Pineapples and cucumbers are both good for treating edema, the accumulation of fluid beneath the skin. English cucumbers have a milder flavor than regular cucumbers.

INGREDIENTS | YIELD: 1 CUP

1 English cucumber, peeled
1 cup pineapple, peeled

Juice cucumber and pineapple. Stir. Garnish with cube of pineapple on a stick.

Per Serving

CALORIES: **99**
FAT: **0.17g**
SODIUM: **5.6mg**
FIBER: **2.6g**
PROTEIN: **2.6g**
SUGARS: **20g**
CARBOHYDRATES: **32g**

Cauliflower Broccoli

» **Good for easing chronic fatigue syndrome and fibromyalgia**

Vitamin B for energy is the key to this juice, and the magnesium in the cauliflower and beet greens will also boost energy.

INGREDIENTS | YIELD: 1 CUP

1 cup cauliflower
4 broccoli spears
2 beet greens

Juice cauliflower, broccoli, and beet greens separately. Stir together.

Per Serving

CALORIES: **78**
FAT: **0.56g**
SODIUM: **213mg**
FIBER: **9g**
PROTEIN: **6.7g**
SUGARS: **3g**
CARBOHYDRATES: **10g**

CHAPTER 12

Juicing for Better Breathing

If you suffer from asthma, allergies, and frequent respiratory problems, you may be able to juice your way to better breathing. A large number of studies show that you can increase your breathing capacity by consuming a diet rich in vitamins A, C, and D; folic acid; zinc; omega-3 fatty acids; and other nutrients. Because these vitamins and minerals are all found in fresh fruits and vegetables, you can create homemade juices that contain concentrated "doses" of natural medicine by mixing and matching those that foster better breathing.

The Best Nutrients for Better Breathing

Although scientists aren't exactly sure why, it appears that a group of allergic problems, including asthma, eczema, and hay fever, often occur together. Fortunately, studies show that basic nutrients play a crucial role in reducing the incidence and severity of these conditions.

The Role of Vitamin D

Researchers from Costa Rica found that many people suffering from asthma and other respiratory conditions were deficient in vitamin D, a vitamin supplied by the sun. Low levels of this vitamin were associated with more frequent hospital visits, increased severity of asthma, and higher levels of the allergy marker immunoglobulin E (IgE).

The Role of Vitamins A and C

Data analyzed from studies conducted over thirty years in England show that relatively low dietary intakes of vitamins A and C are associated with statistically significant increased odds of asthma and wheezing.

The Role of Folic Acid

According to research published in the *Journal of Allergy and Clinical Immunology*, two studies of more than 8,000 people showed that those who consumed high levels of folic acid (a B vitamin) had lower levels of the IgE allergy marker, fewer reported allergies, fewer episodes of wheezing, and a reduced incidence of asthma. Those who consumed the lowest levels of folic acid had a 40 percent increase in risk of wheezing, a 30 percent higher risk of elevated IgE, and a 16 percent increase in risk of having asthma.

The Role of Synergy

Many studies have supported the importance of nutrient synergy in reducing asthma risk. For example, a trial published in the Egyptian nutrition publication *Acta Paediatrica* showed that consuming omega-3 fatty acids, vitamin C, and zinc together was associated with significant improvements in asthma symptoms, lung function, and markers of inflammation in the lungs. While each nutrient alone also yielded benefits, the effects were much greater when the nutrients were consumed together.

The Best Fruits and Vegetables for Better Breathing

You can breathe better by creating juices from a variety of fresh fruits and vegetables that contain high concentrations of these beneficial vitamins and minerals.

- **Vitamin D** is abundant in sunflower seeds, sprouts, and mushrooms.
- **Folic acid** can be found in blackberries, cruciferous veggies, spinach, and kale.
- **Vitamin A** and **carotenes** are found in romaine lettuce, carrots, parsley, kale, beet greens, spinach, and broccoli.
- **Vitamin C** is found in citrus fruits, cruciferous veggies, spinach, parsley, asparagus, and watercress.
- **Omega-3 fatty acids** are found in flaxseed and hemp.
- **Zinc** is found in cruciferous veggies, garlic, carrots, ginger root, parsley, cucumbers, and lettuce.

Addressing Allergies

Allergies, which include hay fever, eczema, and asthma, are all caused by inflammation, the body's way of responding to injury. A recent study in *Clinical & Experimental Allergy Reviews* suggests that the development of allergies over the past few decades may be because of significant changes in diet.

FACT

One in three children suffers from allergies today, and that number is expected to narrow to one in two by 2015. Genetics influence whether a person will develop allergies or asthma, but the drastically increased incidence of these conditions almost certainly has environmental factors.

The Stress Connection

Stress, worry, fatigue, and gastrointestinal upset are believed to trigger or exacerbate allergies by increasing the body's susceptibility to them. If your allergies seem to worsen when you're upset or tired, try getting more rest and eat foods that are known to help alleviate inflammation and fight free radicals, including the following fruits and vegetables:

- **Apples.** High in vitamins A, C, and B, which help cleanse the system and aid digestion.
- **Blueberries.** A good source of tannins that kill bacteria and viruses, and help with digestion. Blueberries are also potent antioxidants that are packed with vitamin C and potassium.
- **Grapes.** A good source of antioxidants, anti-viral properties that can help fight infection, and flavonoids, which help protect the heart.
- **Mangos.** High in vitamins A and C, beta-carotene, niacin, fiber, and potassium to help fight infection and toxins.
- **Oranges.** A good source of vitamin C and choline, which helps promote mental functioning.
- **Raspberries.** A good source of niacin, potassium, and vitamin C, which boost the immune system.
- **Strawberries.** High in vitamin C, antioxidants, and anti-viral properties that help ease allergies and infections.
- **Asparagus.** One of just four veggies high in vitamin E. Also a good source of vitamins C and A, potassium, niacin, iron, and antioxidants.
- **Beet tops.** High in vitamin A, antioxidants, and betaine, an enzyme that strengthens the liver and gall bladder.
- **Onions.** Loaded with antioxidants that help prevent inflammatory responses. Also a rich source of quercetin, a powerful antioxidant.
- **Bell peppers.** High in vitamins C and A and antioxidants that fight infection and inflammation.
- **Spinach.** High in vitamins E, C, and A; lutein; chlorophyll; calcium; iron; protein; and potassium.
- **Watercress.** High in antioxidants and vitamins C and A.

Managing Asthma

Asthma is a chronic condition in which the airways of the lungs become narrow as a result of hyper-reactions to substances that irritate them and cause swelling and inflammation. The resulting symptoms include short-ness of breath, gasping, wheezing, coughing, and bringing up mucus.

FACT

Research shows that the rate of asthma is increasing, especially among children. Researchers speculate that some of the reasons behind the spike in asthma among children include increased air pollution, lack of nutrients, increased stress, and the increase of new allergens, such as genetically modified organisms.

Foods that May Trigger Asthma

Studies show that food allergies can sometimes lead to asthma in a small number of people. Foods that may trigger asthma include the additives ben-zoates, sulphites, or gallates in cider, wine, and beer; foods containing yeast or mold, such as bread and blue cheeses; and foods containing food color-ings, cow's milk, wheat, eggs, fish, soy, and nuts (especially peanuts).

Foods that Help Control Asthma

One of the best-known foods for controlling the severity of an asthma attack is coffee. It contains caffeine, which dilates air passageways by thin-ning the mucus and opening them up for freer breathing. Other foods that alleviate asthma include spicy, pungent foods like chili, hot mustard, garlic, onions, and spicy herbs, such as pepper and cayenne. These hot foods work by stimulating nerves, resulting in the release of watery fluid in the mouth, throat and lungs.

Some foods can control inflammation of the airways because of their anti-inflammatory components. They include onions, fatty fish, and vitamin C-packed fruits and vegetables including citrus fruit, cruciferous veggies, spinach, parsley, asparagus, and watercress.

Foods that May Help Alleviate Asthma

Researchers have found the following nutrients may help control the severity of asthma symptoms:

- **B vitamins**, found in green leafy vegetables, tofu, tempeh, spinach, turnip greens, bell peppers, prunes, wheat bran, brewer's yeast, kale, and many other fruits and vegetables.
- **Magnesium**, which relaxes muscles, helps improve breathing, and thins out mucus; found in carrots, celery, beets, broccoli, spinach, blackberries, cauliflower, and parsley.
- **Vitamin D**, which can help relieve the severity and frequency of asthma attacks; found in sunflower seeds, sprouts, and mushrooms.

Recent studies show that low levels of vitamin D are associated with higher rates of asthma-related hospitalization, inhaled corticosteroid use, and airway hyper-reactivity in children. Low vitamin D levels were also associated with more direct markers of asthma severity.

Juicing for Respiratory Disorders

Respiratory disorders, or lung diseases, are disorders that include asthma, pneumonia, tuberculosis, lung cancer, and others. According to the Centers for Disease Control (CDC), 121,000 Americans die of lung disease every year. It is the fourth leading cause of death overall and the number one reason for death in infants. More than 35 million Americans struggle with chronic lung disease.

FACT

Studies show that broccoli and other cruciferous vegetables, such as cauliflower, kale, Brussels sprouts, and cabbage, have substances that may help protect against respiratory inflammation that causes conditions like asthma, allergic rhinitis, and chronic obstructive pulmonary disease.

Nutrients that Help Alleviate Respiratory Disorders

Studies show that in addition to quitting smoking, consuming foods high in certain key nutrients can help thin mucus and alleviate symptoms. Those nutrients include:

- **L-carnitine.** This nutrient helps improve breathing and thin out mucus. Meat, poultry, fish, and dairy products are the richest sources of L-carnitine, while fruits, vegetables, and grains contain relatively little L-carnitine.
- **Coenzyme Q10.** An antioxidant made naturally by the body that fights free radicals, this nutrient can also be found in spinach, broccoli, sweet potato, sweet pepper, garlic, peas, cauliflower and carrots. Soybean, rapeseed, sesame, cottonseed and corn oils all have high amounts of coenzyme Q10.
- **N-acetyl cysteine (taken in supplement form).** This nutrient breaks up mucus. Double-blind studies show this nutrient improves symptoms and prevents recurrences in people with chronic bronchitis, and reduces the duration of the flu and other infections.
- **Magnesium.** This mineral relaxes muscles, helps improve breathing, and thins out mucus. It is found in carrots, celery, beets, broccoli, spinach, blackberries, cauliflower, and parsley.

How to Eat to Combat Colds and the Flu

Good nutrition is essential for resisting and recovering from a cold. Drink lots of fluids to flush toxic byproducts out of the body as quickly and efficiently as possible. The best way to do this is to drink juice. Avoid tea and coffee, which have diuretic effects, as well as milk and dairy products. Studies show a compound in milk triggers the release of histamine, a chemical believed to contribute to the runny nose and nasal congestion that typifies cold and flu infections. In addition, avoid fatty, hard-to-digest foods such as cheese, red meat, and pastries, which put added strain on the digestive tract.

If you're having trouble breathing because of congestion, stay away from the hot toddy and stick to fresh fruit and vegetable juices. Alcohol not only depletes the body's reserves of fluids, but also robs it of its vitamin C sources. This puts extra strain on the liver, which has to work harder to detoxify the body.

Nutrients that Help Fight the Congestion of Colds and the Flu

Make sure you're getting adequate amounts of vitamin A, the vitamin B complex (vitamins Bl, B2, B3, B6, folic acid), and vitamin C, as well as the minerals zinc and copper, which help your body absorb iron.

Grapefruit helps fights colds because it is packed with vitamin C, which detoxes the liver and is your major defense against immunity. Oranges and other citrus fruits are too sweet to promote proper liver drainage, so stick to grapefruit juices if you have a cold, juicing one or more daily and consuming the white bitter pulp to build immunity. However, grapefruit may interact with prescription medications such as cholesterol-lowering drugs, psychiatric medications, and antihistamines, so ask your physician or pharmacist if grapefruit juice is safe to drink.

To fight colds and the flu, make sure you consume plenty of the following nutrients:

✓ **Vitamin C**. Nobel laureate Linus Pauling swore by the effects of vitamin C to help prevent the common cold, but more recent research indicates that a minimum dosage of vitamin C is most beneficial and that taking mega-doses of vitamin C is not helpful and may, in fact, cause diarrhea. To avoid diarrhea, mix some calcium ascorbate powder (sold commercially as Ester-C) into your juices. It's the form of vitamin C that's least irritating to the digestive tract and least likely to cause diarrhea.

✓ **Zinc**. Zinc contains neutrophils, compounds that help fight infections and colds, and is also necessary for the conversion of omega-3 acids into anti-inflammatory substances called prostaglandins. Recent studies show that zinc significantly reduces the time it takes to recover from a cold. Find zinc in tangerines, cruciferous veggies, parsley, ginger, carrots, grapes, spinach, and lettuce.

✓ **Vitamin A** is vital to the mucous membranes throughout the respiratory system during a cold or flu. Find it in carrot, kale, cruciferous veggies, beets, chard, watercress, spinach, and romaine lettuce.

✓ **Pantothenic acid** supports adrenal function, which is often compromised when you have a cold. It also helps to minimize nasal congestion and fatigue. Find it in cruciferous veggies.

✓ **Bioflavonoids** have anti-inflammatory properties and help ease the course of a cold. Find them in cruciferous veggies, parsley, plums, tomatoes, citrus fruit, cherries, and watercress.

✓ Herbs that help break up congestion and ease breathing include **garlic**, **ginseng**, **green tea**, and **echinacea**. To ease nasal congestion, use steam inhalation with **eucalyptus oil** added to the water.

✓ **Vitamin B** complex helps regulate energy metabolism and boosts the immune system.

✓ **Copper** helps your body absorb iron and also helps build immunity.

Eating to Combat the Flu

Oriental mushrooms such as shiitake, maitake, and reishi contain compounds that bolster your immune system. In addition, spicy foods help promote drainage and thin mucus, so fire up your veggie juice with chili, horseradish, hot pepper sauce, hot mustard, curry, and Mexican and Indian spices.

ALERT

If you have the flu, it's essential to drink lots of hot fluids. These warm your throat and reduce viral replication, and also have a mild decongestant quality that helps reduce nasal stuffiness and congestion. Hot ginger tea can help reduce inflammation and kill viruses.

Avoid sugar. Too much sugar deactivates neutrophils, a special type of white blood cell that destroys cold viruses and other foreign invaders. In one study, people who consumed 100 grams of sugar, the equivalent of two cans of soda, had 50 percent reduced neutrophil activity.

Allergy RX

» **Good for reducing allergies and respiratory disorders**

Select a cantaloupe by smelling it. If it smells great, it will taste good. Give the melon a gentle shake. If you hear sloshing, the seed cavity is separating, which is a sign of overheating or old age.

INGREDIENTS | YIELD: ¾ CUP

½ cantaloupe, rind removed
2 oranges, peeled

Juice cantaloupe and oranges. Stir.

Per Serving

CALORIES: **251**
FAT: **1.4g**
SODIUM: **57mg**
FIBER: **9.2g**
PROTEIN: **6.4g**
SUGARS: **54g**
CARBOHYDRATES: **62g**

Orange Swiss Chard

» **Good for preventing cold and flu**

Vitamin C can help to reduce cold symptoms. Oranges provide you with 20 percent or more of the recommended daily intake of vitamin C.

INGREDIENTS | YIELD: ¾ CUP

2 oranges, peeled
2 Swiss chard leaves

Juice oranges and Swiss chard. Stir.

Per Serving

CALORIES: **148**
FAT: **0.84g**
SODIUM: **203mg**
FIBER: **7.5g**
PROTEIN: **4.7g**
SUGARS: **6.6g**
CARBOHYDRATES: **9.3g**

Raspberry Lemonade

» **Good for preventing cold and flu**

High in potassium and vitamin C, this juice is a great immune enhancer. It's also a tasty way to keep your body hydrated.

INGREDIENTS | YIELD: ¾ CUP

2 pints raspberries
2 lemons, peeled

Juice raspberries and lemons. Stir.

Per Serving

CALORIES: **291**
FAT: **5.3g**
SODIUM: **7.3mg**
FIBER: **38g**
PROTEIN: **6.1g**
SUGARS: **25g**
CARBOHYDRATES: **69g**

Green Carrot

» **Good for reducing asthma**

This is a great juice to help your asthma. Substitute black pepper for the cayenne if you wish.

INGREDIENTS | YIELD: 1 CUP

2 carrots, peeled
1 cup broccoli
1 green onion
¼ teaspoon cayenne pepper

Juice carrots, broccoli, and green onion. Stir and add cayenne.

Per Serving

CALORIES: **128**
FAT: **0,32g**
SODIUM: **108mg**
FIBER: **9.2g**
PROTEIN: **5g**
SUGARS: **15g**
CARBOHYDRATES: **33g**

Vegetables on Fire

» ### Good for reducing asthma

The spiciness of this juice helps clear breathing passages. It gets its heat from the jalapeño pepper, which is dark green and will turn red when overripe.

INGREDIENTS | YIELD: 1 CUP

3 carrots
1 red or green bell pepper
1 jalapeño pepper, seeded

Juice carrots and bell pepper. Juice jalapeño. Stir.

Per Serving

CALORIES: **165**
FAT: **0.36g**
SODIUM: **119mg**
FIBER: **11g**
PROTEIN: **3.9g**
SUGARS: **20g**
CARBOHYDRATES: **47g**

Healthy Lung Tonic

» ### Good for easing respiratory disorders

A boost of magnesium from the blackberries and carrots should have you breathing easier. Vitamin A is good for the lungs and the immune system.

INGREDIENTS | YIELD: 1¼ CUPS

1 sweet potato
2 carrots, peeled
1 pint blackberries

Juice sweet potato, carrots, and blackberries. Stir.

Per Serving

CALORIES: **341**
FAT: **1g**
SODIUM: **159mg**
FIBER: **25g**
PROTEIN: **8g**
SUGARS: **32g**
CARBOHYDRATES: **79g**

Carrot Parsley

» **Good for easing breathing**

Coughing is the body's way of ridding itself of excess mucus in the lungs and bronchial tubes. Lemons and carrots help your body with this task.

INGREDIENTS | YIELD: 1 CUP

4 carrots, peeled
¼ cup parsley
¼ lemon, peeled

Juice carrots and parsley. Juice lemon. Stir.

Per Serving

CALORIES: **197**
FAT: **0.049g**
SODIUM: **164mg**
FIBER: **12g**
PROTEIN: **4.1g**
SUGARS: **26g**
CARBOHYDRATES: **53g**

Kokomo Coconut

» **Good for reducing asthma and respiratory disorders**

This tasty island-style blend has a host of health benefits to go along with its great flavor.

INGREDIENTS | YIELD: 1½ CUPS

1 papaya, seeded
½ lime, peeled
1 cup unsweetened coconut milk

Juice papaya and lime. Stir in coconut milk.

Per Serving

CALORIES: **589**
FAT: **57g**
SODIUM: **39mg**
FIBER: **7.7g**
PROTEIN: **6.5g**
SUGARS: **5g**
CARBOHYDRATES: **24g**

The Leaves Have It

» **Good for easing breathing and asthma**

Green leafy vegetables rich in vitamin B help control your asthma in this easy-to-make juice.

INGREDIENTS | YIELD: 1 CUP

1 cup spinach
1 cup broccoli
2 asparagus spears
2 Swiss chard leaves

Juice spinach, broccoli, asparagus, and Swiss chard. Stir.

Per Serving

CALORIES: **61**
FAT: **0.68g**
SODIUM: **257mg**
FIBER: **5.7g**
PROTEIN: **6g**
SUGARS: **3.4g**
CARBOHYDRATES: **12g**

Grapefruit Star

» **Good for preventing cold and flu**

Vitamin C is just the thing to get you through a bout of the common cold. Do not store grapefruit at room temperature. They are best kept in a plastic bag in the refrigerator's vegetable drawer.

INGREDIENTS | YIELD: 1 CUP

½ pink grapefruit, rind removed
½ white grapefruit, rind removed

Juice grapefruits. Stir.

Per Serving

CALORIES: **89**
FAT: **0.29g**
SODIUM: **0mg**
FIBER: **2g**
PROTEIN: **1.7g**
SUGARS: **16g**
CARBOHYDRATES: **39g**

Popeye's Secret

» ## Good for preventing cold and flu

Almost all vegetables contain at least a little vitamin C, but broccoli and kale are particularly good sources.

INGREDIENTS | YIELD: 1 CUP

2 kale leaves
1 beet top and greens
1 fist of spinach
½ cup broccoli florets

Juice ingredients in order listed. Stir.

Per Serving

CALORIES: **68**
FAT: **0.65g**
SODIUM: **101mg**
FIBER: **3.9g**
PROTEIN: **4g**
SUGARS: **7g**
CARBOHYDRATES: **16g**

Carrot Sweet Potato

» ## Good for easing breathing

This juice is high in vitamins A and C. If you cannot get a sweet potato, try substituting a regular potato. Sweet potatoes may be stored for 3 or 4 weeks if they are in a cool, dark place. Do not refrigerate them.

INGREDIENTS | YIELD: 1 CUP

1 sweet potato
2 carrots, peeled

Juice sweet potato and carrots. Stir.

Per Serving

CALORIES: **206**
FAT: **0.065g**
SODIUM: **150mg**
FIBER: **9.9g**
PROTEIN: **4g**
SUGARS: **18g**
CARBOHYDRATES: **52g**

Mango Kiwifruit

» **Good for easing asthma and respiratory disorders**

Kiwifruit has been shown to be beneficial in reducing asthma and shortness of breath. Kiwifruit contain more vitamin C than oranges, and it's also high in antioxidants.

INGREDIENTS | YIELD: 1 CUP

2 mangos, pitted
3 kiwifruit, peeled

Juice mango and kiwi. Stir well before serving.

Per Serving

CALORIES: **273**
FAT: **3.1g**
SODIUM: **11 mg**
FIBER: **11g**
PROTEIN: **4.4g**
SUGARS: **77g**
CARBOHYDRATES: **95g**

CHAPTER 13

Fighting Infections

The immune system protects the body from infection and from the formation of cancer. If you're abnormally tired or catch frequent colds or other infections, your immune system may not be working as effectively as it should. Fruits and vegetables contain many infection-fighting vitamins and antioxidants, including vitamins A, B6, C, and E, as well as the minerals zinc and selenium. If you're feeling under the weather, get a nutrition boost by combining your favorite fruits and vegetables in nutrient-rich juices.

Nutrients that Fight Germs and Infections

When it comes to fighting infection, more and more studies indicate that diets high in antioxidants reduce colds and flu infections. Antioxidants also intercept and destroy free radicals, improving immune system function and delaying aging.

A Crash Course in Free Radicals

Free radicals—which include the superoxide radical, the hydroxyl radical, and hydrogen peroxide—are highly reactive oxygen fragments created by normal chemical processes in the body's cells. Because they lack electrons, they attempt to steal them from other molecules in a process known as oxidation. While your body needs some free radicals to fight infection and contract smooth muscles, excess free radicals in the body create harmful toxins that can destroy antioxidants.

FACT

Free radicals can be produced in dangerous amounts by irritants such as cigarette smoke, pesticides, air pollution, ultraviolet light, and radiation, which are all too common in most peoples' everyday environments. Stress, anxiety, and exercising to excess can also produce large amounts of free radicals.

An antioxidant neutralizes oxidants, including free radicals. But when the antioxidant systems of the body are overwhelmed, free radicals stabilize themselves by stealing electrons from them and causing more generations of free radicals, which create further damage. As these chain reactions spread through the body, they attack many vulnerable sites and cause infection and even chronic disease.

The Role of Vitamins

Certain vitamins act as antioxidants, or circuit breakers, to the formation of free radicals. They break up the chain reaction that spawns ever-increasing numbers of free radicals, stopping the damage without generating more free radicals.

Free radicals can lower the body's resistance to infection and disease and cause myriad conditions, including birth defects, ulcers, digestive tract disorders, liver damage, arthritis, cardiovascular disease, anemia, cataracts, high cholesterol, premature aging, cancer, and diabetes.

Reducing Free Radical Damage

You can reduce damage from free radicals by eating a diet rich in antioxidants and avoiding pollution, pesticides, cigarette smoke, and other dangerous environmental factors.

ESSENTIAL

If you have a personal history or a family history of disease, are under chronic stress, smoke, or live in a polluted environment, you should make juicing a daily habit and consider taking antioxidant supplements. Even if you don't see the evidence of free radical damage yet, it's never too early to start a healthy routine.

The Most Important Antioxidants for Infections

The following vitamins help reduce the actions of free radicals and prevent the risk of infection or help heal it:

- **Vitamin A** is a fat-soluble vitamin that is extremely important in immune defense. Vitamin A has been shown to enhance white blood cell functioning, which helps the body resist and fight off infection.
- **Vitamin B6** helps the immune system function properly by aiding in the production of antibodies that help the body fight infection.
- **Vitamin C** boosts immunity by increasing the production of white blood cells to help the body fight off infection. It also increases the body's level of interferon, which prevents viruses from even entering the body.
- **Vitamin E** builds a healthy immune system by triggering the production of cells that kill germs and promote the production of B cells, which create the antibodies that destroy bacteria.

- **Beta-carotene** enhances the effectiveness of vitamin C, an important vitamin in preventing infections.
- **Selenium** is a potent antioxidant that helps kill free radicals.
- **Bioflavonoids** have been shown to reduce the inflammation that accompanies infection. They also boost the action of vitamin C.
- **Zinc** promotes anti-inflammatory actions in the body.
- **Omega-3 fatty acids** help decrease inflammation, a reaction to infection that helps rid the body of toxins.
- **Copper** reduces inflammation.

Best Fruits and Vegetables for Fighting Infections

You can find all of the vitamins and minerals that will help you fight infection in delicious fruits and vegetables that are easy to juice. Enhance their infection-fighting qualities by mixing and matching those with the most potent qualities for your needs.

Where to Find Potent Infection Fighters

Here's a rundown of the best produce sources for fighting infections and germs.

Vitamin or Mineral	Food Source
vitamin A	carrots, sweet potatoes, pumpkin, spinach, kale, red bell peppers
vitamin E	almonds, sunflower seeds, olives, blueberries, tomatoes, spinach, watercress, asparagus, carrots
vitamin C	Brussels sprouts, broccoli, cauliflower, papayas, oranges, cantaloupe, strawberries
selenium	cruciferous veggies, garlic, oranges, grapes, carrots, radishes
bioflavonoids	onions, cruciferous veggies, prunes, tomatoes, citrus fruit, cherries, parsley, melons
copper	turnips, garlic, ginger root
zinc	cruciferous veggies, parsley, garlic, carrots, grapes, spinach, tangerines, lettuce, ginger root
omega-3 fatty acids	flaxseed and hemp oils

Best Herbs for Fighting Infections

Echinacea and astragalus are the two most popular herbs used to boost immunity, but they are also supported by the most significant documentation, according to Michael T. Murray, N.D, a leading authority on natural medicine and a professor at Bastyr University in Seattle. Murray claims that both echinacea and astragalus exert broad-spectrum effects on the body's natural defense mechanisms.

Echinacea can be your best friend if you have a bad cold, flu, virus, or other infection caused by a compromised immune system. But taking it on a daily basis can cause your body to become so used to it that it's no longer as effective, so only take it when you're under the weather. Studies show echinacea may give sluggish immune systems a much-needed boost for fighting infections by stimulating the thymus gland.

Echinacea—especially echinacea angustfolia—was used by Native Americans and early healers for a wide range of conditions, including poisonous bites, syphilis, toothaches, enlarged glands, burns, fevers, and the common cold. In fact, Native Americans used it more than any other plant to treat various conditions.

In addition, Murray argues that echinacea also exerts direct antiviral activity and helps prevent the spread of bacteria by blocking a bacterial enzyme called hyaluronidase. This enzyme is secreted by bacteria in order to break through the body's first line of defense, the protective membranes such as the skin or mucous membranes.

Murray says that clinical studies have shown astragalus, another herb used for viral infections in traditional Chinese medicine, to be especially effective when used as a preventive measure against the common cold. In addition, it reduces the duration and severity of common cold symptoms, and raises white blood cell counts in people with chronic leukopenia (low white-blood cell count).

Other herbs that may help fight infection include the following:

- ✓ **Licorice root** is still one of the most used and most important herbs in Chinese medicine, and is used extensively for urinary and digestive tract problems. It has a very wide range of uses, including the treatment of tuberculosis, diabetes, and everyday coughs and sore throats.
- ✓ **Cat's claw** may promote a healthier immune system by helping white blood cells fight infection and disease. It's also an ancient remedy for digestive disorders and viruses. Studies show it helps reduce inflammation and fight damaging free radicals that can trigger cancer and heart disease.
- ✓ **Goldenseal root** was used by Native Americans to fight infections and viruses, disorders of the digestive tract, respiratory conditions, urinary tract infections, and infections of the skin and eye. The root is primarily used today to treat bacterial infections.

Juicing for Bladder Infections

Urine is sterile in the bladder, but bacteria or other organisms can infiltrate the urinary tract and result in a bladder infection, also called cystitis. Bladder infections are more common in women than men—a quarter of all women in the United States get one at some time in their lives—but men with enlarged prostates are also susceptible to bladder infections. People with indwelling catheters are also more prone to bladder infections.

And so are honeymooners! The term "honeymoon cystitis" was coined to refer to the type of cystitis that occurs after rigorous and prolonged sexual intercourse.

How UTIs Happen

Bladder infections most commonly occur when the urinary tract is attacked by the bacteria E. coli, which thrives naturally in the digestive tract. Studies show that about 85 percent of bladder infections are caused by this nasty bacteria.

If you've ever had a bladder infection, you already know the first signs: frequency and urgency! You can't get to the bathroom fast enough, and it seems you're making many repeated trips. Other symptoms include cloudy urine, pain in the lower back, and fatigue.

Unfortunately, antibiotics are not always effective in treating UTIs. To complicate matters, even if the antibiotic does work, it weakens the immune system, making it easier to get a subsequent infection. The good news is that countless studies show that cranberry juice—either enjoyed alone or mixed with other fruit juices—can prevent UTIs before they can take hold.

According to researchers at the Washington University School of Medicine in St. Louis, a urinary tract infection (UTI) starts when E. coli invade the bladder and penetrate a protective coating of the superficial cells that line the bladder. Once the E. coli is established in the bladder lining, the stage is set for infection.

Cranberry Juice to the Rescue

Cranberries have an extremely high oxygen radical absorbance capacity (ORAC). Many scientists believe foods with higher ORAC scores more effectively neutralize free radicals. Raw cranberries have an ORAC score of 9,584, which means they are extremely effective at neutralizing free radicals and even more potent than much-touted blueberries and raspberries. By comparison, vegetable juice cocktails that combine the juice of a variety of vegetables have an ORAC score of just 548.2

Cranberries' high ORAC score means they are powerful antioxidants that fight disease and aging. They slow the oxidative processes and free radical damage that contributes to age-related cellular degeneration and disease. The antioxidants in cranberries can provide protection against everything from loss of coordination to cancer.

A number of recent studies have shown that cranberries are effective in preventing urinary tract and bladder infections. A year-long Canadian study of 150 sexually active women found that cranberry juice significantly decreased UTIs and that it was also much more cost effective than taking antibiotics. Research conducted in 2009 comparing the effectiveness of cranberry extract with a low dose of an antibiotic in the prevention of recurrent UTIs in older women found that while both the antibiotic and cranberry extract successfully prevented recurring UTIs, the antibiotic had more adverse side effects.

France has permitted food, drink, and dietary supplement manufacturers a "function use claim" that highlights the health benefits of products containing cranberry to consumers. Since 2004, the country has allowed the claim that the North American cranberry can help reduce the adhesion of certain E. coli bacteria to the urinary tract walls.

Juicing for Candida Infections

Candida infections are a very common disorder that affect the gastrointestinal tract. The problem arises when there is an overgrowth of the yeast candida, which causes the condition of chronic candidiasis, or yeast syndrome. Infections can occur after taking antibiotics that destroy the friendly bacteria in the gut that keeps candida in check. Pregnancy and birth control pills also inhibit the body's ability to keep candida under control.

Candida overgrowth can occur when other organisms kill off the beneficial bacteria in your gut, allowing the candida to take over. It can also result from more indirect causes, such as a lowered immune system that gives the candida an advantage.

Other causes of candida include eating disorders; laxative abuse; fasting; starvation; and excessive consumption of artificial sweeteners, MSG, sugary foods, refined foods, canned foods, smoked foods, preserved foods, or fried foods.

Foods that Aggravate Candida Infections

Many foods can also exacerbate candida symptoms. Steer clear of anything made with yeast as well as the following foods:

- Pickled, smoked, or processed meat
- Pickled fish, such as herring
- Bread, pasta, and other gluten products
- Vinegars and salad dressings
- Mayonnaise
- Chutney
- Cream of wheat
- Cheese
- Melons and grapes
- Bruised or moldy produce
- Honey and other natural sweeteners
- Mushrooms
- Refined sugars
- Peanuts and peanut butter
- Pistachios
- Tea and coffee, except herbal tea
- Fruit juice

FACT

If you have an overgrowth problem, limit your consumption of non-sugary fruit, such as apples and grapefruit, to two pieces a day. Avoid fruit juice, which is loaded with sugar. Instead, enjoy nutrient-rich vegetable juice, which inhibits the growth of candida.

An excess of candida can result in myriad problems. The symptoms of chronic candidiasis may be vague and may seem unrelated, but if you suspect you have this condition, you may want to consult your doctor.

SYMPTOMS ASSOCIATED WITH CANDIDA INFECTIONS

- Headaches
- Bladder infections

- Mood swings
- Vaginitis
- Fungal infections (e.g. athletes foot)
- Bad breath
- Extensive food allergies
- Anal itching
- Feeling sick after eating yeasty or sugary foods
- Nasal itching or congestion
- Cravings for sugary foods
- Abdominal distension or bloating
- Gas
- Diarrhea
- Constipation
- Belching
- Indigestion
- Heartburn
- Depression
- Fatigue
- Poor memory
- Lack of sexual desire
- Skin rashes
- Cold hands and feet
- Irritability
- Dizziness
- Menstrual cramps
- Muscle aches

Veggies that Fight Candida Infections

Not only do vegetables starve the candida of its sugar and mold diet, they also absorb fungal poisons and carry them out of your body. Vegetables that may actually inhibit the growth of candida include raw garlic, onions, cabbage, broccoli, turnip, kale, cucumber, Brussels sprouts, cauliflower, peppers, celery, radish, eggplant, asparagus, spinach, zucchini, okra, tomatoes, and avocados. Enjoy them in fresh juice to help eliminate symptoms.

ALERT

If you have a candida infection, avoid starchy vegetables such as carrots, sweet potatoes, potatoes, yams, corn, squash (except zucchini), beets, peas, parsnips, and beans (except green beans). They all contain sugar and can lead to candida overgrowth.

Protein to the Rescue

As part of your plan to starve the candida yeast, eat plenty of high-protein meals like organic fresh chicken, beef, fresh fish, and eggs, which are free of sugar and mold and will fill you up while limiting the growth of candida.

If you need to lose weight, low-carb diets can also help reduce or eliminate candida by limiting the amount of sugar you consume. In addition, nuts and seeds can help starve out candida and restrict its growth. Avoid peanuts and pistachios, as they tend to have higher mold content than other nuts.

FACT

Green algae, including spirulina and chlorella, may be the most ancient organisms on earth, but they're also some of the current cures for candida. Scientists now know that green algae can restore balance to your gut and boost your immune system.

Live yogurt cultures, probiotics, are a class of supplement that helps your gut repopulate the good bacteria it relies on to keep candida under control. The live bacteria in the yogurt will crowd out the candida yeast and restore balance to your system.

Juicing for Inflammation

Inflammation is your body's response to infection, toxins, and injury. By soaking up dead cells and tissues, your body helps prevent foreign organisms from entering. Inflammatory responses range from redness and swelling to pain and heat. Everything from minor injuries and infections to more serious conditions such as fibromyalgia, rheumatoid arthritis, and colitis can result in inflammation.

If you suffer from inflammation, be aware that some prescription or over-the-counter anti-inflammatory drugs have adverse side effects, including liver damage, kidney damage and even heart damage. You may want to try increasing your intake of fruits and vegetables that naturally reduce inflammation.

ALERT

Research published in the *American Journal of Clinical Nutrition* shows that drinking one glass of freshly squeezed orange juice a day may cut the risk of developing inflammatory forms of arthritis because some dietary carotenoids, including beta-cryptoxanthin and zeaxanthin, lower the risk of developing arthritis.

Beta-cryptoxanthin is classified as a pro-vitamin A carotenoid. The body can convert it to an active form of vitamin A. Vitamin A is recognized as being important for skin and bone health as well as immune function. Foods highest in beta-cryptoxanthin include peppers, pumpkins, and winter squash, as well as persimmons, tangerines, and papayas. Zeaxanthin, another carotenoid with antioxidant power, is found in green leafy vegetables and yellow and orange fruits and vegetables.

Fruits and Vegetables that Reduce Inflammation

Fill your juicer with the following produce for a delicious drink that also helps reduce inflammation and swelling:

- **Celery:** Celery is loaded with vitamin C, which promotes a healthy immune system.
- **Eggplant and purple cabbage:** The purple colors of these veggies come courtesy of flavonoids—substances that help decrease swelling and inflammation.
- **Lettuce, spinach, and turnip greens:** Studies show the omega-3 fatty acids in leafy greens can calm the most severe menstrual cramps

quickly and naturally by countering the inflammation that causes pain.

- **Oranges, grapefruit, and lemons:** These citrus fruits contain bioflavonoids, which assist in joint collagen.

Juicing for Parasitic Infections

If you've ever had traveler's diarrhea, you already have an intimate knowledge of parasitic infections. Most common in developing countries and rare in developed ones, parasites can infiltrate your body through your mouth or skin, causing myriad symptoms, including diarrhea, constipation, flatulence, fever, skin rashes, anemia, and weight loss. Because parasites can't produce their own food, they use you as a host, and can thrive inside your body for years on end without causing any symptoms. Studies show most Americans are unknowingly hosting at least one parasite in their body because symptoms are often vague or nonexistent.

Parasites cause deficits of vitamins A, B6, B12; iron; calcium; and magnesium. They can diminish immunity, leaving you susceptible to serious diseases. Predisposing factors include malnutrition, a compromised immune system, chemical or metal poisoning, chronic fatigue, and pre-existing viral, fungal, or bacterial infections, especially candida and AIDS.

According to Cherie Calbom, M.S., author of *The Juice Lady's Guide to Juicing for Health* and herself a victim of intestinal parasites, the best natural remedy is a diet rich in vegetable and fruit juices, healthy oils, and no sugars from sucrose. Because parasites feed on sugar, you should also avoid full-strength fruit juices and dried fruit, and eat fresh fruit sparingly. Produce that helps fight parasites include pumpkin, garlic, onions, cabbage, almonds, kelp, and radishes.

For additional protection, Calbom recommends juicing lots of produce high in vitamin A and carotenes, which help increase your body's natural resistance to parasitic larvae. They include carrots, kale, parsley, spinach, chard, beet greens, watercress, broccoli, and romaine lettuce. Herbs that may help parasites include barberry, goldenseal, Oregon grapes, black walnut, citrus seed extract, and pinkroot.

Cabbage Juice

» ## Good for treating parasitic infections and candida

Mixing apples and carrots with cabbage sweetens this juice. Cabbage is high in vitamins C and K, fiber, and detoxifying sulfur compounds.

INGREDIENTS | YIELD: 1¼ CUPS

1 cup chopped cabbage
2 carrots, peeled
2 apples, cored

Juice cabbage, carrots and apples. Stir.

Per Serving

CALORIES: **180**
FAT: **0.38g**
SODIUM: **95mg**
FIBER: **11g**
PROTEIN: **3.3g**
SUGARS: **33g**
CARBOHYDRATES: **54g**

The Canker Sore Connection

Studies show people with celiac disease (an inability to digest gluten) and frequent yeast infections are more prone to canker sores than others. If you suspect you suffer from either condition, see your physician. A positive diagnosis may lead you to change your diet, which will make you feel like an entirely new person.

Cranberry Apple

» ## Good for treating bladder infections

Cranberries are very high in vitamin C. They're only in season for a few months, but fresh berries purchased in November and December can be frozen and used throughout the year.

INGREDIENTS | YIELD: 1 CUP

1¼ cups cranberries
2 red apples, cored

Juice cranberries and apples. Stir.

Per Serving

CALORIES: **76**
FAT: **0.31g**
SODIUM: **1.7mg**
FIBER: **3.6g**
PROTEIN: **0.093g**
SUGARS: **18g**
CARBOHYDRATES: **27g**

Butternut Delight

» ## Good for reducing inflammation

Butternut is a winter squash. It has hard, thick skin and sweet orange flesh. You can substitute acorn squash for butternut squash if you prefer.

INGREDIENTS | YIELD: 1 CUP

2 gala apples, cored
½ butternut squash, peeled and cut into pieces
1 teaspoon pumpkin pie spice

Juice apples and squash. Stir in pumpkin pie spice.

Per Serving

CALORIES: **159**
FAT: **0.42g**
SODIUM: **12 mg**
FIBER: **6.9g**
PROTEIN: **2.8g**
SUGARS: **23g**
CARBOHYDRATES: **57g**

Immune Booster

» ## Good for reducing inflammation and fighting infections

Turnip is a root vegetable whose flavor varies from sweet to woody. It will keep for a long time in the refrigerator. It is a good source of vitamin C.

INGREDIENTS | YIELD: 1¼ CUPS

1 apple, cored
1 turnip
2 carrots, peeled
½ cup watercress

Juice apple, carrots, turnip and watercress. Stir.

Per Serving

CALORIES: **177**
FAT: **0.34g**
SODIUM: **200mg**
FIBER: **11g**
PROTEIN: **3.8g**
SUGARS: **28g**
CARBOHYDRATES: **50g**

Sinus Cleanser

» **Good for reducing inflammation and fighting infection**

The spiciness of the radish should help clear your sinus passages. Radishes are roots in the mustard family that are available year round. Their flavor is somewhat mild but has a peppery finish.

INGREDIENTS | YIELD: ¾ CUP

2 tomatoes
4 radishes

Juice tomatoes and radishes. Stir.

Per Serving

CALORIES: **50**
FAT: **0.31g**
SODIUM: **41mg**
FIBER: **3g**
PROTEIN: **2.7g**
SUGARS: **1g**
CARBOHYDRATES: **9g**

Cranberry Orange

» **Good for treating bladder infections**

Fresh cranberries and oranges are very high in vitamin C. Cranberries have compounds called proanthocyanidins that keep harmful bacteria from sticking to the bladder.

INGREDIENTS | YIELD: ½ CUP

2 cups cranberries
1 orange, peeled

Juice cranberries and orange.

Per Serving

CALORIES: **152**
FAT: **0.56g**
SODIUM: **3.8mg**
FIBER: **12g**
PROTEIN: **2.1g**
SUGARS: **22g**
CARBOHYDRATES: **44g**

Strawberry Papaya

» Good for fighting infections

Papayas and berries are both known to help fight infections. They are high in vitamin C, and the banana provides vitamin B6 for immune system support.

INGREDIENTS | YIELD: ½ CUP

1 cup strawberries, hulls intact
1 papaya, seeded and peeled
1 banana, peeled

Juice berries and papaya separately. Blend juices. Add banana and blend until smooth.

Per Serving

CALORIES: **152**
FAT: **0.87g**
SODIUM: **4.5mg**
FIBER: **7g**
PROTEIN: **3.1g**
SUGARS: **24g**
CARBOHYDRATES: **42g**

Save Your Peels

Papaya peels can be added to meat marinades to help tenderize the meat. They will not impart a flavor to the meat, but they will make it more tender. Papaya juice is used to take the sting out of a jellyfish bite.

White Grape and Lime

» Good for fighting infections

Look for fresh green grapes that have a pale color for this cool summer drink.

INGREDIENTS | YIELD: 1 CUP

1½ cups green seedless grapes
2 limes, peeled

Juice grapes and limes.

Per Serving

CALORIES: **70**
FAT: **0.45g**
SODIUM: **3.6mg**
FIBER: **4.5g**
PROTEIN: **1.8g**
SUGARS: **25g**
CARBOHYDRATES: **38g**

Mexican Blend

» **Good for preventing infections**

This juice is full of vitamin C, thiamine, and riboflavin. Garlic and green onions are rich sources of allium compounds, which can help lower blood pressure and bad cholesterol levels.

INGREDIENTS | YIELD: 1¼ CUPS

1 cucumber
½ lime, peeled
1 clove garlic
1 green onion
½ jalapeño pepper, seeded (optional)
1 avocado, pitted and peeled

Juice lime, garlic, green onion, cucumber, and jalapeño pepper. Add avocado and blend. Stir.

Per Serving

CALORIES: **293**
FAT: **22g**
SODIUM: **17mg**
FIBER: **13g**
PROTEIN: **5.2g**
SUGARS: **8.3g**
CARBOHYDRATES: **32g**

CHAPTER 14

Helping Your Digestive Disorders

Your digestive tract is a twenty-five- to thirty-five-foot-long engineering marvel. It takes food, chops it up, breaks it down, separates the good from the bad and extracts nutrients so they can be delivered to the body. But if just one component of your digestive system malfunctions, it can lead to problems. Fortunately, the fiber in homemade juice adds bulk to stool and sweeps away harmful toxins. The water helps lubricate the digestive tract, while the many healthful nutrients in juice promote digestive health.

Best Nutrients for Your Tummy

Your stomach works something like a washing machine, churning the digesting food into a mush known as chyme. In the stomach, food is further digested by hydrochloric acid and enzymes. The stomach is coated with a thick layer of mucus, which prevents hydrochloric acid from burning a hole through the stomach lining.

Best Nutrients for Tummy Health

To aid digestion, begin by making changes in your diet. Enzymes are a helpful way to start. You can find formula enzymes at the health food store and in fresh juices, including papaya, pineapple, pear, apple, carrot, kale, mustard greens, and dandelion greens, all of which help promote the healthy flow of your digestive juices.

ALERT

Generally, five portions of fruit and vegetables is the official advice when it comes to consuming an adequate amount of produce. Go for a rainbow mix of different colors and types of fruit and vegetables in your homemade juice, and you'll have no trouble meeting your daily quota.

These natural nutrients also cleanse the intestine:

✓ **Aloe vera.** You can find aloe vera drops in the health food store. Diluting four ounces of aloe vera drops in juices daily can help eliminate bleeding ulcers and promote healing.

✓ **Beta-carotene.** It's found in many fruits and vegetables, including watercress, cruciferous veggies, beet greens, carrots, romaine lettuce, and spinach.

✓ **Acidophilus.** This is a general name for a group of probiotics that promote digestion. You can find them in capsule form at your local health food store.

✓ **Rosehips.** These are found in rosehip tea and in your health food store or natural supermarket.

In addition, the fiber in produce aids digestion by adding bulk to foods that keep them moving in the intestine, preventing toxic build up, which can lead to digestive problems.

Finally, water is one of the most helpful aids to digestion. Drinking eight to ten glasses of water each day keeps the body hydrated and aids digestion in the intestinal tract. Aerobic exercise and stretching each day also contribute to healthier digestion. They keep your muscles and organs in good shape and keep things moving.

Benefits of Food Combining

Some nutrition experts believe that following the principles of food combining can also help prevent digestive disorders. According to Paul Pitchford, author of *Healing with Whole Foods*, if you consume only certain foods at the same time, you avoid putting excess stress on the digestive system. The reason is that different foods require different enzymes to be broken down. Although food combining is not recommended by most mainstream nutritionists or the American Dietetic Society, you may find some of their principles helpful.

- Green and non-starchy vegetables can be combined with protein or starch or fat. This includes leafy greens, cauliflower, broccoli, sprouts, celery, cucumber, onion, garlic, green beans, peas, seaweed, and fresh corn.
- Protein can be combined with green and non-starchy vegetables only. This includes beans, legumes, tofu, tempeh, nuts, seeds, cheese, yogurt, eggs, fish, meat, and fowl.
- Starches can be combined with green and non-starchy vegetables and fats and oils. This includes grains, bread, pasta, potato, sweet potato, beet, parsnip, carrot, and squash.
- Fats and oils can be combined with green and non-starchy vegetables, starches, and acid fruits. This includes avocado, olives, butter, cream and oils.
- In most cases, fruit should be consumed on its own. It digests very quickly. Melons, especially, should be consumed alone.
- Sweet fruit can be combined with sub-acid fruit, including fig, banana, dates, and dried fruit.

- Acid fruits can be combined with fats and oils and sub-acid fruits, which include lemon, lime, grapefruit, orange, tomato, strawberry, pineapple, and kiwi.
- Sub-acid fruits can be combined with acid fruit or sweet fruit, including apple, berries, pear, apricot, peach, grapes, plum, cherry, mango, and papaya.

Why Juicing Helps Healthy Digestion

Research shows that diets high in fiber and complex carbohydrates, which are found in abundance in fruits and vegetable juices, and low in refined foods have been shown to reduce many digestive disorders, including indigestion, ulcers, low stomach acid, constipation, diarrhea, motion sickness, colitis, diverticulitis, and diverticulosis.

ALERT

According to the American College of Gastroenterology, consuming a diet high in dietary fiber can help improve a number of digestive disorders, including chronic constipation, hemorrhoids, diverticular disease, elevated cholesterol, irritable bowel syndrome, and colorectal cancer.

Tips for Increasing Your Fiber

The American College of Gastroenterology recommends consuming at least 20 to 25 grams of fiber daily, which is much higher than the 10 to 15 grams most Americans consume. An easy way to increase your fiber intake is to consume a lot of high-fiber fruits and vegetables in juices.

Those highest in fiber include:

✓ Apples, pears (with skin)
✓ Berries (blackberries, blueberries, raspberries)
✓ Dates
✓ Figs
✓ Prunes
✓ Beans

✓ Broccoli
✓ Chickpeas
✓ Lentils
✓ Parsnips
✓ Peas
✓ Pumpkin
✓ Rutabaga
✓ Winter squash

Other foods that will add a boost of fiber to your homemade juice include wheat bran, psyllium, sunflower seeds, hemp, oat bran, coconut, almonds, Brazil nuts, peanuts, pecans, walnuts, brown rice, and pumpkin and sunflower seeds.

ALERT

Don't shock your system by suddenly doubling or tripling your intake of fiber overnight, warns the American College of Gastroenterology. The result could be constipation and cramps. Instead, increase the fiber levels in your diet gradually over the course of a week or so. Increase the amount of liquids you drink and add both soluble and insoluble fiber.

Alleviating Ulcers

Ulcers occur when gastric juice burns a hole in the lining of your stomach. For years, it was believed that ulcers were caused by high stomach acidity and stress. Today, scientists know that most ulcers are caused by the bacteria helicobacter pylori.

Bleeding ulcers occur when ulcers bleed into the gastrointestinal tract. You may vomit bright red blood, brownish blood dotted with partially digested blood, or pass black or bloody stools.

If you have a very serious ulcer, it can cause a narrowing of the outlet between the stomach and small intestine and cause repeated vomiting, bloating, dehydration, weight loss, and feeling unusually full after eating. If an ulcer breaks through the wall of the duodenum, it can cause severe pain.

FACT

Peptic ulcers are often called "stress ulcers" because they tend to occur when you're undergoing severe emotional stress or severe illness. Scientists believe "irritating" agents such as alcohol, cigarettes, and spicy foods can exacerbate ulcers and prevent them from healing, or even contribute to the formation of one.

The good news is that almost all ulcers can be treated successfully, usually without surgery. Many ulcers can also be prevented. Ulcer treatments include antibiotics, agents that neutralize gastric acid or reduce its secretion, natural cures, and drugs that strengthen the resistance of the stomach and duodenum.

ESSENTIAL

Hypochlorhydria, or low stomach acid, is believed to affect more than half of those over age sixty. Low levels of stomach acid can reduce absorption of nutrients, leading to an overgrowth of bacteria and a greater likelihood of food poisoning. To heal hypochlorhydria, eat produce high in digestive enzymes. Chew food thoroughly, eat frequent and small meals, and avoid drinking liquids with meals.

Dealing with Heartburn

Heartburn is a very common problem caused by regurgitation or reflux of gastric acid into the esophagus, which connects the mouth and the stomach. Heartburn can often be eliminated by stopping smoking and by avoiding fatty foods, caffeine, chocolate, peppermint, overeating, bedtime snacks, and clothing that constricts the abdomen.

Certain medications and heavy lifting and straining may also cause heartburn. Also, because heartburn is a symptom of heart disease, see your physician to rule out underlying medical conditions if you suffer from chronic heartburn.

Best Fruits and Veggies for Heartburn and Indigestion

If you suffer from chronic indigestion, try increasing your intake of vitamin A and carotene, which have anti-inflammatory qualities. Good sources include mangos, cantaloupe, apricots, carrots, spinach, chard, beet greens, watercress, cruciferous veggies, and romaine lettuce.

FACT

To ease heartburn, stick to alkaline foods that don't increase stomach acid, including most vegetables, most fruits (with the exception of strawberries and cranberries), olive oil, and sea vegetables. And drink lots of veggie juice. Studies show vegetable juice is a very effective way to reduce indigestion and heartburn.

In addition, bananas may help protect the stomach from acids while cabbage juice helps heal ulcers and eliminate digestive problems. Papaya and pineapple juice both contain bromelains, which are enzymes that digest proteins and help eliminate heartburn. Ginger helps relieve gas, parsley juice is high in beta-carotene, and lemon juice helps stimulate gastric secretions, according to Cherie Calbom, M.S., author of *The Juice Lady's Guide to Juicing for Health*. Bitter herbs like dandelion, gentian, and goldenseal have a bitter taste that stimulates the nervous system and releases the digestive hormone gastrin. Chamomile tea and the spice anise also promote digestion by relaxing the bowels, she says.

Easing Constipation

Dealing with constipation is no fun. If you've gone for a few days without a bowel movement, you're likely to feel lethargic and irritable, not to mention uncomfortable. Fortunately, consuming at least five servings of fruits and vegetables in your diet every day can help prevent constipation by providing lots of fiber, which binds to water and makes the stool softer and bulkier.

Best Produce for Constipation

Many fruits and vegetables help lubricate your intestines, which in turn makes it easier for waste to be eliminated. Helpful foods include alfalfa sprouts, almonds, apples, apricots, bananas, beets, carrots, cauliflower, honey, okra, peach, pear, pine nuts, prunes, seaweed, spinach, sesame seed oil, walnuts, asparagus, bran from oats, rice, and wheat, cabbage, coconut, figs, papaya, peas, and sweet potatoes.

ESSENTIAL

Yogurt is one of the best foods for relieving constipation. Its active cultures help repopulate your digestive system with organisms that aid in breaking down food, and the acidophilus in yogurt encourages healthy bacterial growth and helps diminish the production of bile acid. The more acidophilus you have in your colon, the less likely you'll have colon diseases in general, so include yogurt in your juices wherever possible.

Calcium for Reducing Colon Cancer Risk

Yogurt is also rich in calcium, which is good for your colon. Unlike other dairy products, yogurt does not have a binding effect, and adding calcium to your diet can help reduce the risk of colon cancer by preventing the growth of excess cells in your colon lining.

Research shows that consuming 1,200 milligrams of calcium per day can reduce your chances of developing colon cancer by 75 percent, so try adding yogurt to your favorite juice for a calcium punch that adds flavor and thickness. Having a healthy colon will also help prevent diarrhea and constipation.

Benefits of Purified Water

Purified water can help relieve constipation, so try using it in your homemade juice to help prevent fiber from hardening and causing blockage in your intestines. Drinking enough water to prevent dehydration will ensure an adequate amount remains in your intestines at all times, so aim for eight

eight-ounce glasses (roughly sixty-four ounces) of water every day, including the water you consume in juices and herbal teas.

Dealing with Diarrhea

Many things can cause diarrhea, including diet, medications, and medical conditions such as irritable bowel syndrome and colitis. It is important to watch what you eat if you have diarrhea, since chronic diarrhea can cause serious dehydration. If you have diarrhea, drink at least eight to ten glasses of fluid every day. This will replace lost fluids. Water, juice (except prune juice), broth, ginger ale, sports drinks, Jell-O, and weak tea are all good sources of fluid.

If your diarrhea lasts more than two days, contact a physician. Although everyone responds differently to treatments for diarrhea, it may help to limit foods that contain caffeine such as coffee, strong tea, and cola beverages; avoid milk and milk products such as cheese, pudding, and ice cream, which can make diarrhea worse; reduce your intake of high-fat foods such as fried foods, fatty meats, high fat desserts, excess butter, margarine, higher fat milk products, and greasy snack foods; and curtail the amount of fiber you consume from fruits, vegetables, whole grain breads and cereals, nuts, and seeds.

ESSENTIAL

If eating too much produce has given you diarrhea, try removing the skins, seeds, and membranes from fruits and vegetables to make them easier to digest. You may also want to limit your intake of dried fruits, berries, rhubarb, legumes, lentils, kidney beans, lima beans, peas, corn, broccoli, spinach, and nuts, which exacerbate diarrhea in some people.

If you have gas or cramping, consider reducing your intake of the vegetables that increase the production of gas, including dried peas and beans, broccoli, cabbage, cauliflower, onions, and Brussels sprouts, as well as carbonated beverages, beer, and chewing gum.

Managing Motion Sickness

Nothing ruins a day on the water faster than motion sickness, that feeling of uneasiness, nausea, cold sweats, dizziness, and/or vomiting that can be brought on by the motion of cars, trains, planes, boats, or any other form of transportation—including elevators and bungee jumping!

Research conducted on a cruise ship involving nearly 1,500 people found that ginger was as effective at combating motion sickness as prescription medications. Another study conducted by NASA showed that ginger was as effective as a placebo at reducing simulated motion sickness. New studies show that it also relieves nausea and stomach discomfort caused by pregnancy.

Because of its blood-thinning properties, ginger should not be used two weeks before or after surgery. Also, if you are taking blood-thinning medication such as warfarin (Coumadin), you should not take ginger because it interferes with blood clotting and prolongs bleeding time.

Juicing for Motion Sickness

Use the following tips for easing queasiness, nausea, and vomiting:

- ✓ Make fresh fruit or vegetable juices with ginger.
- ✓ Avoid spicy foods, spices, and alcohol, which may further upset your stomach.
- ✓ Mint can help ease motion sickness, so trying incorporating fresh peppermint or spearmint into your homemade juices.
- ✓ Consume less acidic fruits (apples, bananas, pears, grapes, melons, etc.) instead of acidic ones like oranges and grapefruit. Milk, water, apple juice, cranberry juice and other low acid beverages are also easier on your stomach.
- ✓ Avoid caffeine, including soft drinks, which are diuretics and accelerate dehydration. The gas in carbonated beverages can also cause indigestion.
- ✓ Drink plenty of water. Partial dehydration lowers your body's resistance to motion sickness.

In addition, avoid greasy or acidic foods and caffeine for several hours before motion. Heavy, greasy foods like waffles or pancakes with syrup combined with acidic juices like orange juice can wreak havoc on your system and end up going overboard as lunch for the fish.

Calming Colitis

Colitis is a condition in which the lower bowels or colon are inflamed. Although there are many different types of colitis, ulcerative colitis is by far the most serious. In this condition, the large intestine becomes inflamed and ulcers form in the intestine's mucous membranes. Symptoms include persistent cramping, diarrhea that contains both blood and mucus, hard stools alternating with diarrhea, prolonged and persistent constipation, fever, and physical fatigue.

ALERT

Colitis can lead to nutritional deficiencies because an inflamed colon is unable to absorb water and nutrients effectively. Nausea, poor appetite, and anemia caused by internal bleeding can also aggravate nutritional deficiencies. The emotional stress that often accompanies the disorder can drain the body of nutrients.

Researchers believe colitis is an autoimmune disease that is partially triggered by a poor diet low in fiber and high in sugar and processed foods. Allergic reactions may also cause some types of ulcerative colitis. Some with the disease are sensitive to salicylate, the active ingredient in aspirin and cow's milk, and products containing gluten and/or yeast.

Incorporate the following ingredients into your juices to help alleviate colitis.

- **Essential fatty acids** help ease inflammation. You can find them in flaxseed and hemp oil.
- **Vitamin E** helps minimize the chances of internal scarring. Find it in watercress, spinach, asparagus, tomatoes, and carrots.

- **B vitamin deficiencies** almost always exist in colitis patients, so make sure to boost your intake with turnip greens, bell peppers, prunes, wheat bran, peanuts, brewer's yeast, citrus fruits, tomatoes, melons, strawberries, and cruciferous veggies.
- **Magnesium** helps prevent muscle spasms and weakness. Find it in carrots, beets with greens, lemons, celery, and broccoli.
- **Bromelain**, a digestive enzyme found in pineapple, can help restore normal digestion.
- **Papain**, a digestive enzyme found in papaya, can help ease colitis.
- **Aloe vera** can promote healthy functioning of the colon. Add 1 tablespoon to your favorite juice daily.
- **Stinging nettle** will reduce inflammation in a couple of weeks. Add 2 tablespoons of stinging nettle in juice or water 5 minutes before mealtime.
- **Silica** will strengthen connective tissue in the intestines and reduce inflammation. Open the contents of 2–4 capsules of spring horsetail into your favorite juices.
- **Hops**, used to flavor beer, can also sooth and calm the nerves in your intestines and help promote sleep. Soak 2–3 tablespoons of whole hops in 1 cup of cold water or juice and sip throughout the day.

Diverticulosis and Diverticulitis

Diverticulosis is a condition that causes small sacs or pouch-like protrusions to form in the colon. Common after age sixty, it has many complications, including bright red rectal bleeding with clots, constipation, and hard, dry stools.

Diverticulitis is a more serious complication in which pouches become inflamed or infected. Symptoms of diverticulitis include pain in the left lower abdomen, fever, and a sudden change in bowel habits. If you have any of these symptoms, see your physician immediately.

Treatment of diverticulitis typically includes antibiotics, a special diet, and surgery. This chronic condition impairs absorption of nutrients by the intestine, causing malnutrition. For this reason, it's important to consume plenty of nutrients.

Diverticulosis and diverticulitis can be prevented and managed by increasing your consumption of dietary fiber in fresh juices made with vegetables, fruits, and sprouts, as well as psyllium, oat brain, and acidophilus. Avoid stimulant laxatives and irritating foods, including dairy products, spicy foods, sugar, processed foods, red meat, and fried foods. In particular, stay away from nuts and seeds, which can become trapped in the natural folds of the colon and cause inflammation.

ALERT

Fruits and vegetables rich in beta-carotene, including watercress, spinach, mangos, cantaloupe, apricots, and beet greens, can help heal the mucous membranes lining the intestines. Parsley juice, which is loaded with beta-carotene, is particularly healing.

A lack of vitamin K, found in asparagus, green beans, cruciferous veggies, and spinach, may increase the incidence of intestinal disorders. Pear and apple juice, which are both high in soluble fibers called pectins, also help improve elimination.

Pineapple Greets Papaya

>> **Good for digestion**

Papaya juice can be found at many health food stores, but you can prepare your own very easily with your juicer. Papaya is a good source of vitamins A and C.

INGREDIENTS | **YIELD:1½ CUPS**

1 cup pineapple
½ orange
1 papaya, seeded

Juice pineapple, orange, and papaya. Stir well.

Per Serving

CALORIES: **134**
FAT: **0.42g**
SODIUM: **3.7mg**
FIBER: **5g**
PROTEIN: **2.2g**
SUGARS: **25g**
CARBOHYDRATES: **35g**

Pomegranate Delight

>> **Good for digestion**

Pomegranates have many health benefits. They contain ellagic acid, vitamin C, and potassium.

INGREDIENTS | **YIELD: 1 CUP**

2 pomegranates, seeded
2 red apples, cored

Cut pomegranate into quarters. Juice pomegranate, then apples. Stir.

Per Serving

CALORIES: **275**
FAT: **1.2g**
SODIUM: **10g**
FIBER: **4.3g**
PROTEIN: **2.9g**
SUGARS: **68g**
CARBOHYDRATES: **77g**

Pomegranate Seeds

Pomegranates seeds are great in a salad, but they can impart a bitter taste to the juice. Be sure to remove them before juicing the pomegranate. To remove the seeds, cut the pomegranate in half and soak it in ice water for 10 minutes. The seeds, encased in the pulp, will release in the water.

Citus Cucumber

>> **Good for digestion**

This juice provides a natural diuretic; cucumber is helpful in increasing urination and flushing toxins from the body. Cucumbers are 90 percent water. Their high water content keeps the inside of the cucumber much cooler than the surrounding atmosphere and makes them a good diuretic.

INGREDIENTS | YIELD: 1½ CUPS

1 pink grapefruit, peeled
1 orange, peeled
¼" slice ginger
1 cucumber, peeled

Juice grapefruit, orange, ginger, and cucumber. Stir.

Per Serving

CALORIES: **202**
FAT: **0.73g**
SODIUM: **5.1mg**
FIBER: **7.6g**
PROTEIN: **4.7g**
SUGARS: **56g**
CARBOHYDRATES: **42g**

Italian Carrot

>> **Good for reducing diverticulosis**

Parsley juice is rich in beta-carotene and vitamins A and C. Carrots promote healing of the intestine membranes.

INGREDIENTS | YIELD: 1 CUP

4 carrots, peeled
1 celery stalk
¼ cup Italian parsley

Juice carrots, celery, and parsley. Stir.

Per Serving

CALORIES: **200**
FAT: **0.11g**
SODIUM: **204mg**
FIBER: **13g**
PROTEIN: **4.5g**
SUGARS: **27g**
CARBOHYDRATES: **53g**

Ginger Carrot Apple Ale

» Good for reducing motion sickness

Ginger contains compounds called ginerols, which act like anti-nausea medications and help block serotonin receptors in the stomach.

INGREDIENTS | YIELD: ½ CUP

2 apples, cored
1 carrot, peeled
¼" slice ginger

Juice apples, carrots, and ginger. Stir.

Per Serving

CALORIES: **119**
FAT: **0.36g**
SODIUM: **41mg**
FIBER: **5.7g**
PROTEIN: **1.2g**
SUGARS: **23g**
CARBOHYDRATES: **37g**

Rise and Shine

» Good for reducing heartburn and indigestion

This tropical combination is a great way to start your day off right. Mangos are rich in vitamins A, C, and D, making them a very healthy choice.

INGREDIENTS | YIELD: 1½ CUPS

1 cup pineapple
1 peach, pitted
1 mango, pitted
1 banana

Juice pineapple, peach, and mango. Add banana to juice and blend well to mix.

Per Serving

CALORIES: **346**
FAT: **1.3g**
SODIUM: **6.6mg**
FIBER: **12g**
PROTEIN: **5.3g**
SUGARS: **49g**
CARBOHYDRATES: **66g**

Apricot Apple

» **Good for reducing constipation**

Apples provide an excellent source of both soluble and insoluble fiber, so they're great for helping you resolve constipation issues. After juicing fruits you may blend them with 1 cup plain yogurt. Yogurt is very good for the stomach because it contains "good bacteria" that aids digestion.

INGREDIENTS | YIELD: 1 CUP

4 apricots, pitted
2 gala apples, peeled

Juice apricots and apples. Stir.

Per Serving

CALORIES: **107**
FAT: **0.56g**
SODIUM: **1.1mg**
FIBER: **3.4g**
PROTEIN: **1.6g**
SUGARS: **21g**
CARBOHYDRATES: **27g**

Pear Apple

» **Good for reducing constipation**

The pectin in pears is a diuretic and pears have a mild laxative effect. Drinking pear juice regularly helps regulate bowel movements. The Bartlett is known for being one of the most juicy pears, which is why it was selected for this recipe.

INGREDIENTS | YIELD: ¾ CUP

2 Bartlett pears
2 red delicious apples
¼ lemon, peeled

Juice pears, apples, and lemon. Stir.

Per Serving

CALORIES: **172**
FAT: **0.87g**
SODIUM: **1.5mg**
FIBER: **13g**
PROTEIN: **2.6g**
SUGARS: **35g**
CARBOHYDRATES: **51g**

Apple Cucumber with a Twist

» **Good for colon health**

Apple skins have pectin, which helps remove harmful substances from the colon. Cucumbers contain an enzyme called erepsin that is useful in digesting protein.

INGREDIENTS | YIELD: 1 CUP

2 Granny Smith apples, cored
2 carrots, peeled
1 cucumber, peeled
1 lemon, peeled
1 celery stalk

Juice apples, carrots, cucumber, lemon and celery. Stir.

Per Serving

CALORIES: **263**
FAT: **1.6g**
SODIUM: **226mg**
FIBER: **17g**
PROTEIN: **6.7g**
SUGARS:**39g**
CARBOHYDRATES:**68g**

Pear of Pineapple

» **Good for colon health**

Pears are a great source of fiber and pectin, both of which are highly beneficial to the colon. Pineapple has long been known for its ability to help with digestion.

INGREDIENTS | YIELD: 2 CUPS

½ pineapple, skin and core removed
2 Bartlett pears, cored
1 lemon, peeled

Juice pineapple, pear, and lemon. Stir.

Per Serving

CALORIES: **372**
FAT: **0.94g**
SODIUM: **7.7mg**
FIBER: **18g**
PROTEIN: **2g**
SUGARS:**65g**
CARBOHYDRATES:**98g**

CHAPTER 15

Cancer Prevention and Treatment

Countless scientific studies show that consuming a diet high in fruits and vegetables can help reduce the risk of cancer of the stomach, esophagus, lung, oral cavity, pharynx, endometrium, pancreas, and colon. The types of vegetables or fruit that most often appear to be protective against cancer are carrots, green vegetables, cruciferous vegetables, and tomatoes, which make delicious juices. Substances present in vegetables and fruit that also help protect against cancer include isoflavones, vitamin C, lutein, folic acid, beta-carotene, lycopene, selenium, vitamin E, flavonoids, and dietary fiber.

The Power Foods for Fighting Cancer

A variety of foods are especially effective in helping to combat cancer, according to the National Institute for Cancer Research. The Nurses Study, conducted by Harvard University, showed that you can help reduce your risk of cancer by juicing with organic produce as opposed to commercially grown produce, which contains additives and pesticides that are suspected carcinogens.

ALERT

To prevent ingesting contaminants, especially if you're using nonorganic produce, be sure to wash and peel all produce. Use a vegetable brush to scrub off pesticide residue, which may not rinse off. Pay attention to where your produce was grown; some of it may have been shipped in from countries that have less stringent pesticide regulations than the United States.

Most Potent Nutrients that Fight Cancer

According to the National Cancer Institute (NCI), the following nutrients are most effective in fighting cancer:

- ✓ **Vitamin A**, found in carrots, kale, romaine lettuce, broccoli, beet greens, spinach, watercress, and chard.
- ✓ **Beta-carotene**, found in orange, yellow, and dark green leafy vegetables, including carrots, cantaloupe, apricots, spinach, squash, kale, parsley, broccoli, lettuce, beet greens, watercress, and mangos.
- ✓ **Vitamin B2** (riboflavin), found in brewer's yeast, kale, prunes, collard greens, parsley, broccoli, and beet greens.
- ✓ **Vitamin B6** (pyridoxine), found in bell peppers, prunes, turnip greens, spinach, and kale.
- ✓ **Folic acid**, found in leafy green vegetables such as kale, asparagus, turnip greens, prunes, and peppers.
- ✓ **Pantothenic acid**, found in brewer's yeast, legumes, and whole grains.

✓ **Vitamin C**, found in kale, Brussels sprouts, broccoli, watercress, cauliflower, citrus, strawberries, papaya, mango, turnips, asparagus, berries, peppers, and cantaloupe.

✓ **Vitamin E**, found in spinach, watercress, asparagus, carrots, tomatoes, and wheat germ.

✓ **Selenium**, found in garlic, legumes, asparagus, oranges, radishes, grapes, carrots, cabbage, chard, and turnips.

✓ **Iron**, found in peas, parsley, dandelion, blackberries, beets with greens, carrots, pineapple, broccoli, strawberries, and asparagus.

✓ **Zinc**, found in ginger, garlic, carrots, grapes, spinach, cabbage, lettuce, tangerines, cucumbers, soybeans, and sunflower seeds.

✓ **Magnesium**, found in green leafy vegetables and nuts.

✓ **Manganese**, found in bananas, bran, pineapple, and nuts.

✓ **Protein**, found in legumes, broccoli, and sunflower seeds.

✓ **Antioxidants**, found in citrus fruits, legumes, and whole grains.

✓ **Phytonutrients**, found in all plants, especially dark and brightly colored fruits and vegetables.

Top Super Foods that Prevent Cancer

The National Institute for Cancer Research lists these foods as the top super foods for reducing cancer:

- Beans (or legumes) are rich in fiber and contain several chemicals that boost immunity to cancer, including saponins, which may inhibit the growth of cancer cells in different tissues; protease inhibitors, which reduce the growth of cancer cells and suppress cell destroyers; and phytic acid, which also slows the growth of tumors. Studies show that those who consume at least three servings of legumes on a daily basis are 38 percent less likely to get prostate cancer than those who eat fewer legumes.

- Berries are high in vitamin C and fiber as well as ellagic acid, which helps prevent cancer of the skin, bladder, lung, esophagus, and breast. Strawberries and raspberries are especially high in this substance, and blueberries contain the most antioxidants of all berries.

- Cruciferous vegetables, including broccoli, cauliflower, Brussels sprouts, cabbage, kale, Swiss chard, and bok choy, contain substances that may reduce the growth of cancer by regulating enzymes that help prevent cancer. Eating a lot of cruciferous vegetables has been associated with a decreased risk for lung, stomach, and colorectal cancers.
- Dark green leafy vegetables like spinach, romaine lettuce, leaf lettuces, kale, mustard greens, collard greens, and Swiss chard all contain high amounts of fiber, folate, and a wide variety of antioxidants that fight free radicals. Studies show that the carotenoids in dark green leafy vegetables may help prevent breast, skin, lung, and stomach cancers.
- Flaxseed is the best known dietary source for lignans, which may act like estrogen in the body. Studies show that consuming a diet high in flaxseed modified estrogen metabolism and offered some protection against breast cancer. Flaxseed has also been associated with reduced risks of colon, breast, skin, and lung tumors. Flaxseed is also high in omega-3 essential fatty acids.
- Garlic is a natural antibiotic and immune system enhancer. A potent antioxidant that attacks free radicals, it also increases the enzymes that break down carcinogens in the body. According to the Iowa Women's Health Study, garlic is a super food that can help prevent prostate and stomach cancer. Women who regularly consume garlic showed a lower risk for colon cancer.
- Grapes, especially red and purple varieties, are loaded with resveratrol, which has been shown to reduce the formation of tumors in lymph, liver, stomach, and breast cells.

FACT

Research shows that drinking green tea on a frequent basis can lower the risk of many cancers, including bladder, colon, stomach, pancreatic, and esophageal cancer. It may also help prevent the recurrence of stage 1 breast cancer. Include green tea in your favorite fruit juices to add flavor and nutrients.

- Green tea is loaded with catechins and offers three times the amount of catechins found in black tea. Catechins reduce the formation of enzyme activities that lead to cancer and may also repair cellular damage caused by free radicals. Green tea may also reduce cancer of the colon, liver, breast, and prostate cells.
- Soy foods, which include tofu, soymilk, soybeans, soy nuts, miso, tempeh, and soy burgers, contain phytoestrogens, a plant-derived form of estrogen that some scientists believe replaces the body's stronger form of estrogen at estrogen receptor sites in the breast. Some doctors believe soy reduces the risk of breast cancer, while others believe phytoestrogens in soy may increase the risk of breast cancer in women who have already had the disease. Research shows that men who drank soymilk more than once per day for twenty years had a 70 percent reduced risk of prostate cancer.
- Tomatoes contain the phytochemical lycopene, which is also found in smaller quantities in watermelon, papaya, and pink grapefruit. Numerous studies have shown that lycopene helps reduce the incidence of prostate, stomach, and lung cancer. Tomatoes are most effective at reducing cancer when consumed as tomato sauce, tomato paste, and tomato juice, because nutrients are more easily absorbed when tomatoes are cooked or processed than when they are raw.

FACT

Research shows that those who consume very low levels of lycopene are three times more likely to get lung cancer than those who consume high levels. African Americans were shown to have eight times the risk of developing cancer when their lycopene levels were very low.

- Turmeric, the spice used in curry powder, has an active ingredient, curcumin, that helps reduce colon, breast, liver, oral, skin, and stomach tumors.
- Consuming lots of yogurt may help reduce breast and colon cancers, so be sure to include it in your homemade juices to add nutrients, flavor, and texture.

Using Produce to Reduce Cancer

According to studies conducted by the Australian government, many types of cancer may be prevented by eating a diet high in fresh fruits and vegetables.

✓ **Lung cancer:** Convincing evidence shows that diets high in vegetables and fruits are protective against lung cancer and that compounds called carotenoids, which are present in significant amounts in these foods, are probably responsible for some of this effect.

✓ **Breast cancer:** Consuming a diet high in unsaturated fats, fruits, and vegetables has been shown to reduce the risk of cancer, while smoking and alcohol consumption may increase the risk, according to many studies.

✓ **Prostate cancer:** Consuming a diet high in saturated fats has been shown to increase the risk of prostate cancer, while consuming lots of fruits and vegetables reduces the risk. The antioxidant leucopenia, which is found in tomatoes, watermelon, and strawberries, has been shown to help lower the risk of prostate cancer in many studies.

✓ **Bowel cancer:** Getting regular aerobic exercise and consuming a diet high in produce has been shown to reduce the risk of bowel cancer, while eating a diet high in saturated fats and alcohol has been shown to increase the risk.

Those Amazing Antioxidants

Antioxidants are substances in foods that help protect cells from the ravaging effects of free radicals, or unstable molecules that attack cells and leave them vulnerable to cancer, heart disease, and many other conditions. Fruits and vegetables are a great source of many different antioxidants, including vitamins C, E, and A; beta-carotene; and lycopene.

How Antioxidants Prevent Cancer

A wealth of research from large-scale, randomized clinical trials indicates that antioxidants may slow or possibly prevent the development of cancer, according to the American Institute for Cancer Research. It states that 30 to 40 percent of cancers are directly linked to diet.

Antioxidants neutralize free radicals. Free radicals are molecules with incomplete electron shells that make them more chemically reactive than those with complete electron shells. Exposure to various environmental factors, including tobacco smoke and radiation, can also lead to free radical formation. The most common form of free radicals is oxygen, which becomes electrically charged or "radicalized" when it robs electrons from other molecules, causing damage to the DNA.

Foods Rich in Antioxidants

Antioxidants are abundant in fruits, vegetables, nuts, grains, some meats, poultry, and fish. The following list describes food sources of common antioxidants.

- **Beta-carotene** is found in many foods that are orange in color, including sweet potatoes, carrots, cantaloupe, squash, apricots, pumpkin, and mangos. Some green leafy vegetables are also high in beta-carotene, including collard greens, spinach, chard, watercress, kale, and romaine lettuce.
- **Lutein**, which can help promote healthy eyes, is abundant in green leafy vegetables such as collard greens, spinach, and kale.
- **Lycopene** is a powerful antioxidant found in tomatoes, watermelon, guava, papaya, apricots, pink grapefruit, and blood oranges. Studies show that 85 percent of Americans get their lycopene from tomatoes and tomato products.
- **Selenium** is a mineral rather than an antioxidant nutrient, but it is essential for antioxidant enzymes. You can find selenium in cabbage, oranges, garlic, grapes, carrots, chard, and turnips. Brazil nuts also contain large quantities of selenium.
- **Vitamin A** is found in sweet potatoes, carrots, spinach, chard, beet greens, watercress, mangos, cantaloupe, apricots, broccoli, and romaine lettuce.
- **Vitamin C**, also called ascorbic acid, is found in abundance in mangos, citrus fruit, asparagus, cantaloupe, watercress, Brussels sprouts, cauliflower, strawberries, and papaya.

- **Vitamin E** is found in almonds, mangos, nuts, broccoli, asparagus, carrots, tomatoes, spinach, and watercress. It is also found in several oils, including wheat germ, safflower, corn, and soybean oils.

How Omega-3 Fatty Acids Prevent Cancer

Extensive research shows that omega-3 fatty acids reduce inflammation and help prevent risk factors associated with chronic diseases such as cancer. The body needs these fatty acids, but it cannot make them and must get them from food sources, such as oily fish, avocadoes, nuts, and nut oils.

Because essential fatty acids are highly concentrated in the brain, they also appear to be particularly important for cognitive and behavioral function.

Three Types of Omega-3s

The three major types of omega-3 acids found in foods include alpha linolenic acid (ALA), eicosapentaenoic acid (EPA), and docosahexaenoic acid (DHA). After you consume foods with omega-3 fatty acids, the body turns ALA to EPA and DHA, the two forms of omega-3 acids that the body can most easily absorb and use. It's important to eat a diet that provides a healthy balance of omega-3 and omega-6 fatty acids; omega-3s reduce inflammation, and omega-6 acids increase it.

FACT

A healthy diet should consist of roughly two to four times more omega-6 fatty acids than omega-3 fatty acids. Unfortunately, the average American consumes fourteen to twenty-five times more omega-6 fatty acids than omega-3 fatty acids. Researchers believe this may be responsible for the spiraling rate of inflammatory disorders in the United States.

The Mediterranean diet includes a healthy balance of omega-3 and omega-6 acids, as well as omega-9 fatty acids, which work together to help lower the risk of heart disease and cancer.

Omega-3s and Colon Cancer

Studies conducted on Inuits, who consume a diet that is high in omega-3-rich fish, have a lower incidence of colon cancer than other populations, even though they consume a high-fat diet.

Studies show that omega-3 fatty acids prevent worsening of colon cancer while omega-6 fatty acids promote the growth of colon tumors. Research also shows that low levels of omega-3 fatty acids in the body are a marker for an increased risk of colon cancer.

Omega-3s and Breast Cancer

Women who regularly consume foods rich in omega-3 fatty acids over many years may be less likely to develop breast cancer, according to recent studies. In addition, the risk of dying from breast cancer may be significantly less for those who eat large quantities of omega-3 from fish and brown kelp seaweed. The risks are especially low for women who substitute seaweed for meat products.

FACT

The delicate balance between omega-3 and omega-6 fatty acids appears to play an important role in the development and growth of breast cancer. Researchers speculate that omega-3 fatty acids in combination with other nutrients (namely, vitamin C, vitamin E, beta-carotene, selenium, and coenzyme Q10) may help prevent and treat breast cancer.

Omega-3s and Prostate Cancer

Studies show men who consume a diet rich in omega-3 fatty acids from fish or fish oil supplements and eat a diet that has a healthy balance of omega-3 and omega-6 fatty acids can help reduce their risk of developing prostate cancer.

Good Sources of Omega-3

Good sources of omega-3 fatty acids include oily, cold-water fish such as salmon, tuna, sardines, halibut, mackerel, and herring. Eicosapentaenoic acid (EPA) and docosahexaenoic acid (DHA) are prevalent in fish, while ALA is abundant in nuts and seeds and their oils, including flaxseed, canola, pumpkin, walnut, soybean, and purslane.

ALERT

Make sure to keep flaxseed and flaxseed oil in the refrigerator so they don't lose their potent action. If you're juicing with ground flaxseeds, use them within twenty-four hours or purchase flaxseeds in mylar packaging, which helps them retain their freshness.

In addition to dietary sources, EPA and DHA can be taken in the form of fish oil capsules.

The Anti-Cancer Diet

Over the last twenty-five years, cancer research has produced dietary guidelines that have become conventional wisdom when it comes to cancer prevention. In 1991, the National Cancer Institute (NCI) and the Produce for Better Health Foundation launched a campaign to increase consumption of fruits and vegetables to five to nine servings a day for every American.

While there is no specific fruit or vegetable responsible for reducing cancer risk, research shows that the regular consumption of a variety of fruits and vegetables reduces risk. Five servings are considered the minimum. For men, the recommendation is nine servings per day; for women, it is seven.

Pack in Phytochemicals

The American Institute for Cancer Study also advises eating produce high in phytochemicals, the nutrients in plants that act powerfully to prevent a healthy cell from turning cancerous. (Tomatoes alone contain up to 10,000 different phytochemicals.) Phytochemicals have been shown to boost detoxification of the cells, stimulate the immune system, and to offer anti-bacterial and anti-viral properties that help maintain inner health and reduce the risk of cancer.

Here are just a few of the powerful phytochemicals found in produce, according to Cherie Calbom, M.S., author of *The Juice Lady's Guide to Juicing for Health*.

- ✓ **Ally sulfides**, found in garlic and onions, and believed to lower the risk of stomach cancer.
- ✓ **Indoles**, **isthiocyanates**, and **sulforaphanes** are three phytochemicals found in cruciferous veggies that help break down carcinogens.
- ✓ **Limomene**, found in citrus, stimulates enzymes that break down carcinogens.
- ✓ **Ellagic acid**, found in strawberries and grapes, prevent cancer-forming substances from altering DNA—the first step in cancer.
- ✓ **Curcumins**, found in ginger and turmeric, stimulate cancer inhibitors.
- ✓ **Lycopene**, found in cooked tomatoes, lowers the risk of stomach and prostate cancers.
- ✓ **Monoterpenes**, found in cherries, lowers the risk of pancreatic, breast, skin, lung, and stomach cancers.

FACT

A recent report sponsored by the World Cancer Research Fund and the American Institute for Cancer Study estimated that eating 400 or more grams of fruits and vegetables daily could prevent at least 20 percent of all cancers. In addition, those who eat the highest amount of fruits and vegetables have been shown to have half the cancer risks as those eating the least amounts.

Focus on Fiber

The National Cancer Institute advises eating plenty of fiber. Fiber moves cancer-causing compounds out of the body before they can cause harm. It is also thought to dilute potential carcinogens and may affect hormone production, thus lowering the incidence of hormone-related cancers like breast and prostate cancers. The NCI recommends 20 to 30 grams of fiber per day.

Foods rich in fiber include barley, oats, oat bran, nuts, apples, bananas, blackberries, citrus fruit, pears, prunes, beans (lima, kidney, pinto, and navy), chick peas, black-eyed peas, and especially lentils, Brussels sprouts, carrots, tomatoes, potatoes, and broccoli.

Consume Healthy Fats

Fat isn't really a four-letter word. Some fats are actually good for you when consumed in moderation, and they're essential for the healthy functioning of cells. Studies show some healthy fats, including olive oil, can help reduce your risk of cancer.

Two of the healthiest fats are omega-3 and omega-6 oils, also known as essential fatty acids. Because your body can't manufacture these healthy fats, it is essential to consume an adequate amount in foods that contain lots of these oils, including fish, nuts, avocados, vegetable oils, and leafy greens such as spinach and mustard greens.

Herbal Helpers

While alternative medicine advocates tout the powerful benefits of herbs, research shows otherwise: Most herbs have little or no effect on cancer, although they might be beneficial for other reasons—and a few could be dangerous. This isn't to say that future research won't turn up some winners. After all, the potent anti-cancer drug taxol comes from the bark of the yew tree.

ALERT

The Food and Drug Administration doesn't require testing for herbs and supplements as it does for conventional drugs, so be cautious in the largely unregulated world of herbal medicines. While some may help, others could be worthless or dangerous. Always check with your doctor before consuming an unfamiliar herb.

The Controversy Over Herbs

New studies show anti-cancer effects in ginger, tea made from a Chinese herb called barbed skullcap, and the more traditional green tea.

FACT

The National Cancer Institute continues to study what—if any—effect green tea has on cancer. In the meantime, drinking a few cups of the antioxidant-rich brew each day certainly won't do any harm, but don't overdo it. Consuming too much green tea could cause nausea and diarrhea.

However, beware that many herbs that allegedly help prevent or cure cancer have little or no proven benefits, and may have dangerous side effects. To be safe, consult your physician before experimenting with any herbal cancer remedies.

Vegetable Seven

» ## Good for cancer prevention

This combination is so much fresher than anything you can purchase in a canned juice.

INGREDIENTS | YIELD: 1½ CUPS

2 Roma tomatoes
1 celery stalk, leaves intact
1 fist parsley
2 carrots, peeled
1 green onion
1 cup cauliflower
2 cloves garlic

Blanch tomatoes by placing in boiling water for 30 seconds and then transferring to an ice bath. Juice ingredients in the order listed. Stir.

Per Serving

CALORIES: **188**
FAT: **1g**
SODIUM: **177mg**
FIBER: **12g**
PROTEIN: **7g**
SUGARS: **23g**
CARBOHYDRATES: **50g**

The Benefits of Lycopene
Lycopene is a powerful antioxidant found in tomatoes. It has been shown to reduce the risk of prostate, ovarian, and cervical cancer.

Broccoli Apple Carrot

» ## Good for cancer prevention

Broccoli is now considered one of the top cancer prevention foods by the American Cancer Society.

INGREDIENTS | YIELD: 1 CUP

4 broccoli spears
¼ cup Italian parsley
2 McIntosh apples, cored
¼ lemon

Juice broccoli, parsley, and apples. Juice lemon. Stir.

Per Serving

CALORIES: **114**
FAT: **0.75g**
SODIUM: **47mg**
FIBER: **7.2g**
PROTEIN: **3.7g**
SUGARS: **17g**
CARBOHYDRATES: **27g**

Garlic Delight

» ## Good for cancer prevention

Wild garlic may once have grown in a large area from China and India to eastern Europe and the Middle East. It is one of the oldest domesticated plants.

INGREDIENTS | **YIELD: 1 CUP**

3 Roma tomatoes
2 red apples
1 clove garlic
1 sprig Italian parsley

Juice tomatoes, apples, and garlic. Stir and garnish with parsley.

Per Serving

CALORIES: **114**
FAT: **1.3g**
SODIUM: **18mg**
FIBER: **4.6g**
PROTEIN: **2.4g**
SUGARS: **26g**
CARBOHYDRATES: **44g**

Garlic

Garlic may be one of the healthiest vegetables you can add to your juices. Studies credit it with fighting bladder, skin, colon, and stomach cancer. Eating one to three cloves per day is recommended for optimum results. Placing garlic in your juice is an easy way to meet that requirement.

Strawberry Papaya

» ## Good for colon cancer prevention

Papaya is rich in vitamin C and carotene, which is good for your eyes. Strawberries are very high in antioxidants.

INGREDIENTS | **YIELD: ½ CUP**

1 cup strawberries, hulls intact
1 papaya, seeded

Juice berries and papaya. Stir.

Per Serving

CALORIES: **76**
FAT: **0.58g**
SODIUM: **3.6mg**
FIBER: **4.4g**
PROTEIN: **2.2g**
SUGARS: **15g**
CARBOHYDRATES: **25g**

The Healthy Strawberry

Strawberries contain a range of nutrients, starting with vitamin C. They also contain significant levels of phytonutrients and antioxidants, which fight free radicals. Free radicals are elements that can damage cells, and they are thought to contribute to the formation of many kinds of cancer.

Carrot Cucumber and a Beet

» **Good for prostate and lung cancer prevention**

Carrots can reduce your odds of contracting colon cancer. A compound found in carrots, falcarinol, lowers the risk of tumors. Research points to beets for treating prostate and lung cancer.

INGREDIENTS | YIELD: 1¼ CUPS

3 carrots, peeled
1 cucumber, peeled
2 beets, greens removed
1 celery stalk, leaves intact

Juice ingredients in order listed. Stir.

Per Serving

CALORIES: **244**
FAT: **0.48g**
SODIUM:**292mg**
FIBER: **16g**
PROTEIN: **7.8g**
SUGARS: **38g**
CARBOHYDRATES: **69g**

Super Berry

» **Good for cancer prevention and heart disease**

Blueberries are available from May through October. Store them for up to five days in your refrigerator.

INGREDIENTS | YIELD: 1 CUP

1 pint blueberries, washed.
2 cups red grapes, washed.

Juice blueberries and grapes. Stir.

Per Serving

CALORIES: **288**
FAT: **1.6g**
SODIUM: **6.6mg**
FIBER: **7.5g**
PROTEIN: **4.1g**
SUGARS: **59g**
CARBOHYDRATES: **74g**

Super Blueberries

Blueberries are being touted as one of the new super foods. Their color contains anthocyanin, a phytonutrient that helps reduce cancer risk by preventing cell damage. They are packed with antioxidants and phytoflavinoids and are also high in potassium and vitamin C. Not only can they lower your risk of heart disease and cancer, but they are anti-inflammatory.

Carrots in the Veggie Patch

» **Good for cancer prevention**

Lowly turnips are packed with cancer-fighting compounds, are rich in the minerals calcium and iron, and have two times the vitamin C of orange juice.

INGREDIENTS | YIELD: 1 CUP

2 carrots, peeled
1 cup spinach
1 turnip
1 celery stalk
2 sprigs parsley

Juice carrots, spinach, turnip, and celery. Stir and garnish with parsley sprigs.

Per Serving

CALORIES: **160**
FAT: **0.3g**
SODIUM: **266mg**
FIBER: **11g**
PROTEIN: **5.2g**
SUGARS: **21g**
CARBOHYDRATES: **40g**

Spicy Tomato

» **Good for cancer prevention**

Research shows that drinking a glass of tomato juice as your first course can cause you to eat up to 135 fewer calories in the rest of your meal.

INGREDIENTS | YIELD: 1¼ CUPS

6 Roma tomatoes
¼ red onion
½ jalapeño pepper
1 clove garlic
1 celery stalk

Juice ingredients in order listed. Stir.

Per Serving

CALORIES: **127**
FAT: **2.7g**
SODIUM: **82mg**
FIBER: **6.4g**
PROTEIN: **6.1g**
SUGARS: **20g**
CARBOHYDRATES: **37g**

Tomato Juice

Tomato juice was served for the first time in 1917 at a spa in Indiana. A French chef ran out of oranges for orange juice, so he squeezed tomatoes instead. It was a huge success and tomato juice became a popular morning drink.

Carrots on Fire

>> **Good for cancer prevention**

This delicious carrot juice has a hint of spiciness. You can control how spicy you make this juice. Remove the seeds of the chili to reduce the heat.

INGREDIENTS | YIELD: 1 CUP

4 carrots
½ Serrano chili pepper
1 sprig parsley

Juice carrots and chile. Stir and garnish with parsley.

Per Serving

CALORIES: **197**
FAT: **0.099g**
SODIUM: **159mg**
FIBER: **12g**
PROTEIN: **4.4g**
SUGARS: **27g**
CARBOHYDRATES: **53g**

Bloody Caesar

>> **Good for cancer prevention**

This mocktail is similar to a Bloody Mary, but without the vodka.

INGREDIENTS | YIELD: 1¼ CUPS

1 large tomato
½ green bell pepper
1 celery stalk
1 clove garlic
2 carrots, peeled
1 teaspoon Worcestershire sauce
Splash of Tabasco sauce

Blanch tomato by placing in boiling water for 30 seconds and then transferring to an ice water bath. Juice tomato, bell pepper, celery, garlic, and carrots. Stir in Worcestershire and Tabasco.

Per Serving

CALORIES: **166**
FAT: **0.54g**
SODIUM: **214mg**
FIBER: **10g**
PROTEIN: **5.6g**
SUGARS: **18g**
CARBOHYDRATES: **40g**

Apple Blackberry

» Good for cancer prevention

Blackberries are low in calories and high in vitamin C. They contain ellagic acid, which is the antioxidant known to prevent cancer.

INGREDIENTS | YIELD: ¾ CUP

2 gala red apples, cored
2 pints blackberries
1 lemon, peeled

Juice apples, lemon, and blackberries. Stir.

Per Serving

CALORIES: **353**
FAT: **3.4g**
SODIUM: **8.6mg**
FIBER: **36g**
PROTEIN: **8.6g**
SUGARS: **48g**
CARBOHYDRATES: **87g**

A Pear of Kiwifruit

» Good for cancer prevention

The black seeds of the kiwifruit are edible. It is not necessary to peel the pears before juicing.

INGREDIENTS | YIELD: ¾ CUP

2 pears
2 kiwi, peeled
½ lemon, peeled

Juice pears, kiwifruit, and lemon. Stir.

Per Serving

CALORIES: **222**
FAT: **2.5g**
SODIUM: **6mg**
FIBER: **15g**
PROTEIN: **3.3g**
SUGARS: **34g**
CARBOHYDRATES: **57g**

The Healthy Kiwi

Kiwifruits are rich in many vitamins, flavonoids, and minerals. They contain high amounts of vitamin C and beta-carotene in particular. They have more vitamin C than oranges and just as much potassium as bananas.

Cancer Buster

>> **Good for cancer prevention**

Wheatgrass juice contains thirteen vitamins. The chlorophyll and beta-carotene in wheatgrass juice is beneficial in fighting and preventing cancer.

INGREDIENTS | YIELD: 1 CUP

1 beet, tops removed
1 carrot
1 cup cauliflower
½ cup wheatgrass

Juice beet, carrot, cauliflower, and wheatgrass. Stir.

Per Serving

CALORIES: **153**
FAT: **0.58g**
SODIUM: **183mg**
FIBER: **10g**
PROTEIN: **5g**
SUGARS: **15g**
CARBOHYDRATES: **26g**

Cauliflower

Cauliflower is high in vitamin C and iron. For juicing, it tastes best when it is mixed with other fruits or vegetables, which lessens its strong flavor. Research has shown it to be effective in fighting cancer. Store it for one week, wrapped in plastic, in your refrigerator.

Peach Grape Delight

>> **Good for cancer prevention**

Peaches and grapes are a wonderful combination. You may vary the recipe by using green grapes instead of red.

INGREDIENTS | YIELD: 1½ CUPS

2 peaches
1 cup red grapes
¼ lemon

Juice peaches, grapes, and lemon. Stir.

Per Serving

CALORIES: **188**
FAT: **1.1g**
SODIUM: **2.1mg**
FIBER: **7.5g**
PROTEIN: **3.9g**
SUGARS: **42g**
CARBOHYDRATES: **47g**

Where do Peaches Come From?

Peaches are native to China. They are available from May to October in most parts of the United States. Peaches are classified as free stone when the pit comes away easily from the flesh. In the other type of peach classification, clingstone, the fruit sticks to the pit. Research shows that peaches contain antioxidants that may help inhibit the growth of tumors. Peach pits contain small amounts of cyanide and should be discarded.

CHAPTER 16

Perfect Juices for People with Diabetes

Until recently, experts thought sugar—including most fruits—was strictly taboo for diabetics. But according to new guidelines by the American Diabetes Association, diabetics can eat pretty much anything they like, provided they pay attention to their diet as a whole and monitor their blood sugar level two hours after meals to see whether any individual food elevates it. Studies show that raw produce is an excellent choice for diabetics because it supplies many needed nutrients for health. Unlike cooked produce, raw fruits, vegetables, and juices help stabilize blood sugar levels.

All about Diabetes

Diabetes mellitus was discovered 2,000 years ago by the Greeks, who observed that ants were attracted to the urine of diabetics. For centuries, doctors would taste the patient's urine for sweetness to detect the disease.

According to the American Diabetes Association, the disease is caused by the body's inability to produce enough insulin or to use it effectively. Insulin, a hormone released by the pancreas, helps keep your body sugar, or glucose, at normal, healthy levels. Your glucose levels change throughout the day, depending on what and when you've eaten and whether you've exercised.

Types of Diabetes

There are two major types of diabetes. Type 1, also known as insulin-dependent diabetes, is caused when your body produces little or no insulin. It is far less common than Type 2 diabetes, affecting just 5 percent of people with diabetes. Type 1 diabetes usually develops early in life, and is controlled by daily injections of insulin.

Type 2 (or non-insulin-dependent) diabetes affects 90 to 95 percent of people with diabetes. This type of diabetes usually develops later in life and often goes undiagnosed until symptoms become too troublesome to ignore, according to the American Diabetes Association. In Type 2 diabetes, the pancreas may produce insulin, but the body becomes resistant to it.

FACT

Type 2 diabetes most often occurs in adulthood. Because of America's high-fat, high-sugar diet and inactive lifestyle, it is now home to 13 percent of the world's diabetics, even though it only has 4.6 percent of the world's population. Studies also show that at least 80 percent of diabetics are obese.

Other risk factors for diabetes include having a parent or sibling with the disease; being African American, Asian American, Hispanic, or Pacific Islander; having higher than normal blood glucose levels; and having high blood pressure or cholesterol levels. While you can't change your heritage, lifestyle factors can dramatically lower your risk of diabetes. Studies show that borderline diabetics who lost 7 percent of their body weight, consumed a low-calorie, low-fat diet, and exercised moderately reduced their odds of having diabetes by 58 percent. Many Type 2 diabetics can control their condition without drugs by following a special diet and getting regular exercise.

Symptoms of Diabetes

According to the ADA, diabetes often goes undiagnosed because many of its symptoms seem so harmless. Some of the more common symptoms include frequent urination, excessive thirst, extreme hunger, unusual weight loss, increased fatigue, irritability, and blurry vision. If you have one or more of these symptoms, see your doctor right away. You can also take an online diabetes risk test to find out if you are at risk for diabetes at *www .diabetes.org*.

Still a Serious Disease

While diabetes is more manageable than ever, it's still a serious disease. It is the country's seventh leading cause of death, and it can raise your risk of developing heart disease and stroke, kidney failure, blindness, infections, and serious nerve damage. Fortunately, consuming a diet rich in fruits and vegetables can help you get a handle on the disease.

Best Nutrients for Diabetes

Sugar was viewed as the enemy because it was thought to increase blood sugar more than any other food. Scientists now know that carbohydrates, whether they are found in sugar or starchy vegetables like potatoes, have the same effect on blood sugar levels. How many carbs you need depends on your medical condition, weight, and activity levels. How you spend those carbs is your decision, provided you distribute them evenly to avoid dangerous sugar spikes that can cause surges in your glucose levels.

Drinking at least six to eight glasses of water daily, depending on your weight, also helps lower blood sugars by flushing out toxins.

Vitamins for Controlling Diabetes

You should consume the following vitamins and minerals daily to keep diabetes in check. Remember that most of these nutrients can be found in fresh fruit and vegetable juice:

- **Vitamin A:** Protects the lining of the digestive system and is also vital for growth and night vision.
- **Vitamin B1 (thiamine):** Vital for muscles and heart function.
- **Vitamin B2:** Converts B6 into an active form so the body can more easily use it.
- **Vitamin B6:** Helps reduce stress and anxiety.
- **Vitamin B12:** Helps reduce depression.
- **Pantothenic acid:** Supports enzyme functions. These enzymes are also needed to break down food and trigger energy release.
- **Niacin:** Metabolizes carbs and fat and supports your digestive system. Vital for diabetics.
- **Biotin (vitamin B3):** Essential for digestion and also triggers enzymes.
- **Vitamin E:** Diabetics require more vitamin E than other people. Getting enough can also decrease the amount of insulin you need to take to control the disease.

ESSENTIAL

According to the ADA, diabetics should get as many of their carbs as possible from fruits, beans, peanuts, peas, whole grain foods, and low-fat dairy products. These low-glycemic foods are digested more slowly than high-glycemic foods such as white bread and potatoes, which your body converts to glucose more rapidly than a candy bar.

Minerals for Controlling Diabetes

If you have diabetes, be sure to consume adequate amounts of the following minerals.

- **Iron:** Essential to create energy and transport blood around the body.
- **Sodium:** Regulates and maintains water balance.

- **Potassium:** Helps control blood pressure.
- **Zinc:** Essential for growth and repair. Like the B vitamins, it also supports enzymes.
- **Manganese:** Low manganese levels may aggravate diabetic conditions. Studies have demonstrated that manganese can help decrease insulin resistance and improve glucose metabolism.
- **Calcium:** Essential for strong bones and regulating muscles.

Best Produce for Diabetics

If you have diabetes, one of the best ways to control blood sugar levels is to consume a diet high in fruits and vegetables, especially raw produce or produce consumed in homemade juices. Here's where to find the vitamins and minerals you need to stay healthy.

WHERE TO FIND VITAMINS
- Produce rich in **vitamin A** includes kale, parsley, carrots, spinach, chard, beet greens, watercress, broccoli, and romaine.
- Fruits and veggies with **vitamin B1 (thiamine)** include garlic, sunflower seeds, and buckwheat sprouts.
- **Vitamin B2** is found in broccoli, kale, parsley, beet greens, and prunes.
- **Vitamin B6** is abundant in spinach, turnips greens, bell peppers, prunes, and kale.
- **Vitamin B12** is found in soy and tempeh.
- **Pantothenic acid** is abundant in broccoli, kale, and cauliflower.
- **Niacin (vitamin B3)** is found in brewer's yeast, wheat bran, and peanuts.
- **Vitamin E** is abundant in tomatoes, carrots, watercress, asparagus, and spinach.

WHERE TO FIND MINERALS
- **Iron** is found in pineapple, blackberries, strawberries, parsley, cruciferous veggies, beets with greens, parsley, and chard.
- **Sodium** is found in celery, spinach, beets with greens, cabbage, garlic, sunflower seeds, turnips, and watercress.

- **Potassium** is found in cruciferous veggies, celery, radishes, garlic, asparagus, and chard.
- **Zinc** is found in turnips, parsley, carrots, cucumbers, spinach, garlic, ginger root, and lettuce.
- **Manganese** is found in cruciferous veggies, carrots, celery, garlic, parsley, beet greens, and spinach.
- **Calcium** is found in carrots, celery, broccoli, garlic, spinach, beet greens, lettuce, string beans, and watercress.
- Natural **diuretics** that help control blood pressure include asparagus, cucumber, parsley, and lemon juice.

ALERT

Beets provide essential fiber, phytochemicals, and minerals. Other essential veggies for diabetics include string beans, which support the pancreas and help stabilize blood sugar levels, and cabbage, which has properties that mimic insulin. Garlic reduces blood sugar levels and is also a potent antioxidant that fights infections, which can be especially dangerous for diabetics.

Foods to Avoid

If you are a diabetic, go easy on the following foods, all of which could cause dangerous spikes in blood sugar:

- Sugar, artificial sweeteners, and honey. However, you may use sweeteners like stevia.
- Candy and chocolate. If you're desperate for chocolate, eat dark chocolate, which contains less sugar and at least 70 percent cocoa solids.
- Avoid foods containing fructose, glucose, and dextrose—all forms of sugar.
- Avoid refined, processed grains found in cakes, biscuits, pies, tarts, breakfast cereals, wheat, rye, barley, corn, rice, bread, pasta, and pastry.

- Don't eat large amounts of vegetables that contain high levels of carbohydrates and starches, including potatoes, carrots, peas, beans, parsnips, and beets. Small amounts are healthy and essential.
- Don't consume large amounts of fruit with a high sugar content, including watermelon, grapes, mangos, pineapples, oranges, and strawberries.
- Use milk in moderation. It contains sugar.
- Use yogurt and whole-fat cheese in moderation, as both contain sugar.
- Avoid commercially packaged foods like TV dinners, especially lean and light varieties, as well as snack foods and fast foods. All of them contain hidden sugars.
- Fresh fruit juice is high in sugar, so be sure to dilute it, using one part juice to four parts water.

Herbal Helpers

New studies show that certain herbs can help lower blood sugar levels as well. Remember that herbs are not regulated by the FDA and may cause side effects. Always read product labels, follow directions, and heed all warnings.

Herbs that May Help Control Diabetes

The following herbs may help control diabetes. Remember that herbs are not regulated by the FDA and may vary in potency levels. Talk to your physician first before using herbs.

- **Ginseng** has been shown in recent studies to decrease post-prandial hyperglycemia, an exaggerated rise in blood sugar after consuming a meal, in Type 2 diabetics. Studies show that taking ginseng after meals has been shown to regulate blood sugar levels.
- Various studies show that **chromium** helps insulin metabolize carbohydrates, protein, and fats. Chromium deficiency may help trigger adult-onset diabetes.

- **Alpha lipoic acid (ALA)**, an antioxidant, may have an effect on insulin utilization and blood sugar metabolism in Type 1 and Type 2 diabetes, according to new research.
- **Vanadyl sulfate** is important for proper glucose metabolism and is safe and well tolerated at doses as high as 1,000 mcg daily.
- Individuals with diabetes have impaired intestinal zinc absorption and low plasma zinc levels. **Zinc** supplements have the potential to help individuals with hypoglycemia, impaired gluten tolerance, and diabetes, according to many studies.
- **Gymnema** has been used to manage diabetes in India for centuries. It appears to act in a manner similar to sulfonylurea agents. Gymnema temporarily prevents the taste buds from recognizing sweetness, helping prevent sweetness cravings. It may help inhibit intestinal glucose absorption in Type 1 and Type 2 diabetes.
- A large amount of promising research indicates that **fenugreek** seeds appear to decrease blood glucose, improve glucose tolerance, and decrease cholesterol levels, although side effects may include diarrhea and upset stomach.
- **Indian kino** is a resin used in India that has the ability to rebuild and heal the pancreas.
- **Balsam pear**, a vegetable grown in Asia, has the ability to lower blood sugar naturally and is being used to treat diabetes, as are onions and garlic. Blueberry leaves act like a mild form of insulin and are used as an alternative treatment to ease symptoms of diabetes.

If you have a seriously harmful side effect, adverse reaction, or illness, contact your physician and have her report it to FDA's MedWatch at (800) FDA-1088.

Fresh from the Garden

» ### Good for reducing diabetes

This healthy and easy juice would make a great appetizer or first course for a dinner party.

INGREDIENTS | YIELD: 1¼ CUPS

1 large tomato
2 celery stalks
1 cup broccoli
2 cloves garlic

Juice tomato, celery, broccoli and garlic. Stir.

Per Serving

CALORIES: **99**
FAT: **0.015g**
SODIUM: **126mg**
FIBER: **6.6g**
PROTEIN: **6.3g**
SUGARS: **7g**
CARBOHYDRATES: **19g**

Cucumber Tang

» ### Good for reducing diabetes

Kosher salt is a coarse grained salt that does not contain additives. Use it in this cucumber lemonade with a hint of ginger.

INGREDIENTS | YIELD: ½ CUP

2 cucumbers
1 lemon, peeled
¼" slice ginger
Pinch kosher salt

Juice cucumbers, lemon, and ginger. Stir in a pinch of salt.

Per Serving

CALORIES: **119**
FAT: **1.1g**
SODIUM: **156mg**
FIBER: **12g**
PROTEIN: **7.3g**
SUGARS: **12g**
CARBOHYDRATES: **36g**

Orange Broccoli

>> **Good for reducing diabetes**

This juice is a good source of manganese for glucose metabolism. In addition, broccoli contains a substance called sulforaphane, which produces enzymes that protect blood vessels and help to reduce cell damage.

INGREDIENTS | **YIELD: ¾ CUP**

2 oranges, peeled
1 cup broccoli, washed

Juice oranges and broccoli. Stir well.

Per Serving

CALORIES: **160**
FAT: **0.93g**
SODIUM: **30mg**
FIBER: **8.4g**
PROTEIN: **5.5g**
SUGARS: **27g**
CARBOHYDRATES: **40g**

String Bean Juice

>> **Good for reducing diabetes**

The lemon in this juice will reduce the strong flavor of the beans and sprouts. String beans are an excellent source of vitamin B6; string beans and Brussels sprouts are great sources of insulin.

INGREDIENTS | **YIELD: ¾ CUP**

1 cup string beans
6 Brussels sprouts
1 lemon, peeled

Juice beans, Brussels sprouts, and lemon. Stir.

Per Serving

CALORIES: **118**
FAT: **1.4g**
SODIUM: **44mg**
FIBER: **10g**
PROTEIN: **7g**
SUGARS: **2g**
CARBOHYDRATES: **29g**

Carrot Cauliflower

» Good for reducing diabetes

This tasty juice provides you with iron and vitamins A and C.

INGREDIENTS | **YIELD: 1½ CUPS**

1 cup cauliflower
3 carrots, peeled
1 celery stalk

Juice cauliflower, carrots, and celery. Stir.

Per Serving

CALORIES: **173**
FAT: **0.11g**
SODIUM:**188 mg**
FIBER: **13g**
PROTEIN: **5.5g**
SUGARS: **23g**
CARBOHYDRATES: **45g**

Cauliflower or Cabbage?

Mark Twain said, "Cauliflower is nothing but cabbage with a college education." It is part of the cabbage family and comes from the Latin word *caulis* for stalk and *floris* for flower. Cauliflower comes in white, orange, green, and purple varieties. The green leaves at the base of the cauliflower are edible. They have a stronger flavor than the curd.

Broccoli Carrot

» Good for reducing diabetes

Vary this simple juice by making it with different color broccoli. The purple variety gives it a pretty hue, and it tastes the same.

INGREDIENTS | **YIELD: 1 CUP**

3 carrots, peeled
6 broccoli spears
1 clove garlic
¼ lemon, peeled

Juice carrots, broccoli, and garlic. Juice lemon.

Per Serving

CALORIES: **195**
FAT: **0.92g**
SODIUM:**175mg**
FIBER: **14g**
PROTEIN: **9.1g**
SUGARS: **20g**
CARBOHYDRATES: **48g**

Apple Cabbage

» **Good for reducing diabetes**

Apple and cabbage are a great combination with wonderful health benefits. Cabbage is inexpensive, which makes it a great choice for juicers on a budget.

INGREDIENTS | YIELD: 1¼ CUPS

¼ head red cabbage
1 cup Napa cabbage
2 Granny Smith apples, cored

Juice ingredients in order listed. Stir.

Per Serving

CALORIES: **130**
FAT: **0.68g**
SODIUM: **26mg**
FIBER: **4.9g**
PROTEIN: **1.6g**
SUGARS: **22g**
CARBOHYDRATES: **33g**

Colors of Cabbage

A head of cabbage should feel heavy and have tightly packed leaves. Store in the refrigerator tightly wrapped in plastic for one week. Napa cabbage has a crinkly leaf. It does not have the strong flavor of regular cabbage and is very crisp. Its flavor is mild. It is a good source of vitamin A, folic acid, and potassium.

Asparagus Squash Medley

» **Good for reducing diabetes**

Squash is high in niacin and vitamins A and C. Its high water content makes it perfect for juicing. Asparagus restores normal blood sugar levels.

INGREDIENTS | YIELD: 1 CUP

4 asparagus spears
1½ pound yellow crookneck squash

Juice asparagus and squash. Stir.

Per Serving

CALORIES: **51**
FAT: **0.058g**
SODIUM: **127mg**
FIBER: **5.3g**
PROTEIN: **6.1g**
SUGARS: **1g**
CARBOHYDRATES: **9g**

Glossary

Antioxidants
Substances found in many foods, including fruit, vegetables, seeds, and nuts. The most common antioxidants are beta-carotene, vitamins A, C, and E, lutein, lycopene, and selenium. Antioxidants gobble up and neutralize free radicals in the body, which can lead to serious diseases like cancer, heart disease, and other diseases.

Capsaicin
Found in hot peppers, it protects DNA from carcinogens.

Carbohydrates
The body's major source of energy. They are found in simple and complex sugars, starches, fibers, and starchy vegetables. Simple carbohydrates, including glucose and fructose, are abundant in fruits and vegetables, while the simple sugar, sucrose, is found in beets and cane sugar, and lactose, another simple sugar, is found in milk. Complex carbohydrates, including starches and fiber, are primarily found in whole grains and legumes. Complex carbohydrates provide more nutrients than simple carbohydrates, and are more filling because they take longer to digest.

Cartenoids
The substances in fruits and vegetables that give them their red, orange, or yellow colors. Cartenoids are potent antioxidants that help fight free radicals. Fruits and vegetables that are high in cartenoids include pineapple, citrus fruit, peaches, nectarines, tomatoes, papaya, apricots, carrots, watermelons, pumpkins, squash, and sweet potatoes. Dark green leafy vegetables like spinach, broccoli, collard greens, and kale also contain high amounts of cartenoids, as well as cholorphyll, which masks the bright colors of cartenoids.

Centrifugal
The juicing process that chops and grinds the fruit and vegetables into tiny particles and dispenses a mixture of juice and microscopic particles, producing a very high yield of drinkable juice. However, this is not technically true juice extraction and produces a lower quality of "living juice."

Chlorophyll
A molecule in plants that plays a crucial role in photosynthesis, a process in which plants absorb energy from sunlight and use it to create carbohydrates from CO_2 and water.

Complete protein
A food that contains all the essential amino acids that are essential for the growth of cells.

Dash
A few drops.

Dice
To cut into small cubes, about ¼-inch square.

Dietary minerals
Inorganic elements necessary for body function in humans and animals.

Dry-packed
Storing fruit by freezing it in individual pieces without adding sugar.

Drizzle
To lightly sprinkle drops of liquid over a food.

Floret
The flower or bud end of broccoli or cauliflower.

Free radicals
Substances produced in the body by exposure to environmental toxins such as cigarette smoke and radiation that trigger cellular changes that can lead to cancer, heart disease, and many other conditions.

Fructose
The natural sugar found in fruit, slightly sweeter than table sugar and okay for consumption by diabetics.

Glucose
The simplest natural sugar.

Grate
To shave into tiny pieces using a grater.

Grind
To reduce a large chunk of something to the consistence of sand.

Indoles
Found in cabbages, they stimulate enzymes that make the estrogen less effective and could reduce the risk for breast cancer.

Infusion
A liquid in which herbs, spices, or other flavorful ingredients have been soaked or steeped to extract that flavor into the liquid.

Isoflavones
Found in soy, they imitate human estrogen and help to reduce menopausal symptoms and osteoporosis.

Julienne
To slice into very thin pieces.

Living juice
A concept created by Dr. Norman Walker. According to Walker, when juice heats to 122°F, the enzymes from the fruits and vegetables die. Therefore, "living juice" is juice that comes from raw fruits or vegetables that has never been heated up to 122°F. This juice lasts longer and contains more vitamins and nutrients than "dead juice."

Mastication
A juicing process that mimics the natural process we use to chew food. An auger (or sometimes two augers) rotates and gently chews up the food to extract high-quality "living juice." This difference in juice quality is actually visible—juices are much darker and more flavorful.

Mince
To cut into very tiny pieces smaller than ⅛ of an inch.

Nutrients
An element required by the body for growth and function.

Oxidation
A process that occurs when juice is heated during the juicing process or exposed to open air for long

periods of time. Essential vitamins and nutrients can escape during oxidation. The more a juice oxidizes, the shorter the shelf-life it has.

Photosynthesis

A chemical equation that's the reaction between carbon dioxide and water, catalyzed by sunlight, to produce glucose and a waste product, oxygen. The glucose sugar is either directly used as an energy source by the plant for metabolism or growth, or is polymerized to form starch, so it can be stored until needed. The waste oxygen is excreted into the atmosphere, where it is made use of by plants for respiration.

Phytochemicals

Non-nutritive plant chemicals that have protective or disease preventive properties. There are more than a thousand known phytochemicals. It is well-known that plants produce these chemicals to protect themselves, but recent research demonstrates that they can also protect humans against diseases. Some of the well-known phytochemicals are lycopene in tomatoes, isoflavones in soy and flavonoids in fruits. They are not essential nutrients and are not required by the human body for sustaining life.

Pinch

The amount of a dry substance you can hold between your finger and thumb.

Polyphenols

Antioxidants found in green tea.

Proanthocyanidins

Responsible for the anti-adhesion properties of cranberry. Consumption of cranberries will reduce the risk of urinary tract infections and improve dental health.

Purée

To reduce a food to a thick, creamy texture.

Rhizome

The underground part of a stem of a plant, such as ginger.

Saponins

Found in beans, they interfere with the replication of cell DNA, thereby preventing the multiplication of cancer cells.

Savory

A popular herb with a fresh, woodsy taste.

Slice

To cut into thin pieces.

Steep

To let dry ingredients sit in hot water until the flavor seeps into the liquid.

Whisk

To rapidly mix and introduce air into the mixture.

Zest

Small slivers of peel, usually from a lemon, lime, or orange.

Index of Ingredients and Recipes

General Index

Aches and pains, 128–33. *See also*
  specific aches and pains
Acne, 146–48
ADHD, 102–3, 108, 109
Age spots, 148
Allergies, 199–200, 206
Aloe vera, 76, 232, 242
Alpha lipoic acid (ALA), 44, 115,
  123–24, 276
Alzheimer's disease, 14, 103–5, 106, 108.
  See also Memory
Amino acids, 4, 6
Anemia, 29, 30, 43, 93, 154, 180, 181, 190,
  193, 194, 241
Anti-aging and longevity
  backaches and, 132–33, 135
  benefits of juicing, 12–14, 113,
    121–22
  best fruits/vegetables for, 117–20
  common aches/pains and,
    128–33
  hypertension and, 125–28, 135
  juice recipes for, 134–39
  memory and, 123–25, 136
  menopause and, 122–23, 138
  muscle cramps and, 131, 134, 137,
    139
  nutrients for, 114–16
Antioxidants, 4, 5, 8, 13, 14, 47, 102,
  104–5, 107, 114, 115, 128–29, 136, 142,
  215–16, 251, 254–56
Arthritis, 122, 128, 129, 130, 171, 174, 175,
  178, 224
Asthma, 201–2, 207–8, 209–10, 212

Backaches, 132–33, 135
Benefits of juicing, 9–14
Beta-carotene, 29, 30, 31, 34, 36, 78, 97,

120, 128, 130, 148, 169, 184, 216, 232,
  243, 250, 255
Bioflavonoids, 30, 66, 118, 152, 189, 205,
  216, 225
Biotin, 29, 143, 145, 180, 182, 272
Bladder infections, 218–20, 226, 228
Blood circulation, 189–90, 194
Blood sugar levels, 49
Bone health, 163–78
  acid in diet and, 164, 167
  best fruits/vegetables for, 165–66
  bone loss and, 164
  calcium absorption and, 169
  juice recipes for, 172–78
  nutrients for stronger bones, 164–65,
    166, 168, 170–71
  osteoarthritis and rheumatoid
    arthritis, 171, 174, 175, 178, 224
  osteopenia and osteoporosis, 166–
    68, 170–71
Boron, 122, 165, 166, 170
Breathing, 197–212
  allergies and, 199–200, 206
  asthma and, 201–2, 207–8, 209–10,
    212
  best fruits/vegetables for, 199
  juice recipes for, 206–12
  nutrients for, 198–99
  respiratory disorders and
    (including colds and flu), 202–5,
    206–7, 208, 209, 210–11, 212
Bromelain, 117, 118, 130, 137, 237, 242
Bursitis, 128, 129, 134, 137

Calcium, 7, 43, 95, 99, 123, 131, 132, 151,
  154, 164, 165, 166, 167, 168, 169, 171,
  188, 238, 273, 274
Cancer, 249–68

anti-cancer diet, 258–60
  antioxidants and, 254–56
  calcium reducing colon cancer
    risk, 238
  herbs and, 260–61
  juice recipes for prevention and,
    262–68
  nutrients for fighting, 250–51
  omega-3 fatty acids preventing,
    256–58
  super foods for preventing/
    reducing, 251–54
Candida infections, 220–23
Canker sores, 149–50, 158, 226
Carbohydrates, 5, 95, 98
Carnitine and L-carnitine, 44–45, 184,
  203
Carotenes, 97, 98, 114
Carotenoids, 114–15
Chlorophyll, 5–6
Cholesterol, lowering, 50
Chromium, 44, 46, 47, 95, 142, 147, 148,
  188, 275
Chronic fatigue syndrome (CFS),
  182–85, 192, 195, 196
Circulation, 189–90, 194
Coenzyme Q10, 45, 184, 203, 257
Colds and flu, 203–5, 206–7, 208, 209,
  210–11, 212
Colitis, 241–42
Constipation, 237–39, 247
Copper, 135, 143, 168, 170, 205, 216

Depression. *See* Mental health and
  happiness
Detoxing and cleansing, 73–89
  best fruits/vegetables for, 76–78
  dos, don'ts, and danger signs, 80–83

Find out Everything on Anything at everything.com!

The new **Everything.com** has answers to your questions on just about everything! Based on the bestselling Everything book series, the **Everything.com** community provides a unique connection between members and experts in a variety of fields. Since 1996, Everything experts have helped millions of readers learn something new in an easy-to-understand, accessible, and fun way. And now Everything advice and know-how is available online.

At **Everything.com** you can explore thousands of articles on hundreds of topics—from starting your own business and personal finance to health-care advice and help with parenting, cooking, learning a new language, and more. And you also can:

- **Share advice**
- **Rate articles**
- **Submit articles**
- **Sign up for our Everything.com newsletters to stay informed of the latest articles, areas of interest, exciting sweepstakes, and more!**

Visit **Everything.com** where you'll find the broadest range and most authoritative content available online!